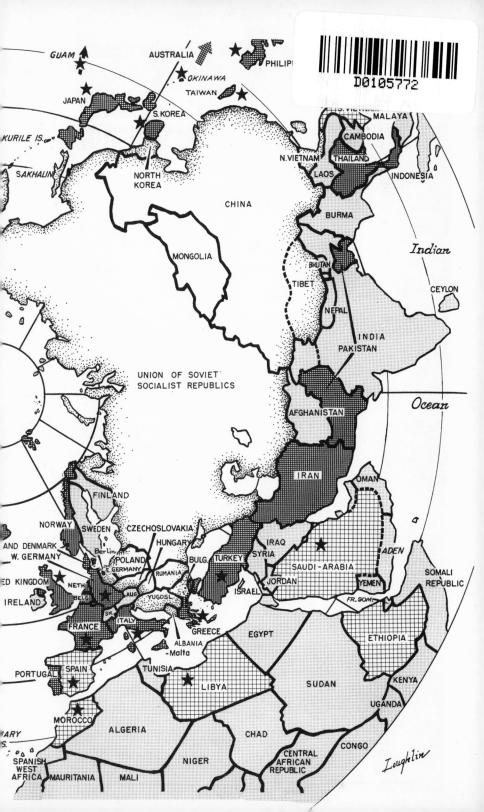

*American Military Forces Abroad*

*A Publication of the Mershon Center for Education in National Security*

# American Military Forces Abroad

## *Their Impact on the Western State System*

*by GEORGE STAMBUK*

OHIO STATE UNIVERSITY PRESS

# Acknowledgments

THE COLLECTION OF MATERIAL for this book was greatly facilitated by a number of people who patiently and competently answered my questions, assisted in establishing the necessary contacts, or made helpful suggestions. I should like to mention, in particular, Mr. William H. Carrol, International Affairs Division, Office of the Judge Advocate General, U.S. Air Force; Colonel William H. Johnson, Staff Judge Advocate, United States Army in Europe; Lieutenant Colonel Roger H. Miller, Office of the Judge Advocate General, U.S. Air Force; Mr. Richard Strauss, Public Affairs Adviser, Office of the European Regional Affairs, and Miss Helen Kavan, Public Liaison Division, Department of State; Mr. Hermann Bünemann, Ministry of Foreign Affairs, Bonn; Hon. William C. Bray, M.C.; Professors Austin V. Clifford and W. Howard Mann, School of Law, Indiana University; and Mr. Charles F. Jones of the John Hay Whitney Foundation. Edward H. Buehrig, Department of Government, Indiana University, read the entire manuscript and gave invaluable advice.

Preliminary research was made possible by a fellowship awarded by the Whitney Foundation in 1957. The Library of Congress and the Max Planck Institute of International Law, Heidelberg, were generous in permitting the use of their facilities and granting office space in the early stages of work.

I am further indebted to the Oxford University Press, London, publishers of the *British Yearbook of International Law* under the auspices of the Royal Institute of International Affairs, for permission to quote several passages from articles by Mr. G. P. Barton, and to the editors of the *Journal of Politics* for permission to include here portions of my article on the present subject published previously in that journal.

Mr. John L. Loughlin, Newport, Rhode Island, drafted the end-sheets map.

With such generous assistance from many quarters, the responsibility for all errors of fact, scope, and judgment can be solely my own.

G. S.

# TABLE OF CONTENTS

# LIST OF TABLES

*American Military Forces Abroad*

# I. Introduction

DURING the decade since the outbreak of the Korean war and the adoption, by the North Atlantic alliance, of plans for an integrated military structure designed to implement a "forward strategy," [1]

[1] "Forward strategy" is the plan, first proclaimed at the meeting of the North Atlantic Council in New York, September, 1950, to defend the NATO area "as far east as possible, in order to assure the defense of all European countries of the Alliance" (*The NATO Handbook* [Paris: North Atlantic Treaty Organization, 1959], p. 22). Military integration began with the appointment of General Eisenhower as Supreme Allied Commander Europe (SACEUR), who activated his headquarters (SHAPE) early in 1951 near Paris. Subsequent NATO decisions, in particular those at the Lisbon Council session in February, 1952, have transformed the original alliance (with emphasis on a promise of assistance in case of aggression) into a military organization relying on forces in being.

the United States has stationed nearly one-half of its active military forces in foreign territory.[2] Indeed, the over-all size of the American military establishment has been determined—aside from financial considerations—largely by the requirements of fulfilling commitments which involve the stationing of American forces abroad.[3] These commitments include collective-defense agreements with forty-three countries,[4] implemented by the stationing of American forces in thirty-five;[5] and further, the training and equipping of local military forces in those countries and elsewhere, which requires the presence of American military personnel in a total of more than seventy countries and territories.[6] The total number of personnel stationed on foreign soil since the reduction following the Korean armistice has been approximately one and one-quarter million,[7] accommodated on "at least 150 air

[2] Secretary Brucker in *Hearings on Sundry Legislation Affecting the Naval and Military Establishments:* [*No. 56*], *Full Committee Hearings on H. R. 8704,* House Committee on Armed Services, 85th Cong., 1st Sess., July 24-August 1, 1957, pp. 3427-3603 (hereafter: *H. R. 8704 Hearings*), p. 3496.

[3] Military spokesmen have testified that in order to maintain an efficient rotation system, "you have to have at least the same number of units at home as you have overseas, or preferably a surplus" (*Study of Airpower: Hearings before the Subcommittee on the Air Force of the Committee on Armed Services,* United States Senate, 84th Cong., 2nd Sess., April 16-July 19, 1956 [hereafter: *Airpower Hearings*], Vol. I, Pt. XVII, p. 1283).

[4] That is, fourteen NATO, twenty Rio Treaty, two ANZUS, three Manila Treaty, and two CENTO countries (duplications excluded) and bilateral agreements with the Philippines, Japan, Korea, and Taiwan. Cf. map, *New York Times,* August 3, 1958, p. E5, and *infra,* Appendix I.

[5] Townsend Hoopes (consultant to the White House on overseas bases, former assistant to the Secretary of Defense), "Overseas Bases in American Strategy," *Foreign Affairs,* XXXVII, No. 1 (October, 1958), 69.

[6] "We are training 200 foreign divisions . . . in 72 countries" (Brucker, *loc. cit.*).

[7] Based on Census Bureau estimates. More specific breakdown of figures at any given time is usually available only for ground forces. Thus, during the fiscal year 1959, the Army stationed "in overseas areas" (out of its total of fourteen divisions and some additional specialized units) eight divisions, seven "battle groups and regiments," and "several" missile commands, including a five-division force in Central Europe, a medium missile command in Italy, two divisions in Korea, "overseas support forces" in Okinawa and Japan, and a "battle group" in the Caribbean (General Taylor in *Department of Defense Appropriations for 1959: Overall Policy Statements,* Hearings, Subcommittee of the Committee on Appropriations, House of Representatives, 85th Cong., 2nd Sess. [1958], p. 252). Out of the total of three Marine divisions, one (and a Marine aircraft wing) was assigned to the Seventh Fleet in the Far East, and a "landing team" of an air-ground Marine force was

and naval bases" in addition to "hundreds of ground installations." [8] The cost of operating overseas bases, including military
pay spent by American personnel abroad, adds some three billion
dollars to the annual dollar outflow of the United States.[9] Another
index of widespread deployment is the existence, in Europe alone,
of 2,918 branches of the Army and Air Force Exchange Service
—now one of the six largest retail chains in the world.[10] Hundreds
of thousands of dependents and civilian personnel [11] accompany
the armed forces, sometimes building their own cities, complete
with schools and industries, giving to the system an unprecedented
air of permanence.

Indeed, while the original deployment of forces and the

afloat with the Sixth Fleet in the Mediterranean (General Pate, *ibid.*, p. 453).
Air Force tactical forces were divided into units stationed permanently abroad,
others "rotating to NATO countries," and still others "earmarked for immediate deployment to NATO if required" (and, presumably, others not committed in either
of the three ways), but no breakdown of figures was made public (General White,
*ibid.*, p. 122). Earlier, an Air Force spokesman had testified that "as it stands today
[1956], there are more units and more aircraft overseas than at home"—a condition expected to be reversed by the introduction of faster deployment methods and
longer-range planes (General Weyland, *Airpower Hearings,* I, Pt. VII, p. 511).
In the cases of the strategic air forces (on a rotation system between the "Zone of
Interior" and overseas) and the Navy ("afloat" rather than "abroad," even when
operating in overseas waters), it is becoming increasingly meaningless to distinguish
between "at home" and "abroad," and reliable figures are not available.

[8] Hanson W. Baldwin, "Overseas Bases Keys to All U.S. Strategy," *New York
Times,* February 17, 1957, p. E5. The distinction between *base* and *installation* is obscure. Earlier figures released by the Department of Defense indicated the existence of 950 "overseas military installations" (*Facts on File,* 1955, 61F-63). Later,
Baldwin found 70 SAC bases "in the United States and abroad," plus 160 NATO
airfields and 250 national airfields available for use in Europe alone (*New York
Times,* February 4, 1958, part of a series of articles reprinted in *Congressional
Record,* CIV [1958], 3160-70). The Air Force construction program, as of 1956,
envisaged the building of 3100 Air Force "installations," of which "360 are classed
as active principal bases, 204 of those in the continental United States and 156
overseas" (*Airpower Hearings,* I, Pt. V, 371). But in 1960, *Time* finds only that
"U.S. planes and ships operate out of 80 U.S. bases in 25 lands and territories";
these bases are supplemented, however, with the "stand-by use of 170 other air
and sea bases" under the terms of NATO and other alliances (July 4, 1960, p. 10).

[9] *New York Times,* October 25, 1959, p. 1.

[10] *Time,* August 15, 1960, pp. 65-66.

[11] During the fiscal year 1959, the Army employed 132,000 "direct-hire civilians"
overseas, the Air Force 63,000, and the Navy 20,000—in addition to large numbers
of "contract-hire indigenous civilians" (Hearings, *supra,* n. 7, pp. 273, 164, 512,
115).

build-up of overseas bases in the early 1950's appeared essentially to be a stop-gap measure, dictated by the military vacuum facing Soviet and Chinese divisions on the perimeter of the Communist bloc, the continued stationing of large American forces overseas increasingly assumes a significance beyond a temporary and strictly military necessity. For, in terms of strictly military consequences, technological development and shifts in the basic American defense posture occurring during the last decade should have affected the overseas component of the American defense establishment much more than they have. Thus, neither the "New Look" policy of 1954 [12] nor the reductions in over-all American military strength, necessitated by increased emphasis on budgetary ceilings during the second term of the Eisenhower administration, have led to significant changes in overseas deployment. Though there was some thinning out of American divisions assigned to Europe, this was presumably offset by increased mobility and new armaments; and the Berlin crisis of 1961-62, aside from effecting an increase in total U.S. military strength by two divisions, resulted in dispatch of an additional 40,000 men. In short, in spite of occasional variations in personnel strength, the number of units deployed overseas has remained essentially at the level determined at the beginning of the last decade.[13] As to the Air Force overseas installations, if some of them recently appeared to be overbuilt, it was only because new airplanes have made faster deployment from the United States possible, and because a new rotation system, of

[12] Proclaimed by Secretary of State Dulles in his famous "Bigger Bang for a Buck" address, when he said: "But before military planning could be changed, the President and his advisers, as represented by the National Security Council, had to take some basic policy decisions. This has been done. The basic decision was to depend primarily upon a great capacity to retaliate, instantly, by means and places of our choosing. . . . As a result, it is now possible to get, and share, more basic security at less cost" (Department of State, *Bulletin,* Vol. XXX, No. 761 [January 25, 1954]).

[13] See the statement of Secretary of Defense Marshall in *Assignment of Ground Forces of the United States to Duty in the European Area,* Hearings, Senate Committees on Foreign Relations and Armed Services, 82nd Cong., 1st Sess., February 1-28, 1951, pp. 40-41, and S. Res. 99 in S. Rept. 175, 82nd Cong., March 14, 1951, pp. 2-3.

smaller units that remain for shorter periods, has reduced the number of personnel and dependents expected to remain overseas under the original plan of rotating entire wings.[14] Partial abandonment of Moroccan bases came only after the completion of the Spanish bases and the expansion of NATO "infrastructure." [15] The Navy can now supply its Sixth Fleet directly from the United States,[16] but the ships, while in the Mediterranean, can rely on allied bases there; moreover, the shift from "soft" missile bases ashore to submarine and surface-craft-based mobile deterrent forces results in additional navy units' operating in overseas areas. Hence, the development of new weapons, significant because of both the newly acquired Soviet capability to destroy the bases and the growing American capability to operate from bases in the United States, has affected only the reasons forwarded in favor of overseas deployment: the reason given at first was the limited combat radius of American bombers; then, the need for dispersal; then, the necessity to offset the Soviet long-range-missile advantage by effective placement of shorter-range American missiles; furthermore, it was necessary to cement alliances both by guaranteeing automatic United States fulfillment of its obligation in case of limited aggression overseas and by strengthening, in the host countries, local determination to resist subversion. Various combinations of these and similar reasons have been constructed by amateur and professional strategists, and it is unnecessary to pursue them here. It is interesting to note, however, that whenever the system of overseas bases is persuasively challenged on technological grounds, its supporters can effectively employ a political argument in its favor; and that although the theories change, the overseas bases and forces remain.

More exactly, what seems to have become a permanent institu-

---

[14] *New York Times,* January 5, 1959, pp. 1, 5.

[15] *Idem,* March 7, 1960, pp. 1, 4. "Infrastructure" is the NATO term for fixed installations, including airfields, telecommunication networks, and fuel pipelines, financed in common according to cost-sharing formulas negotiated in the North Atlantic Council.

[16] *Time,* July 4, 1960, p. 10.

tion—and an unprecedented one—is the stationing of *forces* in the territory of other states in peacetime. Overseas *bases* have been acquired before, by all colonial powers and by the United States, but on terms now outdated. Strictly American bases, even the newly acquired ones, are even now declining in number; only bases belonging to the local states but available for joint use have been increasing. Under the old system, a world power acquired a piece of territory in a strategic area essentially by use of force, though this was often done in the form of a symbolic lease or a similar legal formula other than outright cession. It then built its Gibraltar or Singapore (or Guantanamo or Panama Canal) while occupying the territory and administering it as its own; and it was not concerned with the security of the state from which the base was acquired. Under the new system, the leases, if that form is still retained, are real: there is a *quid pro quo,* and there is no cession of sovereignty. More often, however, forces are not restricted to any particular garrison area. They are in the country at large and they use its military and other facilities as a consequence of their collective-defense function. In such cases, the forces do not own the bases (not even as a real-estate owner, much less in the sense of sovereign rights), though they may build them and use them in the common defense effort. In essence, their status is the same anywhere in the territory of the host state; often it is similar to the status of domestic military forces. Conversely, the host state's sovereignty remains formally in effect inside and outside the military installations. Unless entire countries are considered as American bases, there are no *American* areas; there are, however, *military* areas, some used by domestic, others by American, forces, and still others collectively, perhaps by forces of other foreign nations as well.

Similar situations have occurred before, but only temporarily, in the course of wars fought by alliances, when forces of several nations have operated in the same territory, sometimes under joint supreme command. As a permanent, peacetime arrangement, this system is truly unprecedented. One need not search far in the history of international relations to find the point where permission for permanent stationing of huge foreign forces in the territory of any of a score of countries now under this type of arrangement would have been as inconceivable as would the willingness of the United States to maintain its forces there. Indeed, as late as 1951, opposition leaders in the Senate were horrified at the prospect of sending more troops to Europe as part of an "international army" under NATO command;[17] and there were members of Congress who even refused to admit any knowledge of the fact that American forces, other than occupation troops, already had been stationed abroad.[18] In 1960, at least two presidential aspirants were prepared to propose the inclusion in their party's platform of a plank that would urge not only expanding the process of military integration but working toward a transformation of the Atlantic alliance into a confederation.[19] Though the proposal was not adopted, the fact that it was made seems to indicate that Americans have, however late, learned to live with their peacetime military involvement overseas and are, however reluctantly, getting ready for further steps in recognition of current realities.

Thus, we start from a situation involving huge American forces overseas, not stationed in American or American-occupied territory or taking part in a war or postwar clean-up expedition, but stationed in foreign countries at large, where they perform the normal peacetime functions of a domestic military force. And we find increasing public acceptance of the arrangement as a normal factor in life, presumably to remain indefinitely. There is no need to rehash here the elementary lessons of bipolarity in the world balance of power, which can be inferred from this situation as from any number of others; nor need we expound the belated

[17] Hearings, *supra,* n. 13, pp. 603-18.
[18] *Ibid.,* p. 297.
[19] See report from the Chicago convention by James Reston, New York Times News Service, July 24, 1960.

realization by the United States of its now inescapable role as a "superpower." Instead, this book, on its most general plane, is an attempt to explore the relation of the current pattern of peacetime stationing of military forces in foreign territory to the traditional Western state system and its foundation, the institution known as the sovereign territorial state.

The institution of the sovereign territorial state has for some three hundred years claimed ultimate authority in controlling the activities and aspirations of people within, and in excluding such control from without, its borders. On the whole, the claim has been effective and, indeed, has been accepted as the operating basis of both international politics and international law (and, for that matter, as the orienting concept in the study of international relations) simply because it corresponded to the realities of the era. "There has been no period since Westphalia," we are instructed, "when any other grouping—church, ideological party, international organization, or business firm—could have effectively competed in power with the greatest states." [20] Though individual states have grown and declined in competition among themselves, the institution has remained unchallengeable, expanding from its European place of origin and being duplicated until it has covered the entire inhabitable world. In return, the sovereign territorial state has promised order and prosperity within its territory, and peace and security from without—though it has also acted in ways that "transformed the doctrine of sovereignty from a principle of internal order . . . into one of international anarchy." [21] But there was method in the anarchy—that is, there was as much order as could be had under any *possible* system.

In particular, no single state was ever permitted to conquer all others, for all have at least shared an interest in the survival of the institution as such, and hence, also, of various subsidiary systems

[20] Quincy Wright, *The Study of International Relations* (New York: Appleton-Century-Crofts, 1955), p. 137.

[21] J. L. Brierly, *The Law of Nations: An Introduction to the International Law of Peace* (5th ed.; Oxford: Clarendon, 1955), p. 46.

supporting it. As long as the system of international law, for example, was in its positive content composed mainly of norms which defined the jurisdiction of states, elaborating the general principle of territorial sovereignty, it is not difficult to discover why, contrary to some popular misconceptions, "during the four hundred years of its existence, international law has in most circumstances been scrupulously observed." [22] The Western state system was, of course, not legislated into the world by international law in general or by any particular treaty. The Peace of Westphalia added formal recognition to a gradual development, in the course of which the medieval centers of power—the feudal lord, the emperor, the pope, and the free bourg—had lost out to the monarch of the emerging territorial state. This came about because the units these centers represented had lost viability in several ways but, in the final round, in the field of security. As John Herz has recently pointed out,[23] city walls and feudal manors could offer no protection against new war technology, that is, professional armies equipped with artillery and capable of holding the surrounding territory. But the king had a domain large enough to secure it by placing soldiers and fortifications on its periphery and thus, in contrast to the chaos of the latter Middle Ages, to guarantee relative security from invasions and relative order and prosperity within his territory. Before the king could prove his point and obtain monopoly of the legitimate use of force throughout the new basic unit, it took a protracted period and a variety of steps—the significance of which was not at once obvious. But being able to deliver, he eventually effected a general adjustment in his legal status: he gained the right to reject interference from above, becoming independent from "world government" (the emperor and the pope), and the right to repel penetration of his territory by other states—unconditionally, without the restric-

[22] Hans J. Morgenthau, *Politics Among Nations: The Struggle for Power and Peace* (2d ed.; New York: Knopf, 1954), p. 251.

[23] See his *International Politics in the Atomic Age* (New York: Columbia University Press, 1959), chaps. ii-iv.

tion of the "just war" doctrine. Thus, sovereignty appeared in the end to be exclusive and absolute, just as territoriality and sovereignty appeared to be synonymous.

All this is elementary enough and would not need recalling if the present situation were not so conducive to drawing a parallel to that earlier transitional period in the course of which the sovereign territorial state was born. Threatened by a variety of socioeconomic, ideological, and technological factors that are not easily contained by territorial boundaries, the state is presently faced with tasks which seem to transcend its capacity. Again the ability of the basic units of power (and of the world system within which they operate) to perform their fundamental functions, particularly in the field of security, appears increasingly doubtful. That this condition has been in the making for some time already, is reflected in the founding of the League of Nations and the United Nations—the two attempts to substitute something more secure for the Western state system with its ever more devastating wars. But the original conception of these attempts, based on the hope to change the system by a redefinition of the privileges of the basic units, was obviously misdirected. For, not unlike the Holy Roman Empire after its heyday, the state too has retained enough vitality to refuse to yield to such frontal attacks on its established prerogatives, despite evidence that these prerogatives have lost most of their former rationale. Consequently, the original hopes soon had to be scaled down; and the resulting compromise, an attempt to keep states both sovereign and docile, has become an exercise in futility. In the meantime "the power to go 'vertically' *in medias res*" [24] has grown beyond imaginable proportions, making the search for a viable substitute more pressing than ever.

The collective-defense system of the United States and its allies attempts nothing as magnificent as a redefinition of Westphalian concepts. On the face of it and in official pronouncements, the stationing of American troops and the successive steps in integrating

[24] *Ibid.*, p. 22.

forces and co-ordinating decisions remain within the terms of relations between sovereign territorial states. Yet it is self-evident that the new system could have been adopted only upon the realization, by policy-makers in the United States and abroad, that the state has already undergone a profound change in its presumed role as a workable security-unit against attacks from without, and that it has also lost momentum in its task of maintaining domestic order in the face of new techniques of subversion. Additional changes in the nature of the state are being discovered, or introduced, in the process of putting the new system into effect. Moreover, all this applies to the current condition of the state as an institution, that is, the effectiveness of all—the smaller host states *and* the giant partner. If the presence of American forces in allied countries is predicated on the assumption that the latter cannot be defended by their own forces, there must be a second premise, namely, that the security of the United States has, in the minds of American policy-makers, lost much of its former inseparability from the concept of territory of the United States.

What happens to the sovereign territorial state when its chief function is performed by foreign forces or cannot be performed in its own territory? What, in consequence, may take the place of the territorial state in world politics? These are our general questions. The search for clues is limited to two specific levels: first, the conditions under which the right to penetrate foreign territory— station troops, build or use a base—is acquired (Chapter II); second, the status of the American soldier, once he is in a territory over which his own state *recognizes* the supremacy of local authorities but in which it must also *exercise* acts of sovereignty in order to maintain the ability of forces to perform their function (Chapters III–IV). The current status of American soldiers in foreign territory is compared with the status of forces as defined in the past (Chapter V) before some tentative answers to our general questions are proposed (Chapter VI).

# II. Acquisition of Bases and the Right to Station Forces in Foreign Territory

AMERICAN interest in overseas bases received its first significant impetus during the second half of the nineteenth century; it came from two sources: the world-wide expansion of American commercial interests and the advent of the steamship. Although by 1801 American warships were stationed in the Mediterranean,[1] and during the 1840's, in what might be called an international police action, a naval squadron operated from a foreign base,[2]

[1] To protect American commerce against "Barbary pirates" (Julius W. Pratt, *A History of United States Foreign Policy* [Englewood Cliffs: Prentice-Hall, 1955], pp. 108-12).

[2] The United States participated, without much enthusiasm, in the suppression of slave trade, fulfilling its obligation under an agreement with the British government. The naval squadron was stationed at Cape Verde Islands—too far, most of the time, from where it should have been to perform its function effectively (*ibid.*, p. 197).

overseas exploits of that early period necessitated no nearby fixed installations. The sailship, not restricted by a limited cargo of fuel, could store all its needed supplies for many months of operation and could easily replenish these—if worse came to worse—by raiding an unguarded stretch of coast. Not until the appearance of the armored, fully steam-propelled "New Navy" during the eighties did American warships—to use a celebrated simile—in the absence of "resting places . . . where they can coal and repair," really become "like land birds, unable to fly far from their shores." [3] Bases controlling strategic passages have always been important, but the United States was at first not in a position, and most of the time not inclined, to seek them. "Nothing should ever be accepted which would require a navy to defend it," cautioned Jefferson at the beginning of the century,[4] and "such a scheme of empire," echoed Congress in the 1860's, "if indulged in, will destroy our republican system of government," importing "a military character most destructive of its republican attributes," indeed, signaling "manifest doom." [5]

Pre-Mahanian drives to acquire overseas bases, such as Commodore Perry's in the 1850's and Secretary of State Seward's in the 1860's,[6] failed essentially because of domestic opposition, notwithstanding the fact that the experience of the Civil War, intervening between the two drives, had demonstrated the need for them.[7] Even at the turn of the century, when Mahan's thesis be-

---

[3] A. T. Mahan, *The Influence of Sea Power upon History, 1660-1783* (Boston: Little, Brown, 1890), p. 83. Cf. Duncan S. Ballantine, *U.S. Naval Logistics in the Second World War* (Princeton: Princeton University Press, 1947), p. 10.

[4] Jefferson to Madison, April 27, 1809 (John Bassett Moore, *A Digest of International Law* [Washington: Government Printing Office, 1906] I, 429).

[5] Senators Bayard and Schurz, quoted in Pratt, *op. cit.*, p. 324.

[6] In addition to the feat in Tokyo Bay for which he is better known, Perry negotiated with local authorities of the Ryukyu Islands, securing a supply base in Okinawa, and he took possession of the Bonin Islands, which were later reclaimed by Japan without American protest. Seward successfully negotiated the purchase of the Virgin Islands, a lease of the Samana Bay in Santo Domingo, and protectorates over the entire territories of Santo Domingo and Haiti—all of which was turned down by the Senate.

[7] During the Civil War the United States leased the harbor of St. Nicholas from Haiti (Moore, *op. cit.*, p. 610). The Secretary of the Navy noted the need of

came, for a while at least, all but official policy, Americans preferred to call their bases, inocuously, "coaling stations" and, upon acquiring them, pacified their conscience by refusing to equip them adequately or to fortify them. Though the United States had acquired various islands in the Pacific before giving the coup de grâce to the Spanish empire, Dewey had to sail from Hong Kong to Manila Bay and, had he not annihilated the obsolescent Spanish fleet in the first strike, would have had no base from which to continue his operations.[8] For that matter, as late as 1939, Congress refused to appropriate funds for the development of a base at Guam—in the face of Japanese saber-rattling and secret development of Japanese bases in the mandated islands—because it considered the future achievement of Philippine independence, scheduled for 1946, as a fact relieving the United States from defense responsibilities in the western Pacific.[9]

Characteristically, however, both proponents and opponents of overseas bases thought in terms of annexation of territory. Leases were considered as an alternative to get around refusals of outright

Caribbean and Pacific bases in his Annual Report for 1865 (Pratt, *op. cit.*, p. 321). Haitian offers of a new lease were turned down in 1882 and 1884 because "little hope could be offered that Congress, which must in the ultimate resort be brought to decide the question of such transmarine jurisdiction, would favorably regard such an acquisition as His Excellency proposes" (Freylinghuysen to Langston, June 20, 1882 [Moore, *op. cit.*, p. 432]).

[8] The British closed Hong Kong under their obligations as a neutral. There followed, furthermore, an embarrassingly long waiting period until the arrival of United States forces from across the Pacific to take possession of Manila, during which the German Far Eastern fleet—the strongest one on location—might have grabbed the spoils of American victory, had it not been deterred by the dispatch of British warships to Manila Bay (Thomas A. Bailey, *A Diplomatic History of the American People* [4th ed.; Appleton-Century-Crofts, 1950], pp. 514-15).

[9] See H.R. 4278, 76th Cong., 1st Sess., and *Congressional Record*, LXXXIV (1939), Pt. 2, 1704-22, 1744-82, 1832-44.

The Guam project was first proposed in 1933 because of the weakness of the Philippine position—then subject to the limitations of the Washington Treaty. It became the chief recommendation of the Hepburn Board (Statutory Board on Submarine, Destroyer, Mine, and Naval Air Bases, appointed in June 1938 to report on the need of new naval bases and headed by Rear Admiral Andrew J. Hepburn), other proposals of which, on bases in continental United States and its nearer periphery, were treated more generously. See Buel W. Patch, "American Naval and Air Bases," *Editorial Research Reports*, 1939-I, 109, 121-22; Mark S. Watson, *Chief of Staff: Prewar Plans and Preparations* (*U.S. Army in World War II* [Washington: Department of the Army, 1950]), pp. 453-54, 415-17.

cession or to overcome domestic opposition in the United States, but such schemes were often unsuccessful. The opposition soon learned to refuse to ascribe much significance to the distinction between lease and possession.[10] Nevertheless, there were two pre-Mahanian leases of bases in the Pacific, granted without time limitation, and thus presumably qualifying as servitudes of international law.[11] Both have lost their international character by subsequent annexations. By a treaty concluded on January 16, 1878 with the government of Samoa, the United States acquired "the privilege of entering and using the port of Pagopago, and establishing therein and on the shores thereof a station for coal and other naval supplies"; and the Samoan government renounced "any jurisdiction within said port adverse to such rights of the United States or restrictive thereof." [12] Soon plans were made for the jurisdiction of the United States consul in the Samoan capital to "be increased in extent and importance so as to guard American interests in the surrounding and outlying islands of Oceanica." [13] Samoa granted similar rights to Germany and Great Britain, with the result that "the natives, unaccustomed to a centralized government, were restive under the exercise of authority, and their discontent was ministered to and aggravated by the intrigues and rivalries of foreign interests. This condition of things gave rise from time to time to grave disturbances, and not infrequently to open hostilities, between native factions." In the end, the three lessee powers settled the matter among themselves. The treaty of December 2, 1899 divided the islands into three parts, giving

[10] This was first true of the Senate, when rejecting Seward's and Grant's leases along with their purchases. As the United States grew in power and began to assume the role of a policeman in the Caribbean, the people of the island states and European powers with possessions there, formerly willing to be annexed or to sell out, began to be annoyed at the very sight of American warships and rumors of leases. See correspondence in Moore, *op. cit.*, pp. 432, 580-611 *passim.* Moore himself included the material on leases, together with that on purchases, under the subtitle "Proposals of Annexation."

[11] Helen Dwight Reid, *International Servitudes in Law and Practice* (Chicago: University of Chicago Press, 1932), p. 194.

[12] Moore, *op. cit.,* p. 538.

[13] President Hayes's fourth annual message, 1880.

Tutuila, containing the harbor of Pagopago, and the adjacent islands, to the United States.[14]

Under a convention concluded on December 6, 1884, to extend an earlier "commercial reciprocity treaty" for seven years, the King of Hawaii granted to the United States "the exclusive right to enter the harbor of Pearl River in the island of Oahu, and to establish and maintain there a coaling station and repair station for the use of vessels of the United States." [15] This arrangement was of even shorter life than the Samoan. Although the Secretary of State assured the British that the Pearl Harbor concession "contained nothing to impair the political sovereignty of Hawaii," he rejected their proposal for a four-power guarantee of neutrality and equal *accessibility* of the islands to all nations. The existing treaty, he replied, created "special and important reciprocities," including the fact that "by one of the articles the *cession* of any part of the Hawaiian territory to any other government without the consent of the United States is inhibited." Hence, while the Hawaiians may never have been as confused as the Samoans, when a revolution did take place in Honolulu in 1893, President Harrison could report: "Only two courses are now open: one, the establishment of a protectorate by the United States, and the other, annexation full and complete. I think the latter course . . . is the only one that will adequately secure the interests of the United States." Formal annexation was delayed when Cleveland withdrew Harrison's annexation treaty from the Senate, but from the time the United States had established the exclusive right to a base, there had been little doubt—at least in the analysis of the foreign ministries of the great powers—that the assurances of unimpaired Hawaiian sovereignty were only nominal.[16]

By contrast, the two leases made at the beginning of the twentieth century, which are still in effect, have lost much of their sig-

[14] Moore, *op. cit.*, pp. 539-53.
[15] The treaty was not ratified by the United States, for reasons here irrelevant, until 1889; in the meantime, the Senate inserted as Article II the provisions quoted.
[16] See Moore, *op. cit.*, pp. 494-97. (Emphasis added.)

nificance as bases for intervention in, and never had any as a scheme of future annexation of, the territory of the granting states in its entirety; but they constituted clear transfers of territorial rights as far as the defined base areas are concerned. Cuba leased to the United States "for the time required" certain areas at Guantanamo and Bahia Blanca for naval and coaling stations, including the right to use and occupy adjacent waters and "to do all things necessary to fit the premises for use as coaling or naval stations," with the following provision:

> While on the one hand the United States recognizes the *continuance of ultimate sovereignty of the Republic of Cuba* over the above described areas of land and water, on the other hand the Republic of Cuba consents that during the period of the occupation by the United States of said areas under the terms of this agreement *the United States shall exercise complete jurisdiction and control* over and within said areas.[17]

Similarly, in Panama, the United States obtained "in perpetuity the use, occupation and control" of the Canal Zone, against the payment of a lump sum plus annual rental. The United States received

> all the rights, power and authority within the zone . . . *which the United States would possess and exercise if it were the sovereign* of the territory within which said lands and waters are located to the entire exclusion of the exercise by the Republic of Panama of any such sovereign rights, power and authority.

Furthermore, the United States obtained rights outside the zone, the right to buy or lease land for naval stations at both ends of the canal, and "the right at all times and in its discretion, to use its police and its land and naval forces or to establish fortifications"

---

[17] Agreement signed at Havana, February 16, 1903, and Washington, February 23, 1903 (TS 418; Malloy, *Treaties*, I, 358), Articles I-III. (Emphasis added.)

for the protection of the canal, the railways, and other installations, and ships using the canal.[18]

For pre–World War II theorists of international law, a state's acquisition of a lease of rights "corresponding more or less closely to territorial sovereignty," posed a disturbing problem of classification and reconciliation with the neat theoretical scheme of territorial exclusiveness.[19] Was the relationship a simple contractual obligation to refrain partially from the exercise of local sovereignty, a transfer of territorial rights, or a disguised cession cancelling the original state sovereignty? Various tests were invented to establish whether such leases create the type of relationship, similar to the Roman-law *ius in rem,* which is necessary to constitute a servitude—ranging from absence of a time limit and validity of the lease against successor states of the lessor, to the obligation of third states to acquiesce in the exercise of rights of the lessee in the leased territory (e.g., of his military jurisdiction against their citizens). One ingenious solution distinguishes between "cession" (of territorial sovereignty over the leased area) and "cession of right to administer" ("Verwaltungszession"), the latter transferring only the *exercise* of state power, because the original sovereignty would

[18] Isthmian Canal Convention, signed at Washington, November 18, 1903 (33 Stat. 2234; Malloy, *Treaties,* II, 1349 [emphasis added]); amended by treaties of March 2, 1936 (53 Stat. 1807; TS 945) and January 25, 1955 (6 UST 2273; TIAS 3297); applying to territory described in detail in boundary conventions of 1904 (Redmond, *Treaties,* III, 2752), 1914 (*ibid.,* p. 2770), 1950 (6 UST 461; TIAS 3180), and in the cited treaty of 1955. The latter increased the "annuity" paid to Panama to $1,930,000 (Article I) and, while abandoning some plots of land no longer needed, added to the unlimited general arrangement a fifteen-year lease of a maneuver area outside the Zone and a ninety-nine-year lease of another piece of land. It also authorized the United States to extend certain privileges, formerly reserved to United States personnel, to "military personnel of friendly third countries present in the Zone under auspices of the United States." See *The Panama Treaty,* Hearings, Committee on Foreign Relations, U.S. Senate, 84th Cong., 1st Sess., July 15-20, 1955, for its other provisions, which are mainly concerned with employment conditions and taxing of civilians.

[19] The quotation is from William W. Bishop, *International Law* (New York: Prentice-Hall, 1953), p. 300, where the problem is dealt with laconically. Typical of the earlier theoretical involvement are Perrinjaquet, "Des annexations déguisées de territoire," *Revue générale de droit international public,* XVI (1909), 316-67, and Rudolf Wahl, *Die Kohlenstation* (Greifswald, 1906). See, further, the Bibliographical Note in this volume.

be automatically reactivated if the administering state were to va-
cate the territory or itself cease to exist.[20] It should be clear, however, that the assurances of "ultimate sovereignty" of the local
state, whether express (as in Cuba) or implied (as in Panama),
have no significance when there is an absolute prohibition of its
exercise and the administering state has the right to exercise *all*
rights of a sovereign—"in perpetuity" or at its pleasure. Even the
normative concept of sovereignty is based on effectiveness, that is,
attaches certain legal consequences to the existence of an actual
supremacy. The apparent exceptions in international law—belligerent occupation and governments in exile—are based, as the
war during which they apply continues, on *temporary* physical
impediments and, because there has been no formal renunciation
of rights, the previous legal situation remains in effect until there
is final clarification that its factual basis has been changed. A sovereignty that both "ought not" to be exercised and "is not" exercised does not exist. In sum, as is the case with our specific
examples, pre-World War II bases "abroad" were, in spite of the
attempts of legal construction to the contrary, not abroad at all;
they were cessions of territory, "annexations déguisées," poorly disguised at that, and indeed the ceding state was lucky if nothing
more than the ceded part of its territory was annexed.

### WARTIME ADDITIONS

This section is not concerned with the many hundreds of installations incidental to military operations in progress,[21] established

---

[20] Alfred von Verdross, *Völkerrecht (Enzyklopädie der Rechts- und Staatswissenschaft,* XXX [Berlin: Springer, 1937]), 130.

[21] The Navy alone established in the course of World War II over 400 "advance
bases" which included 152 drydocks, as compared to 15 naval bases and 27 aviation
bases in World War I (Ballantine, *op. cit.,* pp. 287, 22).

on the basis of unpublished *ad hoc* arrangements and rapidly abandoned after 1945.[22] It is necessary, however, to examine several formal acquisitions of bases that constitute transition between the old type, involving annexation of territory, and the current pattern.

At the outbreak of war in Europe, the United States had, all told, two "major" and two "secondary" naval air bases, and six Air Corps stations overseas.[23] "Overseas" meant, of course, outlying United States possessions or the equivalent—Hawaii, Canal Zone, Alaska, Puerto Rico, and the Virgin Islands. Naval stations in the Philippines and Cuba had no flying facilities, while at Midway, Wake, and Guam the Navy had to use the Pan American Airways airports. About one-quarter of the peacetime Army strength was assigned to outlying bases.[24] The function of the Army, however, was limited to the protection of the facilities of the Navy, which, according to official planning, "provided wholly the nation's first line of defense." [25] In effect, as late as October, 1941, total overseas deployment of the Army Air Force's heavy bombers consisted of twelve airplanes in Hawaii, nine in the

[22] In 1951, when General Eisenhower was opening his new headquarters as Allied commander under NATO auspices, American forces had only fifteen airfields in Europe, "and none of them would take jets" (General Gruenther; see Department of State, *Bulletin*, Vol. XXXII, No. 852 [March 28, 1955]).

[23] See *Report on Need of Additional Naval Bases to Defend the Coast of the United States, Its Territories and Possessions* [Hepburn Board report, *supra*, n. 9], H. Doc. 65, 76th Cong., 1st Sess., and *The Army of the United States*, S. Doc. 91, 76th Cong., 1st Sess., June 7, 1939, p. 88.

[24] Approximately 20,000 in Hawaii, 17,000 in the Canal Zone, 4,000 in the Philippine Islands, and token forces of 400 men in Alaska and 900 in Puerto Rico (*Annual Report of the Secretary of War*, 1939, Appendix B, Table C).

[25] Watson, *op. cit.*, p. 454. According to the official Army Air Forces history, the Air Corps was charged with the more ambitious program of " 'the preparation and execution of air operations' in defense of the United States and our overseas possessions, and with similar responsibility for 'operations outside the United States and its possessions as required by the situation' " but "at none of the overseas locations in 1941 was the local air contingent adequate" for that purpose (U.S. Office of Air Force History, *The Army Air Forces in World War II*, Vol. I, *Plans and Early Operations: January 1939–August 1942* [Chicago: University of Chicago Press, 1948], p. 151).

Philippine Islands, six in Newfoundland, seven in Panama, and one in Alaska.[26]

In the expectation that "Britain can do it again," the Navy remained at first concentrated in the Pacific, where it was restricted to the traditional defense position "east of the 180th meridian" or the "strategic triangle" Panama-Oahu-Alaska.[27] Not before June, 1940, was Congress confronted with the unequivocal revelation that a one-ocean navy may not defend two ocean coasts.[28] As the dismemberment of Poland in September, 1939, was followed by a period of military inactivity, the "phony war" in Europe, we are told, lulled Washington into an atmosphere of unwarranted optimism, a sort of "phony peace." [29] The French army, entrenched behind the Maginot line, was presumably able to take care of any contemplated German attack, while British superiority on the sea guaranteed the ultimate victory of the Allies.

The change came after May 10, 1940, when German armies invaded Belgium, Luxemburg, and the Netherlands, and within five weeks forced the French to appeal for armistice. Germany was soon to be in possession of the European coast from Narvik to Bordeaux, with the possibility of extending south to Dakar and to the Spanish islands off the African coast. Atlantic defenses suddenly became a matter of great urgency. At this point President Roosevelt entered, delivering an elementary lesson in technology and geography. With protection of the Western Hemisphere as his guiding principle, he found that the Atlantic and Pacific oceans themselves had at one time provided adequate barriers against

[26] Status map of the War Plans Division for October 17, 1941, in Maurice Matloff and E. M. Snell, *Strategic Planning for Coalition Warfare, 1941-42 (United States Army in World War II: The War Department* [Washington: Department of the Army, 1953]), Appendix.

[27] Military planners accepted as tolerable the loss of Wake, Guam, and the Philippine Islands. See Watson, *loc. cit.* (n. 9 *supra*), and *ibid.*, p. 105.

[28] S. E. Morrison, *The Battle of the Atlantic (History of United States Naval Operations in World War II*, Vol. I [Boston: Little, Brown, 1947]), p. 27.

[29] William L. Langer and S. Everett Gleason, *The Challenge to Isolation, 1937-1940* (New York: Harper, 1952), p. 343.

sail fleets traveling at five miles per hour and steam-propelled convoys at twenty miles per hour. But "new possibilities of the use of nearer bases from which an attack or attacks on the American continents could be made" became apparent as the airplane stepped up the possible speed of an attacking force to two or three hundred miles an hour:

> From the fiords of Greenland, it is four hours by air to New-foundland; five hours to Nova Scotia, New Brunswick and to the Province of Quebec; and only six hours to New England.
>
> The Azores are only 2,000 miles from ports of our eastern sea-board and if Bermuda fell into hostile hands it would be a matter of less than three hours for modern bombers to reach our shores.
>
> From a base in the outer West Indies, the coast of Florida could be reached in two hundred minutes.
>
> The Islands off the coast of Africa are only 1,500 miles from Brazil. Modern planes can be over Brazil in seven hours.
>
> And Para, Brazil, near the mouth of the Amazon river, is but four flying hours from Caracas, Venezuela; and Venezuela is but two and one-half hours to Cuba and the Canal Zone; and Cuba and the Canal Zone are two and one-quarter hours to Tampico, Mexico; and Tampico is two and one-quarter hours to St. Louis, Kansas City and Omaha.[30]

The President's message was delivered in the context of need of additional equipment "to attack the aggressor on his route before he can establish strong bases within the territory of American vital interests," but it also drew attention to the increased need for outlying American bases to put the new equipment to work. Elaborations of the technological argument pointed out that while the airplane had shortened transatlantic distances, it had shortened the operating radius of warships even more than had the transition from sailboat to steamship. Warships could now operate only with adequate, land-based air support. But bombers and transport

[30] Message to Congress, May 16, 1940 (*The Public Papers and Addresses of Franklin D. Roosevelt*, Vol. 1940 [New York: Macmillan, 1941], pp. 199-200).

planes, with an operating radius longer than that of fighter planes needed for fleet support, could attack distant targets. This was especially true when only one-way flights were contemplated, as they may have been, owing to certain geographical conditions that "usually come as a surprise to North Americans." [31] Since South America, as part of the Western Hemisphere, was to be defended with new equipment, the geographical argument ran, it should be clear that it would be "overseas to us" (isolated by jungle and absence of roads) and, consequently, "the problem of defending South America would be a maritime, not a continental problem." [32] Furthermore, the misconception that "South" America lies directly south of the United States tends to create the illusion that it is closer to American bases than to the centers of military power on the other side of the Atlantic Ocean. Actually, almost all of the South American continent lies east of the eightieth meridian passing through Miami Beach. This places Natal, on the eastern bulge of South America, more than twice as far from the United States as from Dakar in Africa. In sailing distance, Brazilian ports south of Natal are about as close to Brest as to Norfolk, and Buenos Aires is farther from New York than the Ukrainian port Odessa, on the Black Sea. Even the easternmost American base, Vieques-Culebra, Puerto Rico, only planned in 1940, was to be a thousand miles farther from the Brazilian bulge than the West African ports, which were presumably within easy reach of the Germans after the defeat of France.[33]

It was this new estimate of the situation that, in addition to effecting Congressional approval of a two-ocean navy and speeding up the development of Atlantic bases in the outlying possessions of the United States, led to the first bases in truly foreign territory.

[31] Buel W. Patch, "Atlantic Islands and American Defense," *Editorial Research Reports*, 1941-I, 442.

[32] Eugene Staley, "The Myth of the Continents," *Foreign Affairs*, April, 1941, p. 489. Cf. Nicholas Spykman, *America's Strategy in World Politics* (New York: Harcourt, Brace, 1942), pp. 407-8, 434-40.

[33] Patch, *loc. cit.*

The new acquisitions had the dual purpose of extending the operating radius of hemispheric defense forces and pre-empting Axis use of bases belonging to weak Allies and to neutrals. The adoption of such an "expansive defense" scheme before the United States became a belligerent meant, in fact, that the hemisphere had been extended far into the ocean. But the terms of these acquisitions also introduced new forms of stationing of forces abroad, tending to reverse the traditional consequences of continued presence of armed forces of one state in the territory of another. The development in this direction is still in process.

The terms of the first acquisition, the "destroyers-for-bases deal" with the United Kingdom,[34] provided that, in view of the British sympathetic interest in the security of the United States and the latter's desire "to strengthen the ability of the United States to cooperate effectively with other nations of the Americas in the defense of the Western Hemisphere," the British government "will secure the grant . . . freely and without consideration, of the lease for immediate establishment and use of naval and air bases and facilities for entrance thereto and the operation and protection thereof" of certain sites in Newfoundland and Bermuda; further, it will "make available" for the same purposes, "in exchange for naval and military equipment and material," certain sites in the Bahamas, Jamaica, St. Lucia, Trinidad, Antigua, and British Guiana.

All the bases and facilities referred to in the preceding paragraphs will be leased to the United States for a period of ninety-nine years, free from all rent and charges other than such com-

---

[34] Exchange of notes, Washington, September 2, 1940 (54 Stat. 2405; eas 181).

I do not propose to deal with the question of "who thought it first up." Churchill may have been interested more in involving the United States than in destroyers by the time the transaction took place; and the bases may have been unnecessary in view of Petain's refusal to permit German use of African bases and Hitler's actual war plans. Historical literature and materials on the legality of Roosevelt's action are abundant, for some of which see the Bibliographical Note at the end of this volume.

pensation to be mutually agreed on to be paid by the United States in order to compensate the owners of private property for loss by expropriation or damage arising out of the establishment of the bases and facilities in question.

His Majesty's Government, in the leases to be agreed upon, will grant to the United States for the period of the leases all the rights, power, and authority within the bases leased, and within the limits of the territorial waters and air spaces adjacent to or in the vicinity of such bases, necessary to provide access to and defense of such bases, and appropriate provisions for their control.

Without prejudice to the above-mentioned rights of the United States authorities and their jurisdiction within the leased areas, the adjustment and reconciliation between the jurisdiction of the authorities of the United States within these areas and the jurisdiction of the authorities of the territories in which these areas are situated, shall be determined by common agreement.

An elaborate implementing agreement defines the rights granted in general and adds special conditions for each territory. It also determines the scope of authority of the United States to exercise jurisdiction over the members of its own forces and persons attacking the security of the base, granting no exemption to American personnel from local law or local jurisdiction; and it prescribes the forms of lease contracts to be concluded, separately for each site. The use of sites for purposes other than those required by military operation is not permitted, and this applies particularly to the establishment of businesses and professions, exploitation of natural resources, and treasure- and antiquities-hunting: these are reserved to the local government and population, and are to be allowed within the leased area insofar as they do not interfere with military necessities. The territorial governments "will take such steps as may from time to time be agreed to be necessary with a view of enactment of legislation to ensure the adequate security and protection of the United States naval and air bases, establishments, equipment, and other property, and the operations of the United States under the leases . . ." and, to the degree that the United

States does not use any part of a leased area, "the Government of the United Kingdom or the Government of the territory may take such steps therein as shall be agreed with the United States to be desirable . . ." including, if necessary, defense measures.[35] Altogether, this is a lease of specific privileges as distinguished from a cession of territory in the disguise of a nominal lease. Furthermore, since the British undertook to procure a lease in Newfoundland, a separate protocol co-signed by Canada assures the participation of the Canadian and Newfoundland governments in the operation of, and future consultation on, the leased sites, thereby in fact validating the agreement, as far as the Canadian territory is concerned, retroactively.[36]

Two other agreements concluded before the official entry of the United States into war authorized a sort of temporary protectorate of the entire territories involved, rather than acquisitions of specified base sites: the agreement with Iceland and the agreement with Henrik de Kauffmann, Danish Minister in Washington, regarding Greenland. In Iceland, which has no military forces of its own, the United States relieved the British force "required elsewhere"; in Greenland, which nobody was eager to occupy, the United States finally had to make the move, chiefly under Canadian pressure, to prevent its occupation by belligerents and the creation of undesirable precedents in the Hemisphere.[37] American forces are still stationed in both places but under new agreements that have changed the character of their presence.

The original agreement with Iceland (whose Parliament had a

---

[35] Agreement signed at London, March 27, 1941 (55 Stat. 1560; EAS 235). This agreement (but apparently not the original lease, *supra,* n. 34) is now in part superseded, as regards the bases in the territories of the new Federation of the West Indies, by the agreement concluded in Port of Spain, February 10, 1961 (TIAS 4734), which is to be valid until 1977 with opportunities for review in 1968 and 1973.

[36] London, March 27, 1941 (55 Stat. 1599; EAS 235).

[37] Occupation by the British or Canadians, that is, who threatened to do it, unless the United States made up its mind to do it itself (Langer and Gleason, *op. cit.,* pp. 429-31; *idem, The Undeclared War,* 1940-41 [New York: Harper, 1953], pp. 428-32).

year earlier suspended the prerogatives of the Danish Crown) declared that the government of Iceland had carefully considered all the circumstances, including the desire of the President of the United States "to ensure the safety of the Western Hemisphere" by immediately sending United States troops "to supplement and eventually to replace the British force." This measure was "admitted" to be in accordance with the interest of Iceland, whose government was "therefore ready to entrust the *protection* of Iceland to the United States." The conditions, including "promises" to recognize Icelandic independence and sovereignty, to withdraw all forces immediately on conclusion of war, and "not to interfere with Government of Iceland neither while their armed forces remain in this country nor afterwards," were accepted. The United States also promised "to undertake the defense of the country without expense to Iceland, . . . to further interests of Iceland in every way in their power including that of supplying the country with sufficient necessities . . ." and to "be strong enough to meet every eventuality and particularly in the beginning . . . to prevent any special danger in connection with change-over." There were no elaborations of the general promises and no provisions regarding the status of forces and specific facilities to be used. The United States merely extended assurances that the inhabitants would suffer minimum disturbance from military activities, "these activities being carried out in consultation with Iceland authorities as far as possible," and, to such ends, "that only picked troops are sent." [38]

In the case of Greenland, the United States and Mr. Kauffmann,

---

[38] Agreement of July 1, 1941 (EAS 232). (Emphasis added.) The matter was first negotiated with the British, and the draft of the Icelandic invitation traveled back and forth until approved by the President, at which point it was decided that the transmission of formal acceptance could be dispensed with. Hence, the original publication (Department of State, *Bulletin*, Vol. V, No. 107 [July 12, 1941]; cf. *American Journal of International Law* [hereafter: *AJIL*], Supplement, XXXV [1941], 194) was simply dated "July 7" (the date of landing of American troops). See *Foreign Relations of the United States* (hereafter: *Foreign Relations*), Vol. 1941-II (Washington: Government Printing Office, 1959), pp. 776-92, for the various steps in adopting the agreement.

who was acting "on behalf of his Majesty the King of Denmark in his capacity as sovereign of Greenland, whose authorities *in Greenland* have concurred herein," [39] agreed, in view of their finding that "the present circumstances for the time being prevent the Government in Denmark from exercising its powers in respect of Greenland," as follows: first, the United States reiterates its recognition and respect for Danish sovereignty but, "recognizing the danger that Greenland may be converted into a point of aggression against the American continent" and having in mind its obligations under the Act of Havana,[40] "accepts the responsibility of assisting Greenland in maintaining its present status"; second, for this purpose the United States shall have the right to "construct, maintain and operate" landing fields and other defense facilities and the right "to lease," for the duration of the agreement (i.e., "until it is agreed that the present dangers to the peace and security of the American continent have passed"), areas of land and water "necessary for the construction, operation and protec-

[39] That is, without authority of the Danish government, which promptly denounced Mr. Kauffmann's action, both openly and in a private message of the King to the President (Perkins, Chargé in Denmark, to Hull, April 26, 1941, *Foreign Relations,* 1941-II, p. 59). The American consul at Gothaab, Greenland, reported on April 9 that one of the two governors of Greenland, "obviously very much agitated," at first drafted a reply "to the effect that he concurred only under protest," but was in the end persuaded to concur "under extreme force of circumstances" instead; and on April 12, that "both Governors were understandably greatly disturbed and resentful over the ultimatum-like manner in which the agreement was presented to them," but that they did not appear to find serious faults with the substance of the agreement (Penfield to Hull, *ibid.,* pp. 44-47).

The agreement was validated in the new agreement concluded pursuant to the NATO defense system (cited *infra,* n. 65), which provides that "upon coming into force of this Agreement, the Agreement Relating to the Defense of Greenland between the two Governments, signed in Washington on April 9, 1941, shall cease to be in force" (Article XII). For a contemporary analysis see Herbert W. Briggs, "The Validity of the Greenland Agreement," *AJIL,* XXXV (1941), 506-13 (Editorial Comment).

[40] Paragraph 14 (I) of the Convention appended to the Final Act of the Second Meeting of Ministers of Foreign Affairs of the American Republics, Havana, July 21-30, provides: "If a non-American State shall directly or indirectly attempt to replace another non-American state in the sovereignty or control which is exercised over any territory located in the Americas, thus threatening the peace of the continent, such territory shall automatically come under the provisions of this convention and shall be submitted to a provisional administrative regime" (*AJIL,* Supplement, XXXV [1941], 30). No such action was ever taken.

tion of the defense facilities specified." The use of such areas, however, "shall not be delayed pending the reaching of an agreement" on the details of leases; instead, their description "shall in each case be *communicated* to the Danish authorities in Greenland." While Denmark retains sovereignty over the defense areas, the United States "shall have exclusive jurisdiction over any such areas in Greenland" and, over its own personnel and dependents, elsewhere as well; but Danish citizens and native Greenlanders will be turned over, and others may be turned over, to local authorities, which will take "adequate measures to insure the prosecution and punishment" of persons turned over to them. The United States agreed further to "respect all legitimate interests in Greenland as well as all laws, regulations, and custom pertaining to the native population and the internal administration of Greenland," and to give "sympathetic consideration to all representations made by the Danish authorities in Greenland with respect to the welfare of the inhabitants . . . ." [41] In sum, the Greenland agreement, while more specific than the Icelandic in its assurances of local rights, constitutes, like the latter, an instance of peaceful occupation. Identical agreements, if the occupying power had a different purpose in mind, would make the two territories permanent protectorates. The breadth of responsibilities of the occupying state is significant, however. Undertaking to promote Icelandic independence at the conclusion of war, holding Greenland "in trust for Denmark," [42] and such commitments as to "provide the necessities" for the population are not features of traditional garrison rights. Nevertheless, while there is a difference in purpose, here in fact whole countries became bases and could have done nothing if they had been used for purposes of which they did not approve.

[41] Agreement Relating to the Defense of Greenland and Exchange of Notes, signed at Washington, April 9, 1941 (EAS 204), Preamble and Articles I-III, X, V-VI, IX. (Emphasis added.)

[42] Roosevelt's message to the King of Denmark, April 19, 1941 (Hull to Perkins, *Foreign Relations*, 1941-II, p. 55).

## CURRENT ARRANGEMENTS

Post–World War II bases were in part acquired through bilateral agreements which, while granting more than purely nominal assurances to the local states, disclose important similarities to the overseas bases of the colonial era. Under other bilateral agreements, however, the authority the host state retains over base areas is sufficient to make a joint effort indispensable for the effective use of bases. There are, further, agreements permitting the disposition of United States forces in the host country at large, as a consequence of a collective-defense agreement. These agreements, in turn, can be either bilateral or multilateral. Finally, combinations of such arrangements can be in effect in the same country, as, for example, when United States troops are in the territory at large, under the terms of an alliance, but use both joint and American facilities.

Among the bilateral agreements that are similar to the old leases, the agreement with Libya is most instructive. The two parties, merely because of a desire to confirm their "determination to cooperate amicably and to support each other mutually in the international field, and to contribute to the maintenance of peace and security within the framework of the Charter of the United Nations" (that is, in fact, without a mutual-defense commitment), agreed that:

(1) The Government of the United Kingdom of Libya grants permission to the Government of the United States *to occupy* and use for military purposes, for the duration of the present Agreement and in accordance with its terms and conditions, those areas which are presently used and occupied . . . .

(2) A particular agreed area shall cease to be considered as such whenever the Government of the United States of America shall notify the Government of the United Kingdom of Libya that it no longer requires such area.[43]

[43] Agreement of September 9, 1954 (5 UST 2449; TIAS 3107), Article I. (Emphasis added.)

What occupancy for military purpose means is made unmistakable
by a further stipulation that "the agreed areas shall be used and
occupied *exclusively* by the Government of the United States"
except that the two governments may agree to joint use, or use by
other nations, "as an element in collective military measures to
maintain or restore international security" (U.N. collective security
system) and that Libya shall examine "expeditiously" requests by
the United States "to permit the use of the agreed areas for training purposes by small groups of military personnel of countries
other than the United States . . ." (Article VI). Within the agreed
areas, the United States government may carry out "construction
and renewal of facilities . . . to improve and adapt such areas for
military purposes and to provide for the *international security* of
such areas" (Article II), and it "may exercise full control over aircraft, ships and water-borne craft, and vehicles entering, leaving
and while within the agreed areas" (Article III). Furthermore, it
may move its own forces, equipment, and supplies not only
"within and between the agreed areas, by land, air, and seas" free
of tolls, pilotage requirements, driving permits, passports, and
customs duties, but "by agreement between the two Governments
. . . shall have freedom of movement in other districts of Libya"
(Articles VIII, XVI, XXI, XXV); and United States public aircraft "may fly over any of the territory of Libya, including territorial waters," except that flying over areas prohibited by the
government of Libya to all foreign aircraft requires an agreement
or an emergency (Article VIII, 3). Finally, the United States may
build wire communications and pipeline facilities; it may construct and maintain necessary roads, bridges, harbors, channels,
entries, and anchorages affording access to the agreed areas (Article
IX); and it may make technical surveys in any part of Libya and
the adjacent waters (Article XIV). Additional land may be rented
directly from private owners, and "if satisfied that there is unreasonable refusal by a private owner, after he has received an offer
of equitable compensation . . . the Government of the United

Kingdom of Libya will take the necessary steps . . ." whereupon the rented lands "shall be regarded as agreed areas for the purpose of this agreement" (Article VII). The United States may also establish its own post offices and other agencies, "including concessions such as sales commissaries, military service exchanges, messes, and social clubs . . . free of all licenses, fees, excise, sales, or other taxes or imports" (Articles XV, XVII). United States personnel and business firms operating as United States contractors are free of Libyan taxation, and within the agreed areas the United States exercises exclusive jurisdiction over its personnel (Articles XXIV, XX).[44] Any individual, however, "whose misconduct renders his presence in Libya undesirable" shall be removed from Libya upon the request of the Libyan government (Article XVI, 5).[45] The agreement remains in effect until the end of 1970, after which date either party may give notice. Thus, what distinguishes this agreement from the old type of lease is its relatively short duration and, of course, the absence of intention of annexation. The latter perhaps can account for the absence of formal assurances of continued local sovereignty and for the lack of insistence on calling the over-all arrangement a lease. Indeed, while there was a payment involved, it was not incorporated in the base agreement.[46] The United States may use the Libyan facilities for whatever purpose it wants, or may turn them back at any time. Needless to say, while Libya cannot remain neutral if the United States is engaged in a war operating from the Libyan bases, the United

[44] Outside the agreed areas there was, originally, a system of concurrent jurisdiction; see however, *infra*, Chapter III, p. 55.

[45] Among the few other limitations upon the United States, an interesting one is that the United States "accepts the principle that military members of the United States forces should wear civilian clothes when in Benghazi and Tripoli in an off-duty status" (Article VII, 5); and that the United States government will not "cut or remove trees in any substantial number . . . without the consent . . . of Libya" (Article II).

[46] An economic-assistance agreement, signed on the same date (5 UST 2435; TIAS 3105), promised: (a) initial assistance for economic development during the United States fiscal year of $7,000,000; (b) up to a total of 24,000 tons of grain for the year; (c) continuation of assistance until 1971 at the rate of $4,000,000 annually for 1955 through 1960, and $1,000,000 annually thereafter.

States may well disinterest itself in the security of Libya per se if it so chooses.[47]

Other bilateral agreements similar to old leases are those concluded with the Philippines,[48] Saudi Arabia[49] and Ethiopia.[50] The Saudi Arabian agreement, renewed at five-year intervals, is the least generous. The stipulation that the Saudi government will only "honor competent United States Government travel orders on condition that such persons are not undesirable" (Article 14), "undesirable" meaning of Jewish religion, is a source of considerable irritation. Another peculiarity of the Saudi agreement is that the facilities installed there immediately become the property of the Saudi government and are then placed, rent-free, at the disposition of the United States. In other countries fixed installations normally become the property of the local state upon the expiration of the agreement. The Philippine agreement is for ninety-nine years and grants extensive privileges, including jurisdiction over local citizens within the base sites. Subsequently, the Philippine Republic has joined the collective-defense system,[51] and there is now reciprocity of defense commitments, if not reciprocity of other rights.

By contrast, the first post-war defense agreement with Japan[52]

---

[47] In a military-assistance agreement concluded in 1957 (8 UST 957; TIAS 3857), Libya undertook to "furnish to the Government of the United States, or such other governments as the Parties thereto may in each case agree upon, such equipment, materials, services, or other assistance as may be agreed upon in order to increase *their* capacity for self defense . . . (Article VI, 2, a; emphasis added) and also agreed "to cooperate with the Government of the United States in taking measures designed to control trade with nations which threaten the maintenance of world peace" (Article VII), thereby accepting the standard Mutual Security Act conditions without the benefit of a mutual-defense commitment on the part of the United States. (Note the distinction, in the State Department's labeling of agreements, between "military-assistance" agreements pure and simple and "mutual-defense-assistance" agreements, some of which are cited below.)

[48] Agreement signed at Manila, March 14, 1947 (61 Stat. 4019; TIAS 1775). See discussion of jurisdictional provisions *infra*, Chapter III, pp. 58-60.

[49] Jidda, June 18, 1951 (2 UST 1466; TIAS 2290), extended April 2, 1957 (8 UST 403; TIAS 3790).

[50] Washington, May 22, 1953 (5 UST 749; TIAS 2964).

[51] Mutual Defense Treaty, Washington, August 30, 1951 (3 UST 3947; TIAS 2529).

[52] Security Treaty, San Francisco, September 8, 1951 (3 UST 3329; TIAS 2491), Article I.

and the agreements with Korea[53] and China[54] simply provided that the host country "grants and the United States accepts the right to dispose United States land, air, and sea forces in and about" that country, as determined by mutual agreement. In the case of China and Japan the purpose is specified:". . . in and about Taiwan and the Pescadores as may be required for their defense"; and "forces may be utilized to contribute to the maintenance of international peace and security in the Far East and to the security of Japan against armed attack from without," respectively. Japan is the only country of the three where the provision on mutual determination of the disposition of forces was further formalized in an Administrative Agreement. This agreement states that the United States shall have the "rights, power and authority" over land, territorial waters, and air space within, adjacent to, *and* in the vicinity of "facilities *and* areas which are necessary *or* appropriate for their [*sic*] establishment, use, operation, defense, and control," thus changing very little in the right to deploy forces in general.[55] But the agreement also establishes a jurisdictional code on the status of personnel (to be considered later), while in the other two countries the United States forces are fully exempt from local legal processes. Conversely, in the Japanese Security Agreement, but not in the agreements with the two other countries, we find an explicit provision for the use of American forces to extend "assistance given at the express request of the Japanese Government to put down large-scale internal riots and disturbances in Japan, caused through instigation or intervention by an outside power or powers." In short, in spite of some differences in detail, the three agreements, formally incorporating "mutual-defense" commitments,[56] represent strictly unequal alliances; mutuality, here, is at

[53] Mutual Defense Treaty, Washington, October 1, 1953 (5 UST 2368; TIAS 3097), Article IV.
[54] Mutual Defense Treaty, Washington, December 2, 1954 (6 UST 433; TIAS 3178), Article VII.
[55] Tokyo, February 28, 1952 (3 UST 3341; TIAS 2492), Article I. (Emphasis added.)
[56] In the case of China and Korea, each party recognizes that an armed attack on the other "would be dangerous to its own peace and security and declares that it

best a matter of common purpose rather than reciprocity of means. In the case of Japan, however, provisions regarding the status of forces and the new defense treaty concluded in 1960 [57] represent steps in the direction of principles which are in effect in the NATO area.

A third type of bilateral agreement is found in the case of Spain. This country has no official place in the collective-defense system insofar as the latter implies the use of American forces in the defense of foreign territory. There is no express commitment to act or consult "in the event of an armed attack." Yet, Spain and the United States have a "Mutual Defense Assistance Agreement," implemented by a "Defense Agreement," concentrating on the crucial efforts before an attack and, thereby, involving an effective collective-defense commitment without the necessity of expressing it in the form of a treaty of alliance.[58] The crucial provisions are found in Articles I and III of the Defense Agreement. The United States and Spain, considering "that the contingencies with which both countries may be faced indicate the advisability of developing their relations upon a basis of continued friendship, in support of the policy of strengthening the defense of the West," agreed that: (1) the United States shall provide "military and item assistance to Spain during a period of several years," that is, until "the minimum requirements for equipment necessary for the defense of Spanish territory" are satisfied, "to the end that should a moment

---

would act to meet the common danger in accordance with its constitutional processes" (Article 3, Korean agreement; Article 5, Chinese agreement). In the case of Japan, "in the event of hostilities, or immediately threatened hostilities, in the Japan area," the two governments "shall immediately consult together with a view of taking necessary joint measures . . ." (Article 24, Administrative Agreement).

[57] Treaty of Mutual Cooperation and Security and Agreement under Article VI . . . Regarding Facilities and Areas and the Status of United States Armed Forces in Japan, Washington, January 19 (TIAS 4509-10; 11 UST 1632 and 1652).

[58] The usual order is reversed: the Spanish defense agreement implements "the principles agreed upon in the Mutual Defense Assistance Agreement." The latter, however, is not the type of agreement that proclaims broad principles. It is based on a routine formula incorporating various statutory conditions for the extension of military aid, and it is normally *the consequence* of a broader "mutual-defense" agreement, in which the principles and a commitment in the event of aggression are expressed.

requiring wartime utilization . . . arrive, from this moment, the requirements are covered to the extent possible as regards air defense of the territory and the equipment of the naval units," and that Army units be equipped "as far advanced as possible" (Article I, 1 and 3); (2) in consequence of the above, Spain authorizes the United States, subject to terms and conditions to be agreed upon,

> to develop, maintain and utilize for military purposes, *jointly* with the Government of Spain, such areas and facilities in territory under Spanish jurisdiction as may be agreed upon . . . .
>
> . . . . . . . . . .
>
> The areas which, by virtue of the Agreement, are prepared for joint utilization will remain under Spanish flag and command, and Spain will assume the obligation of adopting the necessary measures for the external security. However, the United States may, in all cases, exercise the necessary supervision of United States personnel, facilities, and equipment.
>
> The time and manner of wartime utilization of said areas and facilities will be as mutually agreed upon [Articles I, 2 and III].

Within the agreed areas, the United States may station and house the necessary military and civilian personnel and "provide for their security, discipline and welfare"; and it may "fit agreed areas and facilities for military use" in co-operation with Spain. The government of Spain, however, "shall retain ownership of the ground and of the permanent structures which may be constructed thereon" (Articles II and IV).[59] On the occasion of the conclusion of the American-Spanish agreements, the controlled Spanish press could rightfully boast:

> Not one parcel of Spanish land will escape our sovereignty. Our flag will fly over all bases. The status obtained for the joint bases

---

[59] Defense Agreement, signed at Madrid, September 26, 1953 (4 UST 1895; TIAS 2850 [emphasis added]). The agreement remains in force for ten years, with automatic extension for two periods of five years, unless notice is given at the end of the preceding term.

is an undisputable diplomatic success for Spain. No nation has obtained from the United States recognition as complete as this of sovereignty over the strategic points utilized in common.[60]

More important, however, it is evident that this type of agreement requires a high degree of co-ordination between Spanish and American forces, and that the type of aid extended to Spain under this and the Mutual Defense Assistance agreement[61] prepares for joint military operations in the event of war. The working of security arrangements, for example, was recently demonstrated when a Czechoslovakian airliner attempted to fly near the bases and was directed away by Spanish aircraft; American fighters merely stood by for any eventuality. In fact, American and local defense efforts are already integrated to a higher degree in Spain than in at least a dozen countries (e.g., in South America) that have concluded formal alliance agreements with the United States.

An even higher level of integration is found in countries which are parties to the North Atlantic Treaty. While few of the detailed arrangements for the utilization of bases and disposition of forces in member countries have been published,[62] the texts of several agreements that are available indicate an entirely novel development. The Agreement between the United States of America and the Kingdom of Greece concerning military facilities exemplifies

[60] *ABC* (Madrid), as quoted in *Information* (Paris) February 4, 1954; here translated from the French text in Maurice Flory, "Les bases militaires à l'étranger," *Annuaire français de droit international*, I (1955), 2-30, 26.

[61] Madrid, September 26, 1953 (4 UST 1877; TIAS 2849); involving "operations and expenditures effected in Spain by or on behalf of the Government of the United States for the *common* defense effort . . ." and an obligation on the part of Spain to make "full contribution . . . to the development and maintenance of its own defensive strength *and the defensive strength of the free world*" (Article III, 3,a, and 2,a [emphasis added]).

[62] Generally, there is more secrecy about NATO plans on the disposition of forces and utilization of joint bases than about national plans of member states on deployment of their forces in their own territory. For example, lists of SAC bases in the United States, and information on forces and equipment located on them, are released from time to time; no comparable information is officially available on bases abroad, although it is patently impossible to hide any particular air base, in any country of the Western alliance, from the presumed enemy.

this. The two countries, mindful of their responsibilities under the North Atlantic Treaty "to provide for the security and defense of the North Atlantic Treaty *Area,* and under Article 3 thereof to develop their *collective* capacity to resist armed attack . . . ," agree that:

1. The Government of Greece hereby authorizes the Government of the United States of America, subject to the terms and conditions set forth in this Agreement and to technical arrangements between appropriate authorities of the two Governments, to utilize such roads, railways and areas, and to construct, develop, use and operate such military and supporting facilities in Greece as appropriate authorities of the two Governments shall from time to time agree to be necessary *for the implementation of, or in furtherance of approved NATO plans.* The construction, development, use and operation of such facilities shall be consistent with recommendations, standards and directives from the North Atlantic Treaty Organization (NATO) where applicable.

2. For the purpose of this Agreement and in accordance with technical arrangements to be agreed between the appropriate authorities of the Governments, the Government of the United States of America may bring in, station and house *in Greece* United States personnel. United States Armed Forces and equipment under their control may enter, exit, circulate within and overfly Greece and its territorial waters subject to any technical arrangements that may be agreed upon by the appropriate authorities of the two Governments. These operations shall be free from all charges, duties and taxes.

3. The priorities, rates of consumption and charges established for the United States Armed Forces for such services as electric power, sewerage, water supply, communication systems, and freight and personnel transportation by rail, will be *no less favorable than those established for the Greek Armed Forces.*[63]

Thus, forces are deployed in Greece rather than in a leased area; their legal status, to be considered later, is identical throughout the Greek territory; whatever they do in Greece is in implementation of NATO *plans*—not merely reconcilable with the North Atlan-

[63] Athens, October 12, 1953 (4 UST 2189; TIAS 2868), Article 1. (Emphasis added.)

tic Treaty; the conditions of their movements in Greece are comparable to those of Greek forces. Indeed, they perform a function identical to that of Greek forces, inasmuch as both carry the collective responsibility to defend the NATO area. While other agreements extend military aid to Greece in order to foster the same collective-defense capacity,[64] no bribe in the form of a transfer of title to the new installations is needed; facilities erected at the United States' expense may be removed from Greece provided that "no such removal or disposition will be undertaken which will prejudice the mission of the NATO." For the facilities not removed, "the United States will be compensated by the Greek government," but, again, "the method for treating the residual value of these facilities will be without prejudice to agreements with the NATO" (Article II, 2 and 3). The period of validity of the agreement is, likewise, identical to that of the North Atlantic Treaty (Article IV).

Two other examples, both in areas where the United States forces had privileges of pre-NATO standing, may illustrate the change. In the case of Greenland, under the new agreement with Denmark, the United States retained in fact many of its former responsibilities, though a part of the military installations was transferred to the Danish government. This created two types of "military areas": in one the responsibility for the operation and maintenance falls on the American forces and the United States retains its jurisdictional and other privileges, including the right to provide for protection and internal security; in the other the same duties fall on the Danish government, which also retains sovereignty over both categories of military areas and the "natural right of the competent Danish authorities to free movement everywhere in Greenland." The areas were established, however, "on

[64] Cf. Agreement Relating to the Loan of Naval Vessels, Athens, July 26–August 5, 1957 (8 UST 1386; TIAS 3887), extending military aid "for the purpose of promoting an integrated defense of the North Atlantic area in accordance with defense plans formulated by the North Atlantic Treaty Organization" (paragraph 2). Previous aid was extended under legislation covering Greece and Turkey (61 Stat. 103), which imposed different requirements.

the basis of NATO defense plans" (Article II) and, indeed, the entire agreement was concluded because the two parties were "requested by the North Atlantic Treaty Organization to negotiate arrangements under which armed forces of the parties to the North Atlantic Treaty Organization may make use of facilities in Greenland and the rest of the North Atlantic Treaty Area" (Preamble).[65] The development in the case of the Azores, involving several stages, is even more illuminative. An American air base in the Azores was originally acquired in 1944 "for the purpose of facilitating the movement of American forces to the theater of war in the Pacific," as an "indirect participation" of Portugal in the operations "conducted eventually to expel the Japanese from Portuguese Timor." [66] In 1946, the installations in the Azores were transferred to the Portuguese government, which authorized, however, for another period of eighteen months, "the passage in transit through Lagens airfield of American and British aircraft serving the forces of occupation in Germany and Japan." [67] In 1948, still before NATO, there was another extension of the grant of transit facilities, this time as a consequence of the "manifest utility to the Government of the United States, given its international responsibilities with which at the moment it is burdened . . ." and because the two governments had in mind "the advantages which those facilities will achieve for the security of Europe . . . as well as the indirect value which the same may bring about for the

---

[65] "Agreement . . . Pursuant to the North Atlantic Treaty, Covering the Defense of Greenland," signed at Copenhagen, April 27, 1951 (2 UST 1485; TIAS 2292). Cf. *supra*, n. 41.

[66] Agreement and Exchange of Notes, November 28, 1944, published in 1952 (2 UST 2124; TIAS 2338). The Portuguese government conceded, for a period to terminate six months after the termination of hostilities, "the utilization without restrictions of the air base at Santa Maria which shall be, in respect of operations, administration, and control, under the command of the American Air Forces." British forces could also use the field, and assurances were extended that the word "control" in the cited clause "in no way suggests any thought on the part of the United States to seek jurisdiction in matters within the sovereign prerogatives of Portugal."

[67] Exchange of Notes, May 30, 1946 (2 UST 2202; TIAS 2345). Lagens airfield was the British wartime base in the Azores; it was returned to Portugal simultaneously with the American base at Santa Maria.

common defense and security." [68] The North Atlantic Treaty was signed the next year,[69] and the Preamble of the Defense Agreement of 1951 between Portugal and the United States reads:

> The Portuguese Government and the Government of the United States of America:
> Having in mind the doctrine and obligations arising from Articles 3 and 5 of the North Atlantic Treaty signed in Washington April 4, 1949;
> Resolved, in accordance with the preamble of that Treaty, to unite their efforts for the common defense and for the preservation of peace and security;
> Considering the necessity of executing in peacetime the measures of military preparation necessary to the common defense, *in conformity with plans approved by the nations signatory to the referred to Treaty:*
> Taking into consideration that *according to the provisions adopted in the North Atlantic Treaty Organization,* the area of the Azores directly interests Portugal and the United States and that between them they must establish agreements for the determination and utilization of the facilities which it is possible for the first of the mentioned Governments to grant in those islands;
> Agree . . . .

The substance of the provisions that follow is a grant of base rights in case of war, with joint preparation of facilities immediately and Portuguese maintenance once they are completed. American transit rights are extended for the period of construction of installations; thereafter, United States aircraft will continue to use them while "carrying out missions within the framework of the North Atlantic Treaty Organization"; in addition, "from time to time, as may be agreed . . . the Lagens base may be utilized for the exercises of combined training of the appropriate forces of NATO." [70]

---

[68] Exchange of Notes, February 2, 1948 (2 UST 2268; TIAS 2351).

[69] Washington, April 4, 1949 (63 Stat. 2242; TIAS 1964), ratified by the United States July 25, 1949, by Portugal August 24, 1949.

[70] Agreement signed at Lisbon, September 6, 1951 (5 UST 2263; TIAS 3087), Preamble and Arts. 1, 4, 6, and 10. (Emphasis added.)

Thus, an entire spectrum of purposes is found in a series of agreements involving the same limited facilities. The rights of the guests were always narrowly defined in comparison to rights granted elsewhere during the same periods. But the declared purposes reveal in each period more than merely routine invocation of high principles. If the last preamble is as sincere as the three preceding ones, the broad principles of the North Atlantic Treaty have been implemented through several progressively more concrete levels. The final arrangements for the utilization of any particular base, while bilateral in form, are merely the consequence of an assignment of certain tasks to the two nations by the Organization; these two nations, then, acted in implementing the collective decision of the signatories of the North Atlantic Treaty to undertake certain military measures in peacetime without waiting for the *casus foederis* (of NATO, Article 5) to occur.

Do the references to NATO plans and provisions in the examples given above represent reality or merely good intentions? In the absence of published agreements on grants or leases of bases in some of the most important countries of the Alliance in which American and other allied forces are deployed, an elementary inference could be that these forces are there by virtue of collective decisions of the NATO directly. It is possible, however, to conceive of the texts of the implementing bilateral agreements just examined as evidence primarily that the decisions made at the Alliance level *require* similar agreements between the states directly concerned in order to become meaningful and effective; and consequently, it could be at the latter—bilateral—level, while the measures to "implement" NATO plans are negotiated, that the substance of these plans is being *determined*. For in spite of the avowed principle, in the countries of our direct concern here, of making international agreements public, mere absence of publication does not prove that such agreements do not exist. We shall return to some of the speculations of scholars and pronouncements of officials on this matter after we examine the problem of the status of forces once they are deployed in foreign territory. Meanwhile, we have found that the right to station forces and establish bases has evolved from a device of colonial expansion or the equivalent, first, to arrangements involving some sharing of purposes and, finally, to arrangements necessitating a considerable degree of co-ordination and joint action. There is, so far, insufficient evidence that such co-ordination, and perhaps the deployment of forces itself, is in actuality a product of multilateral decisions.

# III. Status-of-Forces Agreements

THE CONTINUED STATIONING of large numbers of American personnel in foreign territory has made it necessary for the "sending" government (the United States) and the "receiving" governments to settle their rights and responsibilities in regard to the "visiting" troops and accompanying civilians. The product of this settlement is the status of American forces abroad.[1] A variety of arrangements,

[1] The terms in quotation marks, originating in British World War I legislation, are now widely used in legal literature on the subject of armed forces in foreign territory. While subsequently used unquoted, they should not obscure the permanent nature of the visit and the fact that the receiving country actually cedes some of its rights.

depending on the sensitivity of the receiving country to the traditional requirements of sovereignty, the circumstances of acquisition of the right to station troops, and the degrees of mutual confidence and interdependence, have resulted. In form they range
from bilateral agreements, which have been concluded by the executive and are still partially classified, to a full-fledged multilateral
treaty covering twelve countries, which has provoked a public controversy over the acceptability of its alleged deviations from the
rules of customary international law and traditional United States
practices. In content they recognize the primacy of the territorial
sovereign as a general principle, but they authorize the exercise of
extra-territorial jurisdiction by the sending state in the receiving
state's territory. Further, they exempt the visiting personnel from
territorial legal processes in various degrees, ranging from liberal
grants of exterritoriality to systems of qualified immunities based
on miscellaneous personal, factual, and geographical criteria.[2]

By 1957, the United States had concluded agreements concerning the status of American forces, civilian components, and dependents with some sixty-five countries.[3] These agreements cover
a wide range of subjects, but attention has been mainly concentrated on their criminal-jurisdiction provisions, particularly in the
case of the NATO Status-of-Forces Agreement[4] and the virtually
identical provisions of the agreement with Japan.[5] During the

[2] To avoid a frequent source of confusion, it is perhaps not idle to clarify that
the term "extraterritorial" will be used only as an adjective showing that jurisdiction is exercised by a state outside of its own territory; the exemption of individuals from the jurisdiction of the state in which they are located will be termed
"exterritoriality."

[3] Senate Report 1162, 85th Cong., 1st Sess., p. 2.
  A list of unclassified status-of-forces agreements will be found in Appendix II
*infra*.

[4] Agreement Between the Parties to the North Atlantic Treaty Regarding the
Status of Their Forces, signed at London, June 19, 1951, effective August 23, 1953
(4 UST 1792; TIAS 2846 [hereafter: NATO-SFA]).

[5] Protocol to Amend Article XVII of the Administrative Agreement [3 UST 3341]
under Article II of the Security Treaty between the United States of America and
Japan [3 UST 3329], signed at Tokyo, September 29, 1953, effective October 29, 1953
(4 UST 1846; TIAS 2848 [hereafter: SFA-Japan]). The same provisions are included
in the new Agreement under Article VI . . . (*supra*, Chapter II, n. 57), effective
June 23, 1960.

Senate NATO–SFA ratification hearings, Senator John Bricker, who had introduced a resolution to delete the criminal jurisdiction provisions, accused the State Department of surrendering established United States rights without a *quid pro quo,* misinterpreting customary international law, violating the congressional right to make rules for the regulations of armed forces, depriving American servicemen of their constitutional rights, and establishing a precedent for the benefit of communism.[6] NATO–SFA was eventually approved by the Senate, 75 to 15, on July 15, 1953, with a reservation more moderate than that proposed by Senator Bricker.[7] The Senate, however, is closely watching the application of NATO–SFA and similar agreements,[8] while bills and resolutions to amend or repeal the criminal jurisdiction provisions of these agreements are being introduced in every session of Congress.[9] The ghost of the mythical citizen, drafted and sent abroad to be subjected to inquisitorial proceedings in unfamiliar and inimical surroundings, finally to be abandoned to the company of low-level criminals in substandard foreign jails or, perhaps, to have his hands

---

[6] *Supplementary Hearing on Status of Forces of the North Atlantic Treaty,* Senate Committee on Foreign Relations, 83d Cong., 1st Sess., June 24, 1953 (hereafter: *Senate Supplementary Hearing*), pp. 3-8.

[7] *Congressional Record,* CXCIX (1953), 8724-28; *infra,* nn. 61, 70.

[8] A subcommittee to review annually the operation of criminal-jurisdiction provisions and their influence on the morale and efficiency of troops was appointed on January 28, 1955. See *Hearings to Review Operation of Article VII of the Agreement between the Parties to the North Atlantic Treaty Regarding the Status of Their Forces,* Subcommittee of the Senate Committee on Armed Services, 84th Cong., 1st Sess., March 29–June 21, 1955; *idem,* 84th Cong., 2d Sess., February 9, 1956; 85th Cong., 1st Sess., April 9, 1957; 85th Cong., 2d Sess., July 29, 1958; and 86th Cong., 1st Sess., August 18, 1959 (hereafter: *Operation Hearings* I, II, III, IV, and V). These hearings are still held every year, but after the original controversy had subdued, they have tended to be a mere formality of accepting the report of the Defense Department. See *idem,* 86th Cong., 2d Sess., June 8, 1960; 87th Cong., 1st Sess., July 19, 1961; and 87th Cong., 2d Sess., September 25, 1962.

[9] During 1957 alone, thirteen resolutions providing for revision of the Status of Forces Agreement to eliminate jurisdiction of foreign courts over American servicemen or to withdraw American forces were introduced in the House, and one in the Senate. Numerous other proposals, ranging from bills that would revise the Uniform Code of Military Justice to resolutions that would require an investigation of the executive responsibility for the "surrender" of individual servicemen to foreign jurisdiction, expressed similar sentiments in both houses of Congress (see the Bibliographical Note).

chopped off for petty thievery, took permanent residence on Capitol Hill.[10] He became soon the *cause célèbre* of self-appointed advocates in spite of contrary evidence submitted by the government and private experts. The controversy naturally resulted in the efforts of the majority of analysts being focused on eliminating public misunderstanding of the jurisdictional provisions of NATO–SFA and of their relation to American constitutional and customary international law—a misunderstanding that both facilitated, and was further stimulated by, the isolationist attack on the entire system under which American forces were stationed in foreign territories.[11] Thus, little energy was left to analyze status-of-forces agreements other than NATO–SFA, or to examine the significance of the entire system as a factor in, or an index of, the current development of international relations in general. The discussion in the present chapter, centering on analysis of the key provisions of various types of current status-of-forces agreements, will also pro-

[10] See, e.g., for the maiming references, *Hearings on Status of the North Atlantic Treaty Organization, Armed Forces and Military Headquarters,* Senate Committee on Foreign Relations, 83d Cong., 1st Sess., April 7 and 8, 1953 (hereafter: *SFA Ratification Hearings*), pp. 50-52; *Senate Supplementary Hearing,* p. 7; *House SFA Hearings,* pp. 36, 306, 362-64, and 460.

[11] For sources on the views of pressure groups and administration officials, see the Bibliographical Note. Legal literature on the subject (cited below in the present and the following chapter) supports on balance the jurisdictional arrangements of NATO-SFA type, from the viewpoint of both the constitutional rights of servicemen and the rights of the United States under general international law; but minor changes are suggested by most authors. The same is true of the *Report on Status of Forces Agreements* of the Committee on International Law, Association of the Bar of the City of New York (New York, 1958), and of the reports of several committees of the Section of International and Comparative Law, American Bar Association, in the *Proceedings* of the Section (Chicago: American Bar Center, 1954 through 1958), none of which claims, however, to represent the official position of the A.B.A.

Concerned with the "operational" aspect of the agreements is another type of literature such as the "Report on the Actual Operation of Article VII of the Status of Forces Agreement" (mimeographed; Washington: Georgetown University Law Center, 1957 [hereafter: *Report*]), and *Status of Forces Agreements and Criminal Jurisdiction* (New York: Oceana Publications, 1957 [hereafter: *Status*]), both by Joseph M. Snee, S.J., and A. Kenneth Pye (these reports are based on a field trip during the summer of 1956 that was sponsored by the American Law Institute in co-operation with the Department of Defense). Like most of the theoretical legal studies, the operational studies support the position of the administration.

vide part of the basis for some broader generalizations, of the kind just indicated, which will be attempted later.

## COMPARISON OF JURISDICTIONAL PROVISIONS

It is axiomatic that if an armed force in foreign territory is to fulfill its purpose, its members must be effectively controlled by its own military rules and enforcement processes. The Uniform Code of Military Justice declares accordingly: "This code shall be applicable in all places." [12]

Conversely, it is an established principle of general international law that "a nation possesses and exercises within its own territory an absolute and exclusive jurisdiction." [13] As a standard text spells out, this means both that "all individuals and all property within the territory of a state are under its dominion" and that "a state must not perform acts of sovereignty in the territory of another state." [14]

Thus, any exercise of authority by the visiting force is necessarily a matter of legitimate concern to the receiving state. This is particularly true in the field of criminal jurisdiction, because the processes of arrest, compulsory appearance in court, and imprisonment, when carried out by a visiting force or on order of a court of the sending state, represent the most tangible examples of performance of acts of sovereignty in the territory of another state. To acknowledge simply that the exercise of extraterritorial jurisdiction by the sending state must be traceable to the consent of the territorial sovereign is far from solving the whole problem. In the

---

[12] Act of May 5, 1950, Public Law 506, 81st Cong. (64 Stat. 108), Article 5.

[13] John Bassett Moore in *S. S. Lotus,* PCIJ judgment of Sept. 7, 1927, Ser. A, No. 10, p. 68. Cf. *Schooner Exchange* v. *McFaddon,* 7 Cranch 116, 136 (1812); Moore, *Digest,* II, 4; Hackworth, *Digest,* II, 1.

[14] H. Lauterpacht, *International Law: A Treatise by L. Oppenheim,* Vol. I (8th ed.; London: Longmans, Green, 1955 [hereafter: Lauterpacht, I]), pp. 287 and 295.

first place, international law authorities differ as to whether and on what conditions such consent is implied in the permission to enter the territory of the receiving state.[15] In the second place, the question must be answered as to whether the receiving state's consent (express or implied) to the exercise of extraterritorial jurisdiction in its territory implies, in turn, the exterritoriality of the visiting soldiers.[16] It appears, therefore, that the cardinal purpose of the status-of-forces agreements should be to establish subsidiary principles for the resolution of the unsolved part of the conflict between the necessary exercise of jurisdiction by the sending state and the territorial jurisdiction of the receiving state, the "absolute and exclusive" nature of which appears to be recognized as the fundamental principle.

The agreements, in effect, reflect the propositions just outlined. They presuppose that the exercise of the sending state's jurisdiction requires the consent of the receiving state;[17] they define the scope of immunities from local proceedings granted to the force (which is not a license to the servicemen to disregard local law);[18] and sometimes even the sending and the receiving states' mutual interest in defining the scope of both the exemption and the au-

[15] See Chapter V *infra.*

[16] *Supra,* n. 2.

[17] Thus, expressly, e.g., Agreement between the Republic of the Philippines and the United States of America Concerning Military Bases (cited *supra,* Chapter II, n. 48), Article XIII, Section 1: "The Philippines *consents* that the United States shall have the *right to exercise* jurisdiction over the following offenses . . ." (emphasis added).

[18] Thus, NATO-SFA, Article II: "It is the duty of a force and its civilian component and the members thereof as well as their dependents to respect the law of the receiving State . . . ." Likewise, agreements granting more liberal immunities, e.g., Agreement Relating to the Use of Facilities and Services at Dhahran Airfield (cited *supra,* Chapter II, n. 49), paragraph 13(a): "All United States military personnel, members of the Mission, and all civilian employees of the Mission who are United States nationals or the nationals of other friendly states and their dependents at Dhahran Airfield shall obey all applicable laws and regulations of the Kingdom of Saudi Arabia." The local authority is further confirmed by the retention on the part of the receiving states of the so-called supervisory jurisdiction over various aspects of the exercise of jurisdiction by the sending state (see *infra,* Chapter V, n. 12) and by the fact that even the most liberal grants of immunities exclude certain types of offenses, with the decision to assume jurisdiction essentially a matter of the discretion of the receiving state (cf. *infra,* nn. 29 and 31).

thorization, once the issue of the presence of the force has been decided upon, is spelled out in the terms indicated above.[19]

Going beyond such general presuppositions, one can find that both the scope of the privileges of the visiting forces and the criteria used to define them show countless variations. It is possible, however, to abstract three basic types of arrangements. Type I approaches full exterritoriality, allowing the exercise of the jurisdiction of the receiving state only under exceptional circumstances. Type II distinguishes between the area of the base and the remaining territory of the receiving state; along with other criteria that may possibly be used, the location is fundamental in determining which state shall have jurisdiction in a given matter. Type III recognizes coexistence of the jurisdictions of the sending and the receiving states regardless of geography but introduces other methods to determine which state shall have priority in exercising its concurrent right in various situations.

*Type I* occurs most frequently, inasmuch as it applies to most of the countries in which only advisory personnel or minor units are stationed. In such countries, visiting personnel is often given quasi-diplomatic status by a military-aid agreement or by some other agreement that was not concluded specifically for the purpose of defining the status of an actual military force.[20] The status of forces is similar in countries, such as those of Central America, in which the United States has special privileges of long standing, or in which the theory of exterritoriality of friendly foreign forces is the accepted legal doctrine.[21] Few post–World War II agreements

---

[19] Thus, Understanding between the United States and Libya, signed at Tripoli, February 24, 1955 (7 ust 2051; tias 3607), paragraph (d): "The two governments recognize that it is in their common interest to take steps to ensure the continuation of the good relations . . . and also to ensure the effective discipline and security of the United States forces. To this end, the Government of the United Kingdom of Libya, in response to the desire of the Government of the United States of America, henceforth undertakes to waive its criminal jurisdiction . . . ."

[20] See Appendix III A.

[21] In the latter case, of course, no agreement should be needed. It is doubtful, however, that full immunity would today still apply anywhere without an agree-

fall within this category. In Germany[22] and Japan,[23] exclusive jurisdiction of the sending states carried over from the earlier occupation periods until the two countries acceded to agreements of Type III. Greenland[24] and Korea[25] appear to be the only other two countries in which substantial forces were granted full exterritoriality, although American officials suggest that among the agreements that remain classified are some that are particularly favorable.[26] In Ethiopia, the United States has exclusive jurisdiction

---

ment to that effect. A Panamanian decision, often quoted in support of the theory of automatic immunity of visiting foreign forces (*infra,* Chapter V, n. 58 and the text there), did not prevent Panamanian trials of a considerable number of American servicemen in recent years (*Operation Hearings* V, p. 26). In Brazil the situation is obscured (*idem,* I, p. 39) in spite of a similarly invoked decision of Brazilian courts (*infra,* Chapter V, n. 57).

[22] See Convention on the Rights and Obligations of Foreign Forces and Their Members in the Federal Republic of Germany, Bonn, May 26, 1952 (6 UST 4278; TIAS 3425), as amended by the Protocol on the Termination of the Occupation Regime, Paris, October 23, 1954 (6 UST 4118; TIAS 3425), both effective May 5, 1955, for the transitional period. Article 8(1)(b) of the Convention on Relations Between the Three Powers and the Federal Republic, Bonn, May 26, 1952 (6 UST 4251; TIAS 3425), effective simultaneously, committed the Allies to conclude an agreement "based on" NATO-SFA.
The agreement on the accession of Germany to NATO-SFA has not been published, but Germany and six NATO countries signed an agreement on August 3, 1959, "designed to implement the NATO Status of Forces Agreement on the accession of Germany to it" and containing "an arrangement similar to our bilateral agreement with the Netherlands" (*Operation Hearings* V, p. 4). Under the new formula, Germany has "general right of jurisdiction over all non-military offenses" but has waived its right "in all cases but those involving the death of a person, robbery, and rape" (Associated Press dispatch from Bonn, August 3, 1959).

[23] Article XVII of the Administrative Agreement under Article III of the Security Treaty, Tokyo, February 28, 1952 (3 UST 3341; TIAS 2492), obligated the United States, upon the coming into effect of NATO-SFA, to "conclude with Japan, at the option of Japan, an agreement on criminal jurisdiction similar to the corresponding provisions of that Agreement," which was done in 1953 (*supra,* n. 5).

[24] Agreement cited *supra,* Chapter II, n. 65, Article VIII.

[25] Agreement between the United States of America and the Republic of Korea, Taejon, July 12, 1950 (5 UST 1408; TIAS 3012).

[26] House SFA Hearings, pp. 34-35. In the case of Taiwan, the Agreement Relating to the Presence of United States Forces in China, exchange of notes, Nanking, August 29 and September 3, 1947 (61 Stat. 3755), still listed in the current edition of Treaties in Force, states laconically that "all armed forces of the United States now stationed in China are so stationed with the consent of the Chinese Government." Consecutive reports of the Department of Defense in *Operation Hearings* I-V indicate that no cases of exercise of Chinese jurisdiction over American servicemen have occurred.

over its personnel, but their number is probably insignificant.[27] Somewhat less than full immunity is granted in countries such as Spain, where offenses punishable under the United States Code of Military Justice are exempt from local jurisdiction.[28] Libya waived its primary right to exercise jurisdiction in a supplementary exchange of notes[29] amending the original agreement based on concurrent rights,[30] thereby moving from Type III to Type I. NATO-SFA was similarly, though not as radically, modified for Greece[31] and the Netherlands.[32] Finally, similar broad immunities apply under other types of agreements in the event of war,[33] or the agreements stipulate an immediate renegotiation of the status in the event of war, presumably to grant exclusive jurisdiction to the

[27] Agreement cited *supra*, Chapter II, n. 50, Article XVII.

[28] *Operation Hearings* I, p. 34. The Defense Agreement between the United States of America and Spain (cited *supra*, Chapter II, n. 59) states only that the United States is "authorized . . . to station therein the necessary military and civilian personnel and to provide for their security, discipline and welfare" (Article II) and that "the United States may, in all cases, exercise the necessary supervision of United States personnel, facilities and equipment" (Article III).

[29] *Supra*, n. 19, *in fine*. Note, however, paragraph (c) of the same agreement: "The Government of the United States of America recognizes the interest of the Government of the United Kingdom of Libya in exercising the jurisdiction reserved to it in cases of particular importance to the United Kingdom of Libya." Under (d), *ibid.*, offenses against the safety and sovereignty of Libya or "an offense which the Libyan State considers to be of serious public concern, including sexual offenses which cause serious public concern," are given as examples.

[30] Cited *supra*, Chapter II, n. 43.

[31] Agreement between the United States of America and the Kingdom of Greece Concerning the Status of United States Forces in Greece, Athens, September 7, 1956 (7 UST 2555; TIAS 3649), Article II (1), commits the Greek authorities to waive their primary right under NATO-SFA "upon the request of the United States authorities . . . except when they determine that it is of particular importance that jurisdiction be exercised by the Greek authorities." The United States practice is to request waivers in all cases subject to foreign jurisdiction (*infra*, Chapter IV, nn. 68 and 72).

[32] Agreement, with Annex, Relating to the Stationing of United States Armed Forces in the Netherlands, exchange of notes, The Hague, August 13, 1954 (6 UST 103; TIAS 3174), Annex, paragraph (3), identical to the provision quoted in the preceding note.

[33] Thus, the Agreement Amending Articles IV and VI of the Leased Bases Agreement of March 27, 1941, Washington, July 19, and August 1, 1950 (1 UST 585; TIAS 2105), contains three sets of jurisdictional provisions covering the following situations (in order of increasing jurisdiction of the United States): (a) when a state of war exists in which the United Kingdom is and the United States is not engaged; (b) when a state of war does not exist; (c) when a state of war exists.

sending state.[34] In peacetime, however, recognition of exclusive jurisdiction is becoming exceptional, although nearly complete immunity may still be granted in classified agreements or with reference to situations not involving substantial forces.

*Type II* agreements grant broad privileges to the visiting force within camps, bases, and other defined areas. Outside such areas, concurrent jurisdiction is the general rule, with priority depending on the contracting parties' relative interests in the matter at hand; in some cases, however, the agreement is not specific as to who has the prior right. It is at once evident that this type of agreement allows for considerable variation from country to country in the actual scope of immunities and in the scope of the right of the visiting forces to exercise their own jurisdiction. In the case of *extra-castral* offenses, jurisdiction may turn on the personal status of the offender or on the identity of the person or object that he has offended. Within the area of the base, the rights of the visiting force may, likewise, depend on various personal and substantive criteria, inasmuch as the receiving state may exercise jurisdiction over certain types of offenses committed outside the base area. The criterion of location seldom stands alone. *Inter se* offenses,[35] offenses against the security of the sending or the receiving state, and acts committed while "on duty" or "in the line of duty," [36] constitute the most frequent exceptions to the general rule. Furthermore, the jurisdictional rights of the sending state may apply only to military personnel, or to persons subject to its military law,[37] or to dependents along with military and civilian

[34] See, e.g., NATO-SFA, Article XV(1).

[35] That is, offenses committed by the members of the visiting force against the person or property of other members or against the force.

[36] Strictly speaking, "in-the-line-of-duty" offenses need no conventional immunity (*infra*, text at n. 65). The agreements nevertheless frequently include some special provision for one or the other type of "on-duty" offense.

[37] Military personnel plus civilian employees of the force. Congress added dependents ("persons . . . accompanying the armed forces without the continental limits of the United States . . .") to the category of persons subject to military jurisdiction (UCMJ, Article 2[11]), but the Supreme Court has ruled first that a

personnel, with or without exclusion of persons who are normally residents of the receiving state. In some cases, the agreements permit the visiting authorities to exercise jurisdiction even over local residents and transient civilians who are neither employed by nor accompanying the visiting force. Any combination of the subsidiary criteria is possible and not a few have been used. Thus, the agreement with Saudi Arabia[38] is relatively uncluttered. It provides:

13 (c). Depending on international authority, the Saudi Arabian Government agrees that:

(i) If any member of the armed forces of the United States commits an offense inside Dhahran Airfield he will be subject to United States military jurisdiction.

(ii) In the case of any offense committed by a member of the armed forces of the United States outside Dhahran Airfield at Al Khobar, Dammam, Dhahran, Ras Tanura, the beaches south of Al Khobar to Half Moon Bay, and the roads leading to these places, the Saudi Arabian authorities will arrest the offender and after promptly completing the preliminary investigation will turn such person over to the mission at Dhahran Airfield for trial and punishment under American military jurisdiction.

(iii) Any offense committed by a member of the armed forces of the United States outside the places mentioned in (i) and (ii) will be subject to the local jurisdiction of the Kingdom of Saudi Arabia.

This, in effect, is a grant of exterritoriality to the military personnel within a defined area, and paragraph 13(b) makes clear that no exemption from local jurisdiction applies to non-military

---

dependent cannot be tried by courts-martial for a capital offense committed abroad (*Reid* v. *Covert*, 354 U.S. 1 [1957]) and eventually that courts-martial have no jurisdiction over any civilians in time of peace (*McElroy* v. *U.S. ex rel. Guagliardo*, 361 U.S. 281 [1960]).

[38] Cited *supra*, Chapter II, n. 49.

persons anywhere. There is no reference to on-duty status as a basis of immunity outside the defined area.[39]

By way of contrast, the agreement with the Philippines[40] is much more detailed. Its secondary criteria have failed, however, to make the situation clearer or to satisfy either side. It first authorizes the United States to exercise jurisdiction over:

(a) Any offense committed by any person within any base except where the offender and offended parties are both Philippine citizens (not members of the armed forces of the United States on active duty) or the offense is against the security of the Philippines;

(b) Any offense committed outside the bases by any member of the armed forces of the United States in which the offended party is also a member of the armed forces of the United States; and

(c) Any offense committed outside the bases by any member of the armed forces against the security of the United States.

Second, the agreement assigns to the Philippine jurisdiction all other offenses committed *outside* the bases. It goes on, in Section 3, to allow the exercise of Philippine jurisdiction in all cases, including wartime offenses by military personnel, when "for special reasons the United States may desire not to exercise the jurisdiction reserved to it . . ." and, vice versa, in Section 4, when the Philippines may desire not to exercise their jurisdiction. Finally, the agreement exempts from the Philippine jurisdiction *extracastral* offenses committed by a member of the armed forces of the United States "while engaged in the actual performance of a specific military duty," or when either government declares a period of

[39] A State Department spokesman made clear, however, that "as a practical matter" it is not possible for a member of U.S. Forces to find himself outside of the area in which the United States has exclusive jurisdiction, unless he be absent without leave. Even then, he added, chances are that the Saudis would turn him over to United States authorities (*House SFA Hearings*, pp. 378 and 380).

[40] Cited *supra*, Chapter II, n. 48.

national emergency. The decision as to whether the offense has occurred on duty is left to the Philippine prosecuting attorney, whose decision may be appealed to the Secretary of Justice. Thus, *intra-castral* offenses fall within the United States jurisdiction even when the offender is a United States civilian, or when he is a Philippine citizen—unless he attacks another Philippino or the security of the Philippines is involved;[41] but there is no *extra-castral* immunity for the civilian component of the armed forces and dependents, nor *extra-castral* jurisdiction of the United States over offenses committed by American civilians *inter se* or against the security of the United States, although the *intra-castral* jurisdiction of the Philippine authorities over security offenses extends, by implication, to "any person." The phrase exempting on-duty offenses is rather ambiguous, inasmuch as an offense, although committed during the performance of a specific military duty, may well not be in the line of duty. To leave the determination of this matter to the discretion of an administrative officer of the host country is not the best protection of the rights of the accused and is, further, questionable, considering that according to general international law the responsibility for this type of offense falls on the sending state. The accused is also confronted with the fact that the two states can cede their jurisdictions arbitrarily, since the nature of the "special reasons" that should serve as the basis of such cession is not disclosed. Conversely, to exempt from local jurisdiction *intra-castral* offenses committed against a local national by a visiting serviceman or civilian who is not on duty appears absurd to Philippino spokesmen, particularly where the camp area "includes a town of several thousand inhabitants with an organized government . . ." and where the local "rules and procedures

---

[41] This provision produced the anomalous situation in which the United States was authorized to exercise jurisdiction which it did not have. (See *Operation Hearings* I, p. 37). In 1950, the United States military jurisdiction was expanded to include "all persons within an area leased or otherwise reserved . . ." that is subject to United States jurisdiction by virtue of a treaty or the general international law (UCMJ, Article 2 [12]).

of the courts are patterned after those of the United States and the English language is officially and universally spoken." [42]

Other examples may illustrate the variety of the arrangements based on special status in a defined area. The agreement covering the Azores allows the exercise of exclusive jurisdiction over United States personnel and nationals serving with the United States forces in the case of offenses that occur within the area where they are quartered or in defined areas outside;[43] but in 1958 a Defense Department spokesman indicated that the arrangement in force "permits local courts to exercise jurisdiction over United States personnel when a Portuguese national is the offended party, or when the punishment for the offense alleged is 5 years or more." [44] Thus, aside from the criteria already seen in the other examples, the gravity of the offense, even in cases of *inter se* offenses, can constitute an exception to the general arrangement. The agreement with the Dominican Republic extends the immunities granted to all persons subject to the United States military law with the exception of Dominican nationals and local residents. There is exclusive United States jurisdiction for *intra-castral* offenses and for *inter se* offenses committed by the privileged persons outside the defined areas. For *extra-castral* offenses against a Dominican national or local alien, there is concurrent jurisdiction with *ad hoc* negotiations to determine priority: "In each such case,

[42] Urbano A. Zafra, Minister Counsellor, Philippine Embassy, in the annual meeting of the American Society of International Law (*Proceedings* of the Society, 1958, pp. 192 and 193). He went on to say that "the Philippine military agreement, compared with NATO agreements, is very much less favorable to the host country and very much more favorable to the United States."

By January, 1959, the Philippine agreement had been amended twelve times, mainly to redefine and reduce the base areas.

[43] Text not published. The information is from *Operation Hearings* I, p. 38. The Defense Agreement between Portugal and the United States of America (*supra*, Chapter II, n. 70) merely authorizes the conclusion, by the ministers of defense of the two governments, of "technical arrangements" to determine, *inter alia*, "the number and missions of the personnel" and "the legal statute to which they will be subject, as well as the exemptions which the personnel and material will enjoy in time of peace and in time of war" (Article 6, in connection with Article 1).

[44] *Operation Hearings* IV, p. 56. A "technical arrangement" on the matter of jurisdiction came into force March 1, 1956 (*idem*, III, p. 38).

the Mixed Military Commission shall decide which Government shall exercise jurisdiction and shall give consideration to whether the offense arose out of any act or omission done in the performance of official duties." [45]

The most complex jurisdictional arrangement among those founded on the distinction between the base area and the territory outside the base concerns the bases leased from the United Kingdom in 1941. The original agreement [46] gave to the United States "the absolute right in the first instance to assume and exercise jurisdiction" in two cases. *Within* the base area, the United States had jurisdiction over persons other than British subjects with respect to all offenses, and over British subjects with respect to military and security offenses if the offenders were apprehended within the base or if they could not be tried in the area outside the base because the offense was not punishable under the law of the territory. The United States had jurisdiction both *within and without* the base over United States military personnel with respect to discipline and internal administration, and over persons other than British subjects with respect to security offenses and offenses of a military nature. The right to exercise jurisdiction could be waived, but if the United States elected to exercise it over a British subject, the trial could be held only in the territory.

The 1950 amendment [47] to the Leased Bases agreement intro-

[45] Agreement for Extending the Long Range Proving Ground for the Testing of Guided Missiles, Ciudad Trujillo, November 26, 1951 (3 UST 2569; TIAS 2425), Article XV(1).

[46] Cited *supra,* Chapter II, n. 35, Article IV.

[47] Cited *supra,* n. 33. This agreement concerns the leased sites in Bermuda, the Bahamas, Jamaica, St. Lucia, Antigua, Trinidad, and British Guiana. Identical provisions were adopted for the "Bahamas Long Range Proving Ground" on July 21, 1950 (1 UST 545; TIAS 2099), and, subsequently, for the extensions of the proving ground to the Turks and Caicos Islands (January 15, 1952 [3 UST 2594; TIAS 2426]), St. Lucia (June 25, 1956 [7 UST 1939; TIAS 3595]), and Ascension Island (June 25, 1956 [7 UST 1999; TIAS 3603]), and for the oceanographic-research stations in the Barbados (November 1, 1956 [7 UST 2901; TIAS 3672]), Turks, and Caicos Islands (November 27, 1956 [7 UST 3169; TIAS 3696]), and the Bahamas (November 1, 1957 [8 UST 1741; TIAS 3927]), Articles V and VI corresponding in each case to Articles IV and V of the Leased Bases agreement as amended.

The jurisdiction over Newfoundland bases included in the 1941 lease agreement

duced additional criteria and differentiated between two degrees of jurisdiction, "exclusive" and "concurrent," giving special meanings to both terms. It also divided all persons potentially subject to the United States jurisdiction into five categories, for each of which the right to exercise jurisdiction varies not only according to the location and the kind of offense, but also according to the condition of the authorities of the contracting states at the time jurisdiction is to be exercised. Listed in the order of decreasing rights of the United States, these categories are: (1) members of the United States forces (including any British subjects)[48] who are entitled to wear the uniform; (2) persons subject to United States military or naval law, with the exception of British subjects and local aliens; (3) persons not subject to the United States military or naval law who are neither British subjects nor local aliens; (4) British subjects and local aliens; (5) members of a United Kingdom Dominion or Colonial armed force. Stripped of the special provisions applicable when one or the other or both contracting parties are involved in a war, the agreement authorizes the United States to exercise:

1. *Intra-castral* exclusive jurisdiction with respect to:
   a) "United States interest offenses" committed by United States military personnel;
   b) Security offenses committed by all persons except members of United Kingdom Dominion or Colonial forces, provided that a civil court of the United States is sitting in the territory to try any of the civilian categories of persons. In the

---

was modified by an agreement with Canada of February 13 and March 19, 1952 (3 UST 4271; TIAS 2572), and later, along with the Goose Bay area leased directly from Canada (3 UST 5295; TIAS 2730), changed to NATO-SFA status, which applies as of September 27, 1953, to all United States forces in Canada (Exchange of Notes, Washington, April 28 and 30, 1952 [5 UST 2139; TIAS 3074]). NATO-type of jurisdiction was also introduced in the 1961 agreement with the Federation of the West Indies (cited *supra*, Chapter II, n. 35).

[48] The agreement explicitly provides for the interesting case of the local citizen who becomes a member of the visiting force without a change in his citizenship. His position is identical with that of other military personnel of the sending state.

absence of such court, the United States has nevertheless jurisdiction over security offenses committed by civilians subject to United States military or naval law (with the exception of British subjects and local aliens) if the offense is not punishable under the law of the territory.

2. *Intra-castral* concurrent jurisdiction with respect to:
   a) All other offenses by persons subject to United States military or naval law (members of forces and others except British subjects and local aliens) ;
   b) All other offenses committed by persons (other than British subjects and local aliens) who are not subject to the United States military law;
   c) Security offenses committed by members of United Kingdom Dominion or Colonial forces.

3. *Extra-castral* exclusive jurisdiction with respect to:
   a) Security offenses committed by United States military personnel;
   b) If not punishable under local law, (i) "United States interest offenses" committed by United States military personnel, and (ii) security offenses committed by persons in any of the civilian categories, provided that to try a British subject or local alien or a person not subject to United States military law, a civil court is necessary.

4. *Extra-castral* concurrent jurisdiction with respect to:
   a) All other offenses committed by United States military personnel;
   b) All other offenses committed by persons (other than British subjects and local aliens) who are subject to the United States military law, if a civil court of the United States is sitting in the territory.[49]

"United States interest offenses" are defined as offenses *solely* against the interest of the United States or against property and persons (other than British and local) present in the territory *solely* by reason of service in the operation of the bases. Security

[49] For text of relevant sections, see Appendix IIIB.

refers to the security of the United States and its bases in the territory, and the types of offenses falling under this category are specified. Exclusive jurisdiction may be assumed unilaterally and merely requires notification of the local authorities to prevent them from assuming jurisdiction. Concurrent jurisdiction requires in every case a joint decision of the two contracting parties to determine who shall exercise it; after that, there is protection against double jeopardy only if the offense falls in both cases under the jurisdiction of civil courts.

The concept of exclusive jurisdiction has, normally, two facets. One is the authorization to exercise the jurisdiction of the sending state. The other is the exemption from local jurisdiction. Concurrent jurisdiction usually has only the first feature; but to be meaningful, it must be possible to exercise it unilaterally. The possibility of granting jurisdictional rights by means of *ad hoc* negotiations is, of course, always open, whether foreseen in an agreement or not. This being the case, it is evident that behind the complicated formula of Article IV there is very little substance with regard both to authorizing the exercise of jurisdiction of the sending state and to granting immunity from the jurisdiction of the receiving state. It is, for instance, obvious that the grant of exclusive jurisdiction over certain offenses when they are not punishable under the law of the territory means nothing more, in terms of immunity, than the truism that no court can exercise more jurisdiction than is authorized by the legal order of its own state. Neither is there much meaning in unqualified immunity from the exercise of local jurisdiction in cases of security offenses and *intracastral* offenses committed by the military personnel *inter se,* insofar as states hardly ever, in the absence of an agreement, punish offenses directed against the security, or "solely" against the interests, of other states. It is true, however, that Article V obligates the governments of the territories to adopt legislation "to ensure the adequate security and protection of the United States naval

and air bases . . . and the punishment of persons who may con-
travene any laws and regulations made for that purpose." To the
degree that such legislation is adopted, the agreement grants a real
immunity, but only with respect to matters that have come under
local jurisdiction in consequence of the same agreement. At the
same time, moreover, the adoption of such legislation reduces the
area of exclusive jurisdiction of the United States with respect to
*extra-castral* United States interest offenses committed by the military personnel and with respect to security offenses committed by
civilian personnel in or out of camp.

An analysis of concurrent jurisdiction under the present agreement leads to similar conclusions. It shows, first, that—unlike the
situation in the Philippines—an offense against a local resident
can never be tried by the United States nor exempted from the
local jurisdiction by way of a unilateral decision of the United
States, no matter where or by whom the offense is committed. Nor
can the United States ever exercise military jurisdiction over a
local resident, even if the offense is committed within a base and
is directed solely against the United States or its personnel, and the
offender is a person subject to United States military law. If there
is no civil United States court available locally (which is the actual
situation), civilians in general, including Americans, are well protected against the exercise of American jurisdiction. It would be a
mistake, however, to assume that the need to reach an agreement
in every case of concurrent jurisdiction restricts the local courts
the way it restricts the American authorities. With respect to civilians generally, only the establishment of United States civil
courts in the territories under the lease would have such an effect.
With respect to military personnel and non-local civilians on trial
in a military court, no restraining effect on the local authorities
results from the need for a bilateral decision on the exercise of concurrent jurisdiction, because an agreement on the trial in a military court does not exclude subsequent trial for the same offense

in a civil court of the territory. Altogether, the Leased Bases agreement grants less immunity and substantially less authority to exercise American jurisdiction than NATO-SFA.

Thus, that NATO-SFA should become the focal point of the dispute between the opponents and the defenders of the status-of-forces agreements in the United States was certainly illogical. Indeed, there is no reason to assume that any agreement, merely because it differentiates between the general territory of the receiving state and a defined area under a special regime (our Type II),[50] accords a better status to the visiting force than agreements based on systems of concurrent jurisdiction applying uniformly throughout the territory of the receiving country. In fact, the scope of immunities under the agreements of Type II varies. In the case of agreements approaching Type I, the *intra-castral* immunities are liberally granted and it is almost impossible for visiting personnel to find themselves outside the defined area. Other Type II agreements grant *intra-castral* rights so broad as to include substantial powers over the local residents, although the immunities of the visiting personnel are not the broadest. And still others restrict both the immunities and the right to exercise the jurisdiction of the sending state to the minimum—whether or not the agreement is based on a long-term lease of the camp area.

*Type III* agreements, as opposed to the largely bilateral agreements of the preceding categories, originate in the multilateral status-of-forces convention of the Brussels treaty powers, which never came into effect.[51] Its basic formula, however, was adopted

[50] Particularly if it is a *leased* area, a term which, as we have seen in Chapter II, suggests territorial rights in semi-dependencies. In this context it is interesting to note that in 1948 the United States Supreme Court held (not with reference to criminal jurisdiction, and reversed the following year) that one of the leased bases is a "possession" of the United States (*Vermilya-Brown Co.* v. *Connel,* 338 U.S. 217).

[51] Agreement Relative to the Status of Members of the Armed Forces of the Brussels Treaty Powers, December 21, 1949 (Cmd. 7868; see Department of State, *Bulletin,* XXII [1950], 449-53), signed by Belgium, France, Luxembourg, the Netherlands, and the United Kingdom; superseded by NATO-SFA.

for NATO-SFA,[52] which, in turn, has served as the model for another multilateral and at least four bilateral status-of-forces agreements.[53] The most striking feature of Type III agreements is the fact that they use none of the criteria found in other agreements as the basis of a definitive system of immunities. Instead, some of these criteria are employed in a novel way. Generally speaking, the full extent of jurisdiction conferred by the laws of the sending and receiving states respectively—as applied to certain categories of persons defined by the agreement—is recognized in principle. In the overlapping area, which is labeled "concurrent," there is a system of priorities: the sending state has the "primary right" to exercise jurisdiction essentially in "on-duty" and *inter se* offenses; the receiving state in all others. The waiving of the primary right to exercise jurisdiction is then encouraged in cases considered by the requesting state to be of particular importance; a double jeopardy provision, however, makes it difficult for the sending state and impossible for the receiving state to exercise concurrent jurisdiction if the other party has already exercised its primary right in the case at hand. The key provisions are Sections 1 and 3 of Article VII, NATO-SFA, and of the corresponding articles of the two Japanese agreements:

1. Subject to the provision of this article,
   (a) the military authorities of the sending state shall have the

[52] Cited *supra*, n. 4. Concluded and ratified by Belgium, Canada, Denmark, France, Italy, Luxembourg, the Netherlands, Norway, Portugal, the United Kingdom, and the United States. Greece and Turkey acceded. Iceland, from among the original signatories, failed to ratify. Portugal excluded its adjacent islands and overseas provinces. See *supra*, n. 31 and 32 for the special cases of Greece and the Netherlands, and n. 22 for Germany.

[53] That is, Article XVI of the Agreement Regarding the Status of United Nations Forces in Japan, Tokyo, February 19, 1954 (5 UST 1123; TIAS 2995), Article XVII of SFA-Japan (*supra*, n. 5), Article 2 of the Annex on the Status of United States Personnel and Property in Iceland, Reykjavik, May 8, 1951 (2 UST 1533; TIAS 2295), and the new arrangements regarding the status of forces in the Leased Bases in Newfoundland and the Federation of the West Indies (*supra*, n. 47) correspond to Article VII, NATO-SFA. The agreement on the status of United States forces in Morocco, among those that remain classified, seems to be similar (*Annuaire français de droit international*, I [1955], 27-29; Snee and Pye, *Status*, p. 55, nn. 253 and 254).

right to exercise within the receiving State all criminal and disciplinary jurisdiction conferred on them by the law of the sending State over all persons subject to the military law of that State;

(b) the authorities of the receiving State shall have jurisdiction over the members of a force or civilian component and their dependents with respect to offences committed within the territory of the receiving State and punishable by the law of that State.

. . . . . . . . . . . . .

3. In cases where the right to exercise jurisdiction is concurrent, the following rules shall apply:

(a) The military authorities of the sending State shall have the primary right to exercise jurisdiction over a member of a force or of a civilian component in relation to

(i) offences solely against the property or security of that State, or offences solely against the person or property of another member of the force or civilian component of that State or of dependent;

(ii) offences arising out of any act or omission done in the performance of official duty.

(b) In the case of any other offence the authorities of the receiving State shall have the primary right to exercise jurisdiction.

(c) If the State having the primary right decides not to exercise jurisdiction, it shall notify the authorities of the other State as soon as practicable. The authorities of the State having the primary right shall give sympathetic consideration to a request from the authorities of the other State for a waiver of its right in cases where that other State considers such a waiver to be of particular importance.

It will have been noted that the jurisdiction of the receiving state extends specifically to dependents according to Section 1(b), while the jurisdictional provisions for the sending state only mention persons subject to its military law in Section 1(a) (which may or may not include the dependents) and assign priority under Section 3 with respect to military and civilian personnel, but not with respect to dependents.[54] Section 2, omitted above, calls the jurisdiction over offenses punishable only under the law of the one *or* the other state "exclusive"—an unilluminative point, since nothing prevents either party from expanding its penal law to additional offenses. This section repeats the distinction of Section 1 as to the personal spheres of competence. Thus, the intention of the negotiators apparently was to equip the sending state with authority over the accompanying civilians in matters of the discipline and security of the visiting force (which would normally, though not necessarily, be covered only by the legislation of the sending state) but only insofar as the civilians could be tried in the military courts under the legislation of the sending state. In matters covered by the laws of the receiving state, the sending state has no jurisdiction whatever over the dependents. Over civilian personnel the sending state has concurrent jurisdiction subject to the system of priorities established under 3(a) and (b), but again only to the extent to which they can be subjected to military jurisdiction. Section 4 prohibits, furthermore, any military trials over the nationals of, and persons "ordinarily resident in," the receiving state, unless they are actually members of the visiting military force. Hence, a security offense committed by a local resident against the sending state will normally have no forum, although a person not a national of the sending state, if brought into the territory as a consequence of his association with the visiting force, would be subject to the same provisions as the nationals of the sending state. It is also evident from the text of Section 3 that offenses committed by the personnel of one sending state against the personnel, property, or security of another sending state are subject to local jurisdiction. Section 8 forbids trial "for the same offense within the same territory" when an accused "has been tried . . . and has

---

[54] An offense committed by a member or civilian component against a dependent qualifies as *inter se,* apparently. Based on a study of *travaux préparatoires,* Snee and Pye (*Status,* pp. 35-39) conclude that the differences are not due to faulty drafting.

been acquitted, or has been convicted and is serving, or has served his sentence, or has been pardoned . . ." by the authorities of a contracting party; however, the sending state is permitted to try its military personnel for any violation of the rules of discipline arising out of the act that constituted an offense already tried by the authorities of another contracting party. There is, further, a separate paragraph requiring mutual notification about the disposition of all cases falling under concurrent jurisdiction (Section 6b), which creates a problem in view of a similar provision in Section 3c.[55] Two provisions impose standards of treatment of the personnel subject to actual exercise of jurisdiction under the agreement: the sending states are prohibited from executing a death penalty in the territory of a state whose law does not provide for capital punishment in a similar case (Section 7a); and the receiving states are obligated to observe specified minimum procedural rights in trials of members of the visiting force and the accompanying civilians (including dependents) before their courts (Section 9). The remaining sections deal with legal aid and arrangements for policing and the execution of sentences.[56]

Literature expounding the meaning of the criminal jurisdiction provisions of Type III agreements[57] began to accumulate soon after NATO-SFA came into force. In addition, the ratification debate had stimulated publications that were centered on the broader issues of the legitimacy of the new agreements in the light of the American constitutional system and the rules of customary international law.[58] The growth of this interpretative material should not be surprising, since the text of NATO-SFA is indeterminate enough to leave ample room for speculation and may have created more problems than it has settled.[59] Furthermore, as the first multi-

---

[55] See *infra*, n. 72, and the second section of Chapter IV.

[56] For full text of Article VII, see Appendix IIIC *infra*.

[57] See the Bibliographical Note in this volume.

[58] *Supra*, pp. 49-50.

[59] A panel of American and foreign experts, meeting five years after NATO-SFA came into force, focused its discussion on the failure of the status-of-forces agree-

lateral agreement on the peacetime status of friendly forces in foreign territory, NATO-SFA became at once applicable to a larger number of American personnel (and, at the same time, had consequences for a larger number of local civilians in the receiving countries) than any other agreement on a similar subject.[60] Inevitably, the early cases under its provisions set closely observed precedents, as has the very fact of the conclusion of the agreement—a Senate resolution to the contrary notwithstanding.[61] Small wonder that, aside from theorists of international and constitutional law, a large number of people involved in the application of NATO-SFA had to be concerned, for professional reasons, with the exact meaning and validity of key clauses of its Article VII and that another series of publications, centering on individual cases arising under it, resulted.[62]

Government spokesmen have in the meantime reiterated that NATO-SFA "does not contain every single right and exemption desired by the armed services . . ." and that it "does not fully satisfy all that the United States or any other country might desire." Rather, it is, like other status-of-forces agreements, "the best we could obtain today," and represents "the best common denominator of conflicting national requirements which could be agreed upon

---

ments to contribute to the "juridification of international relations" and on consequent "fragmentation of general international law." See paper read by Professor R. R. Baxter, "Jurisdiction Over Visiting Forces and the Development of International Law," *Proceedings of the American Society of International Law,* 1958, pp. 174 ff., especially 179-80, and the discussion on pp. 183, 185, 189-90.

[60] Defense Department statistics reveal that slightly over one-half of cases subject to foreign jurisdiction and three-fourths of those actually tried by foreign courts occur in NATO countries. Of the remainder, more than two-thirds occur under the identical Japanese agreements (see Tables 1 and 2 in Chapter IV *infra*).

[61] The Senate ratification resolution (4 UST 1828) reads, in part: "In giving its advice and consent to ratification, it is the sense of the Senate that: 1. The criminal jurisdiction provisions of article VII do not constitute a precedent for future agreements." The agreement, as indicated already (*supra,* nn. 5 and 53), was duplicated at least five times and has recently been extended again (n. 22), and it is only natural that other allies of the United States press for the adoption of similar arrangements. Article XVIII, 3, of NATO-SFA opens the agreement to accession by new members of NATO "subject to approval of the North Atlantic Council and to such conditions as it may decide."

[62] See the Bibliographical Note, *infra.*

by the NATO nations." At the same time, however, the appropriate cabinet member declared that NATO-SFA and the related agreements, though not containing "the absolute solution for every problem," are "operationally sound" and "provide the essential framework in which these problems can be solved." Moreover, the State Department declared that the legal arrangements on the status of forces are "reasonable and practicable and represent considerable concessions to the viewpoint of the United States," and that they would constitute a "firm basis for the rights of our troops abroad . . ." and a "uniform basis . . . in place of the varied interim arrangements . . . ." [63] Evidently, some of these authoritative statements should be viewed in light of the threat to the United States system of bases and alliances, which, the administration thought, was arising from the growing domestic opposition to the status-of-forces agreements at the time of NATO-SFA ratification hearings and in the early period of application of the treaty.[64] The statements asserting the firmness and the uniformity of the legal basis provided by the agreements appear to be particularly open to doubt. In fact, some of the immediately apparent difficulties in the adopted wording of Article VII suggest that the "best common denominator" was a compromise achieved largely at the expense of clarity and certainty; hence, also at the expense of the affected individuals, visiting and local, and of the con-

[63] See the statements of Generals Ridgway and Bradley and Secretary of Defense Wilson in *SFA Ratification Hearings,* pp. 33, 36, and 11; Deputy Under Secretary Murphy in *House SFA Hearings,* p. 160; and "Information supplied by State Department," *SFA Ratification Hearings,* p. 28.

[64] "Quite apart from the question as to what the correct rule of international law is, the practical consideration which influences my judgment is the undoubted fact that no country need allow any of our troops to enter its territory, or to fly from air bases on its soil, or to conduct maneuvers across its countryside, or to allow American naval activities to be based at its seaports. . . . [The] denunciation of the status agreement *would in many cases automatically constitute a denunciation of the right . . . to use these vital military installations. What could be more self-defeating to the basic national security interests of the United States . . . ?"* —Wilson to Gordon, July 1, 1957 (H. Rept. 678, 85th Cong., 1st Sess., pp. 9, 11 [emphasis added]). Cf., in the same vein, General Norstad's statement before the Foreign Affairs Committee (quoted *ibid.,* p. 14) and the message of General Gruenther to Chairman Richards (*ibid.,* p. 13).

tracting party with the weaker bargaining position at the time a case with conflicting claims to jurisdiction arises.


A PRELIMINARY EVALUATION


The point just made will be further substantiated in examining the actual application of the status-of-forces agreements. But a theoretical analysis reveals at once the main difficulties arising out of the adopted formulation of Article VII. First, the precise scope of the two exceptions to the principle of priority of the local right to exercise concurrent jurisdiction is an unsolved puzzle. It is evident that a conflict of jurisdictional rights over the ever reappearing soldier who commits, negligently perhaps, an offense *while* performing an official function cannot be resolved by reference to the text of the agreement: there is neither an indication as to what constitutes an act "done in the performance of official duty," nor designation of an authority to decide on the matter in case of doubt. The definition of a visiting "force" makes clear that the treaty applies to the personnel of a contracting party only "when in the territory of another Contracting Party in the North Atlantic Treaty area in connection with their official duties . . ." (Article I, Section l[a]). This excludes from treaty provisions personnel present in a receiving state while on leave from duty that takes place in another receiving state; but it also indicates that a closer relation to duty than mere presence in connection with duties is required to place the priority of the right to exercise jurisdiction in the hands of the authorities of the sending state according to paragraph 3(a)(ii) of Article VII. How close? If it is not to be presumed that visiting personnel will be ordered to commit acts that would constitute offenses against local law (although, if that should happen, there would be no question of the personnel involved being exempt from local jurisdiction), the solution must be somewhere in between. Private Smith may be driving an official vehicle on an ordered mission and injure a fellow serviceman—to compound the ground for exemption—but he may have been speeding because he took a detour for his own pleasure rather than the direct route. Was he on duty at the time the offense occurred? Is the receiving state obligated to accept as conclusive a certificate of on-duty status issued by his commanding officer if the offense occurred in the local red-light district, out of the way of any military installations? Or, should the local authorities disinterest themselves in the case, and in the driving habits of visiting servicemen in general, as long as the actual victim is, incidentally, another member of the force? Suppose Smith has accomplished his mission and makes the detour on his way back. Or, suppose he is driving his private vehicle to his post and the accident happens before he is assigned to an actual mission for the day. Unless there is clarification in supplementary agreements, the decisions that have to be made in these and similar situations must be arbitrary and may be capricious and a cause of irritation for everyone concerned.

The criterion of national attachment of the person or object against which the offense is directed will, likewise, yield only inadequate guidance. Few offenses will qualify as "solely" *inter se,* and it may be difficult to determine the difference between two aspects of the same offense and two offenses arising out of a series of events. In the case of Smith, who violated a local traffic ordinance along with the military code and perhaps his specific orders, a strict application of the treaty would place the case in the hands of the local authorities—at least as far as the *inter se* aspect is concerned—although this would probably run against the spirit of the treaty, which, in the section at issue, was obviously inspired by the theory of predominant interest. If Smith is convicted, or acquitted, or pardoned by the local authorities, he will be protected against court-martial proceedings within the same territory for the injury of the fellow serviceman, which happens to be the most substantial of the offenses involved. The disciplinary aspect could be pursued after he has served the sentence imposed by the local court for speeding and injury to the fellow serviceman, and he will, of course, ask for leniency in local proceedings in view of the prospective disciplinary action. He has nothing to rely on, however: if his military superiors are dissatisfied with the action of the local court, he can be taken across the border and subjected to court-martial on all counts—if need be, under the omnibus article of the Uniform Code of Military Justice which threatens unspecified offenses with unspecified punishment (Article 174).

Second, the implications of the terms "concurrent jurisdiction" and "primary right to exercise jurisdiction" are not clear. Does the primary right mean that a secondary right exists which becomes operative whenever the primary right is not used, or is not used promptly, or is not used in the precise way that would constitute protection against double jeopardy under Section 8? Or, is the "concurrent" jurisdiction conferred to both contracting parties in Section 1 cancelled in Section 3 for the state not having the primary right? If the first interpretation is the correct one, the difficulty with "on-duty" offenses is increased. The immunity of individuals on military duty, acting as agents of their state, has been an unchallenged principle of international law ever since the McLeod case of 1840.[65] NATO-SFA, in its claims provisions, recognizes that principle (Article VIII, Section 5[g]) as well as the complementary legal responsibility of the sending state for acts done in the performance of official duty by its subordinates.[66] The primary right to exercise jurisdiction in on-duty offenses, if it implies the existence of a secondary right, means something substantially short of the kind of immunity that was traditionally recognized in such cases—and Article VIII seems to indicate that it was not the intention of the contracting parties to upset the general inter-

[65] See Moore, *Digest*, II, 24-28. We need not be concerned in the present context with the one possible exception, the war-crimes trials after World War II.

[66] Article VIII, Section 2(a) with respect to property owned by the receiving state; Section 5 with respect to tortious acts vis-à-vis individuals. For claims purposes, there is also an arbitrator to decide disputes regarding the "on-duty" status.

national law on this matter. As one authority, otherwise holding highly restrictive views on exemptions from territorial jurisdiction under the rules of customary international law, tersely remarks, "It is evident that the terminology of primary jurisdiction is inappropriate in this situation." [67] If, on the other hand, the correct interpretation is that which would cancel any right to exercise the "concurrent" jurisdiction of the state not having the primary right—whether or not the state having it makes use of it—what, then, prevented the drafters from calling the "primary right" unequivocally "exclusive jurisdiction," and why was it felt to be necessary or even helpful to include the double jeopardy prohibition in Article VII? [68] The first interpretation leads to a result contrary to the established practice of states—which, of course, was within the power of the contracting parties to agree upon. The second interpretation contradicts the other provisions of the treaty itself. This, too, was within the power of the contracting parties to agree upon, but accepting it as the *intended* solution is predicated on the assumption that it was also the intention of the drafters to befuddle the matter.

The last difficulty to be mentioned in the present context arises out of the provision for waiving the primary right to exercise jurisdiction. Again, there are two facets to the problem. In the first place, the necessary standards are as lacking as in the previously discussed provisions of Article VII. The obligation to give "sympathetic consideration" in cases considered "important" by the requesting party simply takes the cases out of the treaty framework and transfers them to the area of *ad hoc* negotiations. As a consequence, the consideration extended will necessarily vary, depend-

---

[67] G. P. Barton, "Foreign Armed Forces: Qualified Jurisdictional Immunity," *British Year Book of International Law*, XXXI (1954), 341-70, on p. 367.

[68] A double-jeopardy situation is, of course, possible only if all of the following occurs: (1) the state having the primary right of jurisdiction makes use of it rather than waiving it or disposing of the case without trial; (2) the state not having the primary right nevertheless uses its concurrent jurisdiction in the same case. The drafters must have assumed that in the absence of the double-jeopardy prohibition the situation just described could occur.

ing on the level at which the requests are made, the authority of local courts and prosecutors, the relations between them and the officers of the visiting forces, the presence or absence of supplementary agreements, and various other factors.[69] And with regard to the requesting end of the matter, one can only find that the relevant part of the Senate ratification resolution,[70] combined with the requesting policy of the Defense Department,[71] adds insult without solving the fundamental problem—that of the vagueness of the treaty. In the second place, it is unclear what kind of action constitutes a waiver and what exactly is effected by such action. The inclusion, in the paragraph on the waiving procedure (Article VII, Section 3[c]), of the clause requiring prompt notification in the event of a decision not to exercise jurisdiction—which seems to add little to the broader obligation of notification about the disposition of all cases in paragraph 6(b)—may indicate that the notification is equivalent to a waiver, the latter being the term for notification of non-use by request.[72] Be that as it may, what does the waiving state retain? The difficulty at this point is equivalent to the one discussed in the preceding paragraph. If the second hypothesized solution was the correct one, the waiving state, by analogy, divests itself completely of its jurisdiction—even if the state to which the right was waived makes no use of that right and so notifies the first state, unless the second state actually waives the right back to the first. It should then follow that (1) what the waiver accomplishes is the creation of exclusive jurisdiction in the hands of the state that originally lacked even the right to exercise

[69] See Chapter IV *infra;* also *supra,* nn. 31-32.

[70] Paragraph 2 requires the commanding officer to study local laws with reference to the procedural rights contained in the United States Constitution. Paragraph 3 requires that the commanding officer request a waiver if in his opinion "there is danger that the accused will not be protected because of the absence or denial of constitutional rights he would enjoy in the United States." In case of failure to obtain a waiver, diplomatic action and notification of the Senate are required.

[71] That is, the policy to try to obtain waivers "whenever possible" (*infra,* Chapter IV, n. 68).

[72] Conversely, it could be argued that Section 6(b) indicates that waivers are granted on condition that the case will be tried.

its "concurrent" jurisdiction; (2) the duplicate notification clause has no purpose. As it happens, in the current stage of the actual controversy on the matter of waived rights, it is exactly this interpretation, requiring a return-waiver before the first state can reclaim its "concurrent" jurisdiction, that has been adopted in the highest court of a major receiving country.[73] At the same time, however, arrangements that are in effect in another area allow the assumption that the waiver is granted if within a certain period there is no notification that the primary right will be exercised.[74] In any event, the matter is far from being "uniformly" or "firmly" settled, or even from being susceptible to such settlement under the current basic provisions. More generally, it appears that the waiving feature may not be the panacea which would take care of all other difficulties in the application of the agreement; on the contrary, the problems that arise out of the application of the waiving clause seem to be as substantial as those which the clause was expected to alleviate. There is no doubt that such a clause would be an extremely useful feature as a "safety valve" in an agreement otherwise highly specific, particularly if the only nations involved were sharing standards that could lead in its use. Here, at least in the case of some countries, there may be a question as to the presence of equal standards; furthermore, the fundamental difficulty of Type III agreements—excessive vagueness—can hardly be remedied by a general escape clause.

It will have been noted that some of the ambiguities pointed out in the discussion of provisions of NATO-SFA are not peculiar to that agreement and its duplicates. The "special reasons" for waiving in the Philippine agreement; the matters of "serious public concern" and similar phrases used to define exceptions to the general provisions in several agreements; the possibility of automatic extension of competence by way of unilateral legislative action in the Spanish, the Azorean, and the Leased Bases agreements—these

---

[73] In France (*infra*, Chapter IV, n. 59).
[74] In Japan (*infra*, Chapter IV, text at n. 82).

are some of the counterparts of the "matters of particular importance," the "sympathetic consideration," and the distinction between the "concurrent" and "exclusive" jurisdictions of NATO-SFA. Offenses "solely" against the sending state are found in the Leased Bases agreements, and so is the need for *ad hoc* negotiations, only, in contrast to NATO-SFA, they are expressly provided for in all cases falling under the concurrent jurisdiction. On-duty offenses, finally, are seldom defined with any precision. From a legal point of view, what is perhaps more disturbing in the case of NATO-SFA than in the case of other agreements—particularly in view of the wide and still-increasing domain covered by agreements of this type—is that the ambiguities are compounded and there is, in effect, no criterion present to provide more than the most general guidance for the solution of specific cases of conflict of jurisdiction. To the degree that under NATO-SFA and its duplicates the separation of jurisdictional rights depends on unilateral legislative action, the details must necessarily differ between different contracting parties. The answers to most of the other problems must be found in day-to-day negotiations. The separation of competences of the contracting parties and the position of the individuals involved become thereby a matter of political rather than legal determination.

It should not be overlooked, however, that the method in this chapter has been restricted to an examination of representative texts of the current status-of-forces agreements. As will be seen in the following chapter, some of the difficulties inherent in the wording of these agreements are in effect worked out in practice to mutual satisfaction; others are merely worked out. In some respects, the practice compounds the uncertainty found in the texts. Yet, the system is by no means on its way to collapsing—in spite of the fact that occasionally a case arising under it stirs up widespread unfavorable reaction. It seems to be legitimate to conclude at this point only that, insofar as the system is working, it must be for reasons other than the clarity or solidity of the legal basis provided by the agreements.

Meanwhile, it may also be remembered that the purpose of the preceding discussion has been not merely to find out exactly who gets what under the agreements in force, nor even whether it is possible to find that out from their wording. It will be shown later that the first conclusion of this subsection has implications reaching further than may be evident at this point. Furthermore, the review of representative texts of the agreements reveals another tendency in the over-all status-of-forces pattern, a tendency perhaps more significant than the contracting parties' increasing propensity for vagueness. It may be useful to recollect here our basis for classification of the current agreements. An attempt was made to observe the significance ascribed in the agreements to the various criteria for separating jurisdictional rights and immunities. Inasmuch as one of three such criteria was found to be fundamental in every agreement concluded, three main categories resulted. Thus, one category (Type II) included all agreements in which the basic allocation of authority occurs *ratione loci,* the place of the offense either being the sole criterion or modifying the role of whatever additional criteria are employed. Another category (Type III), to the degree that it clarifies the matter of jurisdictional rights at all, does so on the basis of the nature of the offense, that is, *ratione materiae,* the relevant aspects of that nature being the interest offended, the author of the law violated, and some less tangible factors, such as the importance ascribed by the two states to the matter at hand. It will now be seen that a substantive criterion also underlies the agreements placed in a separate category on the basis of the quantitative criterion of granting maximal privileges (Type I): these agreements determine jurisdictional rights, in effect, *ratione personae,* applying an equal (in this case nearly complete) measure of exemption from local jurisdiction to all persons covered by the agreement, irrespective of elements of place or the nature of the offense. Disregarding for the moment the possible existence of some ultimate principle, which may underlie the agreements in all categories, it should be noted that, in determining the status of visiting forces, the involved states increasingly rely on systems of division of competences *ratione materiae*. Not only are the agreements of Type III, which employ principally this method today, applicable to the largest number of forces (and setting a pattern most likely to be followed in concluding future agreements) but the nature of facts in relation to which jurisdiction is to be exercised is an increasingly important factor under the agreements of Type II as well, while agreements of Type I are restricted to small units and special situations. The implications of this trend, however, can also be explored more profitably after examination of the operational aspect of NATO-SFA and the relation of the current conventional status of visiting forces to the rules of customary international law.

# IV. Status of Forces in Practice

THE ACTUAL STATUS of American forces stationed in foreign territory is not revealed by an analysis of the texts of the status-of-forces agreements. This is so for more reasons than the vague wording of their key provisions. Department of Defense statistics on the "operation" of the status-of-forces agreements, submitted semiannually to a subcommittee of the Senate Committee on Armed Services, disclose year after year that the theoretical authority to exercise jurisdiction over members of visiting forces, even when clearly stated, is in practice waived more often than it is used.[1] Therefore, without examining implementing practices

---

[1] World-wide, the exercise of jurisdiction of the receiving states has been waived in about two-thirds of cases occurring during five years (*Operation Hearings* V, pp. 15 and 20).

in the receiving countries, it is impossible to ascertain whether or not some of the agreed principles merely serve to obscure a pattern of relationships developing independently of formal provisions.

Moreover, if we focus on the implementation of Type III agreements, we can see that identical provisions mean different things in different countries or even different provinces, depending on local constitutional and political structures as well as on the nature of relationships in general between the sending and the receiving state. Nevertheless, the scope of immunities actually asserted and granted, the differences in the interpretation of identical provisions, and the intensity of the feed-back impact of the application of the status-of-forces agreements upon the constitutional structures of the participating states appear to be correlated. They reveal a certain pattern in spite of the fact that the actual status of forces depends more on *ad hoc* negotiations, unilateral legislative actions, and a varying amount of pressure from the sending state than on the provisions of the agreement.

### PRIMARY JURISDICTION OF THE SENDING STATE

It will be remembered that NATO-SFA provides for two exceptions to the principle of local jurisdiction that applies, in general, whenever a situation is covered by laws of both the receiving and the sending state. One of the exceptions, concerning offenses "arising out of any act or omission done in the performance of official duty" (Article VII, 3a[ii]) raises, as has been pointed out by several commentators on the text of the agreement, two distinct questions: first, what standards are to be applied to determine how close to the ordered mission an offense must lie to fall under the exception; second, who shall have authority to determine whether the requirements of the exception are present.[2] American authori-

---

[2] *Supra,* Chapter III, p. 73; cf. Snee and Pye, *Status,* p. 46.

ties have tended to identify the latter question with a third one, namely, who shall decide whether the offender was on duty at the time the offense occurred. Taken by itself, this third question creates very little difficulty, since the authorities of the receiving state can have no firsthand knowledge in the matter. However, if the right to determine whether the serviceman was "in an on-duty status" at the time of the offense is identified with the determination of whether the offense was an act close enough to the ordered mission to be an offense "arising out of" it, it is evident that the officers of the visiting force can retain virtually exclusive jurisdiction without even establishing or publishing a set of criteria for asserting jurisdiction. Since NATO-SFA foresees exclusive jurisdiction of the sending state only in matters not involving an infraction of the local law (Article VII, 2a), the American endeavor to maintain in principle that the certificate of duty status issued by the commanding officer is conclusive has been regarded by local authorities as an attempt to restrict local jurisdiction beyond the terms of the agreement and as a threat to the integrity of the legal system of the receiving state. Consequently, instead of a joint effort to clarify the term "arising out of," there has been a series of controversies about the validity of the certificate. The matter has been pursued with varying degrees of insistence at various levels of the governmental structures of the contracting states. The American interpretation has prevailed in some cases and has been qualified or withdrawn in others.

Thus, although British negotiators of NATO-SFA seem to have accepted the American proposition that the certificate of duty status be considered conclusive,[3] legislation implementing the agreement

---

[3] The implementing bill was amended when debate in Parliament disclosed that "the dignity of the British Empire would not allow the certificate of a commanding officer of some other nation as to facts occurring on British territory to be conclusive" (*Testimony of Department of Defense and Department of State on the Case of United States Army Specialist Third Class William S. Girard, Involving the Death of a Japanese Woman on January 30, 1957*, Hearing, Subcommittee of the Senate Committee on Armed Services, 85th Cong., 1st Sess., June 5, 1957 [hereafter: *Girard Hearing*], p. 14).

in the United Kingdom makes the certificate sufficient evidence only "unless the contrary is proved" in local court.[4] The British interpretation also applies in Canada,[5] and State Department spokesmen have assured Congress that it would also apply in American state courts in cases of foreign servicemen who committed an offense while on duty in the United States.[6] In France, on the other hand, the Ministry of Justice instructed local *procureurs* to accept the certificate as binding on condition that it is issued by a legal officer of the visiting force (i.e., a staff judge advocate rather than the commanding officer).[7] A similarly qualified version of the American view is now in effect in Turkey, after several years of insistence by local authorities that they have the final word in the matter of the relation of offense to duty.[8] In Italy, in the absence of implementing instructions on the national level, the validity of certificates has generally depended on the discretion of local prosecutors, but the American commanders have been able in most cases to have their way.[9] The problem has not arisen in other NATO countries because of the small number of troops on duty there or because a different device, the general waiver, has served to retain American jurisdiction in practically all cases.

Although attention has been focused on the conclusiveness of the commanding officer's certificate, the parties to the status-of-forces agreements have also held conflicting views on substantive standards for determining the degree of closeness of offense to

[4] Visiting Forces Act, 1952, 15 and 16 Geo. VI and 1 Eliz. II, c. 67, s. 11(4).

[5] *Girard Hearing, loc. cit.*

[6] *SFA Ratification Hearings*, pp. 70-71.

[7] Ministry of Justice, First Bureau, Circular 56 R 85 G. 1, June 27, 1956 (translation supplied by USAREUR Com Z, Office of the Staff Judge Advocate [Orléans]).

[8] The certificate must be signed by the highest ranking American officer (Chief, JAMMAT) and presented to the prosecutor in the district where the offense was committed (Exchange of notes, July 28, 1956 [not published in the UST collection]). This is considered highly inconvenient in view of the widely scattered military installations in Turkey (*Operation Hearings* II, pp. 17-18; Snee and Pye, *loc. cit.*). For previous status see *Operation Hearings* I, p. 28; *idem*, II, p. 24.

[9] *Operation Hearings* IV, p. 52; Snee and Pye, *op. cit.*, p. 53. Implementing provisions are now in effect (*Gazette Ufficiale della Republica Italiana*, No. 70, March 16, 1957).

duty that is necessary to transfer jurisdictional priority to the sending state. The authoritative American field study on the application of NATO-SFA in Europe finds that "the United States has consistently adhered to the position that any act or omission occurring incidental to the performance of official duty is within the meaning of paragraph 3(a)(ii)." [10] Local authorities, when in a position to apply their own standards, have often required a much closer relation of offense to duty, and both sides have, on occasion, pressed their position to absurdity. In one case, occurring in Japan, a certificate of duty status was issued to exempt from local jurisdiction an M.P. accused of entering a house and raping a girl while he was on duty patrolling the streets.[11] Turkish authorities have held that there can be no question of exemption from local jurisdiction if a local resident is killed in an accident occurring in the course of an official mission "because the official duty did not contemplate the killing of a Turk." [12] American observers have criticized the acquiescence of American military authorities in France in the subjection to local jurisdiction of offenses involving specific intent that is inconsistent with acting in the line of duty. One such case was that of embezzlement of money collected for a French bus company by a member of the visiting force, whose duty consisted of arranging tours for the visiting servicemen.[13] In another case occurring in Turkey, the duty status of a sergeant accused of an offense committed while working for extra pay for the Armed Services Motion Picture Service, after his normal duty hours, was

[10] Snee and Pye, *Report,* p. 44.

[11] The certificate was eventually withdrawn "because what he was doing was so far removed from the duty obligation that even though he was at the moment in a duty status he was off on some enterprise of his own" (*Girard Hearing,* p. 22).

[12] Joseph H. Rouse and Gordon B. Baldwin, "The Exercise of Criminal Jurisdiction under the NATO Status of Forces Agreement," *AJIL,* LI, No. 1 (January, 1957), 29-62, on p. 42. Turkey was later persuaded to adopt legislation expanding the wording of Article VII, 3(a)(ii) by adding "or done in connection with the performance of official duty" (Law of July 16, 1956; see Snee and Pye, *Status,* p. 48).

[13] Snee and Pye believe that this case did arise out of an act done in performance of official duty (*Report,* p. 45) and that the specific intent criterion is "artificial and undesirable" (*Status,* p. 48).

questioned. A Defense Department spokesman explained later: "The Turks said it wasn't official duty. We said it was. They won." [14] In short, the criteria of the duty-based exemption from local jurisdiction appear often to be chosen in a hit-or-miss fashion. Where the commanding officer's certificate is conclusive, it may well be issued with little justification. Where local authorities have retained the final word in the matter, the outcome seems to depend more on the amount of pressure considered feasible by the authorities of the sending state than on the objective application of agreed principles. Often, the duty issue seems to be raised merely to provide additional argument in favor of a waiver, a dropping of charges, or a nominal sentence. In such cases, there is a better than even chance that somewhere in the various stages of the proceedings the insistence of local authorities on exercising their primary right of jurisdiction will be overcome, though both sides will continue to insist that their interpretation of the agreement is the only correct one. Upon seeing the instructions given to American negotiators in a case that had aroused unfavorable world-wide attention, the chairman of the investigating subcommittee of the Senate Committee on Armed Services described the implementing policy of the United States pointedly: "In other words, that means to me, you insist on maintaining our position unless the other side refuses to accede to it, then agree to their position." [15]

The case Senator Ervin referred to was that of Specialist Third Class William S. Girard, who early in 1957, *while* he was on duty, shot and killed a Japanese woman. That this case should have created such a problem is perhaps surprising, for of all countries under a jurisdictional regime of Type III, Japan is the one in which the smallest percentage of offenses subject to local jurisdiction under the terms of the agreement actually result in trials in local courts—a fact suggesting that borderline cases should be easily resolvable in favor of the United States. Furthermore, SFA-

[14] *Operation Hearings* I, p. 28.
[15] Senator Ervin in *Girard Hearing*, p. 24.

Japan[16] is supplemented by formal procedural agreements that eliminate some of the difficulties found elsewhere. In the Girard case, however, the insufficient substantive criteria for determination of jurisdictional rights invited the assumption, on the part of American military authorities, of an untenable position, resulting in a prolonged deadlock and, eventually, under the fire of public opinion abroad, in a retreat—only to provoke an equally critical public reaction in the United States. The incident occurred on a part-time firing range during a break in military exercises when Girard and another soldier were left in the area to guard military equipment which remained there while the units engaged changed their positions. The woman was one of a group of Japanese civilians who came to the firing range to gather scrap brass—a regular practice generally tolerated by American officers, except that there was concern about keeping the scavengers out of the line of fire. On the day of the incident, when the Japanese disregarded warning signs and local police summoned to remove them did not show up, live ammunition was withdrawn, apparently to prevent harming them. The two soldiers left on duty during the break allegedly first threw some expended cartridges towards the scavengers, inviting them to come closer for more. When some of them approached, Girard fired two expended cartridges in their direction, using blank shots to propel the cartridges from the grenade launcher attached to his rifle, and hit a fleeing woman in the back. The commanding officer issued a certificate stating that the shot was fired as a warning while Girard was on duty, and that the United States intended to exercise jurisdiction in the case.

Supplementary agreements to SFA-Japan declare that the certificate of the commanding officer is conclusive "unless the contrary is proved." [17] The adopted procedure authorizes American assumption of jurisdiction unless the local procurator notifies the com-

---

[16] Cited *Supra,* Chapter III, n. 5.

[17] "Agreed Official Minutes" of September 29, 1953 (appended to the Protocol, 4 UST 1851, TIAS 2848). Further, "Agreed Views" (the part relevant here is printed in *Girard Hearing,* pp. 18-19).

manding officer within ten days of receipt of the certificate that he is in possession of contrary proof, in which case the matter is referred to the Joint Committee.[18] One of the supplementary provisions protects the final authority of Japanese courts to determine the scope of their own jurisdiction; but the original Administrative Agreement (of which the jurisdictional provisions are a part, amended by a Protocol to incorporate the NATO type of provisions) declares that "any matter" which the Joint Committee is unable to resolve shall be referred to the respective governments for further consideration. Another supplementary provision defines the term "official duty," [19] but there is no clarification as to what constitutes "arising out of" duty.[20] In the present case, the Japanese informed the commanding officer that contrary proof existed and submitted a statement to the Joint Committee that the incident arose out of a material deviation from the performance of duty. The following excerpt from the discussion in the Joint Committee demonstrates the main difficulty in applying the on-duty exemption from local jurisdiction under NATO-SFA and its derivatives:

> U.S.: Do you agree that Girard was on duty as a guard, and that the incident arose while he was on such duty?
>
> JAPAN: We admit that he was on duty, but it is our position that the shooting had no connection with his duty of guarding the machine gun. The act of Girard in throwing out brass and enticing the victim toward him had no connection with guarding the machine gun.
>
> U.S.: Your statement of fact does not take into account Girard's statement of his intent. That is, that he fired for the purpose of

[18] Established by the Administrative Agreement (*supra*, Chapter III, n. 5), Article XXVI. No such committee exists in NATO countries.

[19] Defined as "any duty or service required or authorized to be done by statute, regulation, the order of a superior, or military usage" (Agreed View No. 39).

[20] This is so in spite of the fact that a circular of the United States Army Forces, Far East, specifies: "The term 'official duty' . . . is meant to apply only to acts which are required to be done as a function of those duties which the individuals are performing" (*Operation Hearings* IV, p. 21). The circular seems to contradict the general implementing policy of the United States and, for that matter, the actual practice of United States authorities in Japan.

scaring the Japanese away and thus insure the safety of the machine gun.

JAPAN: The evidence shows that there was no danger to the machine gun. Nickel made a statement to this effect. Thus, we do not consider that Girard actually fired to protect the machine gun. The Japanese were only picking up brass in the vicinity; they were not interfering in any way with Girard's mission to guard the machine gun. There was thus no necessity or reason for Girard to shoot at them to insure the safety of the machine gun. Its safety was never in danger. Further, according to the statement of Lt. Mahon, firing an empty cartridge from a grenade launcher is not authorized, and any superior of Girard observing such an action by Girard would have been obliged to interfere and prevent Girard from firing his weapon in this manner.

U.S.: However, if we give full weight to Girard's statement, we must conclude that he did, in fact, fire to scare the Japanese away and thus insure safety of the machine gun. . . . If you were to believe Girard's statement, would you consider that he was acting in the performance of official duty?

JAPAN: Your question is based on a supposition that is not supported by the evidence, and we are not prepared to answer it.

U.S.: In determining official duty in this case, is it not important to consider Girard's intent as disclosed by his own statement?

JAPAN: In determining that the incident did not arise in the performance of official duty, we considered all the evidence . . . . It is our position that the evidence shows that the firing had no significant connection with the guarding of the machine gun.[21]

After three months of this, the American representative on the Joint Committee was instructed to *waive* the American primary right if the deadlock continued.[22] He did so after an additional three weeks of negotiations, whereupon the Secretaries of State and Defense in a joint statement urged the American public to acquiesce in this "completed action." [23] Since the adopted course

[21] *Operation Hearings* IV, pp. 19-20.

[22] That means, in fact, *not* to agree that Japan had the primary right in the case according to the terms of the treaty.

[23] News Release, Office of Public Information, Department of Defense, June 4, 1957.

left room for speculation that something was relinquished which belonged to the United States by right, the isolationist attack against the status-of-forces system was revived, and the Senate Committee on Armed Services scheduled special hearings on the case. Following an unsuccessful appeal to American courts,[24] Girard was tried in Japan and received a suspended sentence.[25] But the commanding officer's certificate was never withdrawn.[26] Furthermore, a Defense Department spokesman explained that the provision of the supplementary agreement protecting the right of Japanese courts to determine their own jurisdiction had been agreed upon because "our effort was to prevent our appearing as the dictator in these places where we were embarked around the world in a joint enterprise," though it was known all the time that other provisions can be used to block any case before it reaches a Japanese court.[27] In the Girard case, these provisions were not exploited to the limit[28] but far enough to miss the opportunity for yielding gracefully. All of this happened merely in order to assert a theory whose value is best demonstrated by the fact that it had to be by-passed by waiving what it purported to establish.

The second exception to the principle of primacy of local jurisdiction—"offenses solely against the property or security of [the sending] state, or offenses solely against the persons or property of another member of the force or civilian component or of a dependent" (NATO-SFA, Article VII, 3a[i])—raises the problem of separating two aspects of the same wrongful action when both the sending

---

[24] *Wilson* v. *Girard,* 354 U.S. 524 (July 11, 1957), reversing the decision of the District Court for the District of Columbia that the waiver was unconstitutional.

[25] *Operation Hearings* IV, p. 4.

[26] *Girard Hearing,* pp. 22-23.

[27] *Ibid.,* p. 15.

[28] The Joint Committee did not formally abandon negotiations and refer the matter to the two governments according to Article XXVI(3) of the Administrative agreement, mainly because it was eventually realized that "such reference would result in a still further postponement of the trial and still further inflammation of the situation in Japan" (*Girard Hearing,* p. 24).

and the receiving state or their subjects are injured. Strict interpretation of the agreement would place all such cases under the
jurisdiction of the receiving state. In practice, however, it has been
recognized that the sending state has a reasonable claim to exercise
jurisdiction when the offense is directed primarily against a fellow
serviceman, although it causes a minor injury to a local interest as
a by-product. This would include, for example, a case of man-
slaughter, when the victim is another member of the visiting force,
but the offense occurs in the course of a brawl in a local tavern,
causing a breach of the peace; or a traffic offense resulting in an
accident in which a fellow serviceman is injured, but the lives of
local residents are also endangered by reckless driving; or a case of
wrongful appropriation and disposal of property of the sending
state in violation of local customs and currency regulations. In
similar situations, the desirability of dealing with all aspects of
the same chain of events in one trial is a convincing argument, and
the receiving states have generally been willing to concede that
the weightier aspect of the wrongful conduct should determine
jurisdiction over the entire set of circumstances.[29] The exception
is the United Kingdom, where the courts have insisted on their
right to protect the integrity of domestic regulations adopted for
the safety of the public, especially traffic regulations, even if the
only actual victim is a member of the visiting force.[30]

A different type of deviation from the text of the agreement occurs when the injuries to both sides are substantial and neither is
willing to relinquish jurisdiction. The solution is often sought in
forgetting the argument about the desirability of sound legal practices and reading two distinct offenses into the same wrongful
course of action. The American concept of double jeopardy (based
on the legal definition of the wrongful act rather than on the act
itself) is readily accepted by the receiving states to get around Arti-

[29] Rouse and Baldwin, *op. cit.*, p. 40.
[30] Snee and Pye, *Status*, p. 57.

cle VII(8) of NATO-SFA.[31] In some cases, however, the local authorities have, as a matter of principle, considered a single trial under
the jurisdiction of the sending state preferable to two trials, although the injury to the local interest would have appeared to an
American judge to be the more substantial one.[32]

In sum then, it is clear that no uniform standards exist for the
application of either the on-duty or the *inter se* exception from
the principle of primacy of local jurisdiction under NATO-SFA and
its derivatives. It has been asserted that the main sources of difficulty in the administration of NATO-SFA can be found, first, in
"grafting the treaty provisions upon the body of internal law of
the country, whose procedures were not designed to meet the new
needs of Article VII"; second, "in the lack, in many instances, of
any uniform directives from higher military authorities establishing accepted interpretations of the Agreement and policies and
procedures to be followed." [33] If these two main sources of difficulty are the reasons for the differences in the application of the
key provisions, the role of the first is more readily ascertainable,
but both require some redefinition. More than the problem of
antiquated procedures is involved in the role of the local law. For
example, the constitutional privileges of Italian prosecutors, not
necessarily an antiquated feature, aggravated the difficulty arising
out of the lack of national implementing laws, thus making the

---

[31] In a case under the Moroccan agreement with France (reported by Snee and
Pye, *op. cit.*, p. 55), American authorities tried *inter alia* for "wrongful sale" (of
stolen American pistols) while the French asserted their jurisdiction in trying for
the "illegal trafficking in arms"—a procedure difficult to reconcile with the *ne bis
in idem* principle. Article VII(8), NATO-SFA, states that "where an accused has
been tried in accordance with the provisions of this Article by the authorities of
one Contracting Party . . . he may not be tried again for the same offense within
the same territory by the authorities of another Contracting Party."

[32] An Italian prosecutor waived the trial over a serviceman who had killed a
local resident in the course of a joy ride in a wrongfully appropriated American
vehicle. The wrongful appropriation was regarded as a more serious offense than
the negligent driving (Snee and Pye, *op. cit.*, p. 57).

[33] Snee and Pye, *Report*, p. 98.

early application of NATO-SFA in Italy an erratic undertaking. Or, to offer a different illustration, the premium placed on the availability of inexpensive remedies to the injured individual in France (in contrast to the situation in the United Kingdom, where the main consideration is the integrity of the legal system and the role of the judge as protector of the general public interest) lessens local pressure to assert the punitive aspect of jurisdiction once an adequate way of settling the private claim is assured. More generally, the exemption of foreign military persons from the jurisdiction of local courts is easier to effect where the exemption of domestic military persons (and of military-type offenses by whomever committed) from the jurisdiction of civilian courts is a feature not unknown to the existing legal system or, at least, recent legal history. This feature accounts for much of the less reluctant acceptance of American interpretations of NATO-SFA in the so-called civil-law countries, but it sometimes leads to unexpected difficulties: under a system of special jurisdiction for offenses of a military type, a member of the visiting force may have to face trial in a local military court.[34] Thus, different priorities assigned to the values protected by local law, different legal connotations of the terms of the agreement, constitutional obstacles, and different methods of translating an international obligation into domestic law—all have a part in the "grafting" process.

The second major difficulty involves, similarly, more than an omission on the part of higher military authorities in providing uniform instructions concerning accepted interpretations, policies, and procedures. Although in some cases the only policy demonstrated appeared to be lack of any policy, and there was a shortage of instructions on various aspects of the agreement, the total out-

---

[34] The offense could be theft of a military vehicle owned by the receiving state. If stationed in an area in which martial law has been proclaimed, a member of the visiting force would also fall under the local court-martial jurisdiction. NATO-SFA does not exclude military tribunals from the concept of "authorities of the receiving state," which have jurisdiction in all offenses against local law. The case mentioned *supra*, n. 31, was tried in a French military tribunal. See Snee and Pye, *Report*, pp. 40-41.

come indicates that in actuality there always was an American implementing policy in effect. In line with negotiating policy, which left some of the key provisions of the agreement too vague,[35] this implementing policy pursues maximum immunity of the visiting forces; but it also differentiates between the various receiving countries in the intensity with which the declared general objective is pursued. In other words, the variations in implementation of the provisions on the primary right of the sending state are not the result solely or even primarily of different local situations or conceptions. They reveal the existence of what might be called a graduated implementing policy of the United States—a point that should become even clearer after a review of the application of another key provision of the agreement.

### WAIVERS OF JURISDICTIONAL RIGHTS: WHAT IS BEING WAIVED?

As was suggested in the preceding chapter, the provision incorporating a system of waivers into Type III status-of-forces agreements also has two major weaknesses: first, lack of standards for the requesting and granting of waivers; second, lack of clarity as to the exact consequences of a waiver. The uncertainties arising from the latter are now somewhat lessened as a result of the conclusion of prolonged litigation in French courts in a case waived by the French prosecutor but reopened by the private claimant when American authorities failed to make use of their jurisdic-

---

[35] What has become known about the negotiating history of NATO-SFA (see Snee and Pye, *Status,* pp. 12, 38, 51, 65, *et passim*) indicates that it was usually a representative of a smaller country who brought up hypothetical problems and asked for the inclusion of appropriate provisions in the text. These proposals were, however, brushed off in the hope that such problems would never arise, or that they could be solved in the spirit of mutual trust without specific provisions. Later, in bilateral settlement of actual cases under an agreement lacking specific provisions, the spirit of alliance turned out to be—as will be demonstrated in the last subsection of the present chapter—more often than not identical with the viewpoint of the larger partner.

tion.[36] Besides clarifying the consequences of a waiver granted by French authorities, the case involved several related problems of interpretation of NATO-SFA. Two in particular were the meaning of the concept "concurrent jurisdiction," and the relation between the distribution of jurisdictional rights under the treaty and the distribution of legal functions in criminal proceedings under French national law. In its various stages, the case has stimulated comment in professional literature in France and in the United States, and the final decision of the French Court of Cassation will doubtlessly be referred to by American authorities in the application of Type III agreements elsewhere.[37]

The facts of the case involved an accident in the course of which a car, driven at excessive speed in bad weather conditions by an American Air Force officer stationed in France, Major Jack Whitley, crashed into a tree. A passenger, Squadron Leader Aitchison, a Canadian officer attached to the same NATO headquarters, was killed. Upon the request of Air Force authorities, the French Ministry of Justice and the local prosecutor waived jurisdiction over the matter, but no court-martial proceedings were instituted because an informal Air Force investigation led to the conclusion that evidence was insufficient. The widow of the Canadian officer, not entitled to pension under Canadian law because the accident did not occur while her husband was on duty, sued thereupon as a *partie civile* in the French criminal court of Corbeil, in order to establish Whitley's liability and thus force his insurance company to pay compensation.

The argument brought forward on behalf of the American officer that the waiver had divested France of any jurisdiction in

[36] *Aitchison c. Whitley,* Tribunal correctionel de Corbeil, 5 avril 1954, *Revue critique de droit international privé,* XLIII (1954), 602, *Annuaire français de droit international,* I (1955), 579; *Whitley c. Aitchison,* Cours d'appel de Paris, 16 mai 1956, *Revue critique . . . ,* XLVI (1957), 100, *Annuaire . . . ,* III (1957), 721; reversed, Cours de cassation, Chambre criminelle, 1958 (see *Revue générale de droit international public,* LXIII [1959], 17-18, and *Operation Hearing* IV, p. 43, for the substance of the last decision).

[37] See the Bibliographical Note at the end of this volume.

the matter was rejected by the French court essentially on two grounds. In the first place, relying on domestic legal principles, the court pointed out that the French legal system does not assign the monopoly of criminal prosecution to the government. Since nobody can renounce more rights than he possesses, all that the public prosecutor can waive is his own right to initiate criminal proceedings. The concurrent right of the private party to set in motion the wheels of justice remains intact. This, the court thought, is entirely reconcilable with NATO-SFA, because its Article VII implicitly recognizes the possibility of assumption of jurisdiction by the state not having the primary right to exercise jurisdiction in that it requires the contracting parties to "notify one another of the disposition of all cases in which there are concurrent rights" (Article VII, 6b). Second, the court interpreted the waiving provision of NATO-SFA as conditional upon the exercise of jurisdiction by the other state. This, the court thought, followed *a contrario* from the double jeopardy provision of NATO-SFA. Since a person who "has been tried in accordance with the provisions of this article by the authorities of one Contracting Party and has been acquitted, or has been convicted and is serving, or has served his sentence, or has been pardoned" may not be tried again within the same territory by the authorities of another contracting party (Article VII, 8), a person who has not been subject to any of these actions by the state holding the primary right may well be tried by the other state. As the purely administrative determination of American authorities not to proceed to a trial was not an act of "jurisdictional significance," [38] the concurrent French jurisdiction was revived and there was nothing to prevent the injured party from making use of its right of prosecution under French law. Jurisdiction is thus "concurrent" because both states hold it all the time, and what is waived is at most the priority in the use of

---

[38] That is, it did not constitute even a *res judicata*, in the sense of a formal sentence or acquittal, much less fulfil the requirements of Article VII, paragraph 8, that a "sentence" be "served" (or pardoned) to bar further prosecution. Indeed, not even a formal investigation under Article 32 UCMJ was held.

jurisdiction. Indeed, whether priority is the original one, based on the agreement, or is acquired by the waiver, the outcome is still the same: jurisdiction cannot be held suspended, for the other state still retains its jurisdiction and can make use of it as soon as the state holding the primary right decides not to act.[39]

The first ground the Corbeil court put forward for resumption of jurisdiction, restricting the scope of the waiver to the renunciation of the right of the public prosecutor to institute criminal proceedings, was considered improper even by French observers who agreed with the outcome of the case; but the remainder of the court's reasoning is more convincing. Thus, Professor Jacques Léauté, although he urges that the decision be "generalized" if erosions of the sovereignty of the receiving states continue, rejects the court's narrow conception of waivers on the ground that it contradicts both traditional French practices in the field of so-called international criminal law and the text and spirit of NATO-SFA.[40] However, he considers the second ground forwarded by the

[39] This proposition is also supported by the first sentence of paragraph 3(c) of Article VII, NATO-SFA, which requires that the state having the primary right notify the authorities of the other state as soon as practicable if it decides not to exercise its right.

[40] In his comment on the Corbeil court's decision (*Revue Critique, supra,* n. 36), Léauté makes clear (p. 610) that (1) the text of NATO-SFA refers to the waiving of state jurisdiction in its entirety, which effectively bars private as well as public prosecution simply because what is waived is the authority of the *state* to make its judges conduct the judicial proceedings; that (2) in analogous situations where an exemption from local jurisdiction is granted (such as in the case of diplomatic immunities and offenses committed aboard men-of-war), French legal practice knows only of a renunciation of the right of the French state to judge the matter, not merely of the right of the ministry or the prosecutor to initiate criminal proceedings; and (3) that Article VII, paragraph 6(b) is not intended to confirm the coexistence of two jurisdictions but merely to organize further the matter already introduced in paragraph 6(a), i.e., co-operation between contracting states in carrying out investigations into offenses that are to be prosecuted under the terms of the agreement.

See also comment of Luc Muracciole on the decision of the appellate court in the same matter in his report, "Jurisprudence française relative au droit international public," *Annuaire français du droit international,* III (1957), 686-772, paragraph 143, p. 722, where he points out that domestic allocation of authority to proceed has little weight in the face of an international agreement and that the appellate court, although not retracting from the position of the court of first instance, appears to have recognized its weakness.

court quite sufficient. Assuming that the basic purpose of Article VII is to resolve conflicts of jurisdiction (and thus contradictory judgments in the same matter), it follows that its various provisions—those allocating original jurisdictional priorities, the system of waivers, and the double-jeopardy prohibition—all have to be interpreted with reference to this basic purpose. The intention was to guarantee that there shall be only one proceeding followed by a single judgment. Consequently, there is little sense in waiving the exercise of one jurisdiction unless the other is exercised; for in the absence of a positive conflict of jurisdictions, why should rules designed to resolve such conflicts be applied? [41]

American commentators welcomed Léauté's criticism of the court's first ground for resumption of jurisdiction, but they criticized the court's second ground as well. Moreover, they drew a different conclusion from the purpose of the agreement. Thus Rouse and Baldwin observed that, to accomplish the purpose of NATO-SFA, it is necessary that the conflict of jurisdiction be resolved "quickly and with finality," and that "the waiver is purposeless unless it is an insulation from the waiving state's exercise of criminal jurisdiction." [42] Snee and Pye,[43] and Schuck,[44] suggested the application of Article XVI of NATO-SFA,[45] but Schuck at the same time went overboard in his criticism of the French decision. Having noted, first, that any argument based on *French* municipal law is irrelevant,[46] he went on to criticize the rationale of the decision on the ground that it must ultimately generate a theory which would mean nothing less than "to advocate the violation of

---

[41] Léauté, *op. cit.*, p. 611.

[42] *Op. cit.*, p. 49.

[43] *Status*, p. 72.

[44] Edwin G. Schuck, "Concurrent Jurisdiction under the NATO Status of Forces Agreement," *Columbia Law Review*, LVII, No. 3 (March, 1957), 355-71, on p. 371.

[45] Providing for direct negotiations to settle differences in the interpretation and application of the agreement and, in case of failure to reach a settlement, referring of the matter to the North Atlantic Council.

[46] *Op. cit.*, p. 364.

*United States* law as well as the misuse of the judicial machinery in the interests of political expediency." [47] American military authorities in Europe, apparently conceding that the waiver is conditional upon the exercise of American jurisdiction "in some manner," took the position, not endorsed by the Departments of State and Defense, that a determination not to proceed to a trial (whether made after formal procedure under Article 32 of the Uniform Code of Military Justice, or on the basis of an informal investigation) is an exercise of jurisdiction and bars subsequent trial by the receiving state.[48] It is difficult to conceive how this position could have been taken in the face of the specific wording of Article VII, paragraph 8, of NATO-SFA and its negotiating history.[49] Indeed, an interservice legal committee, convening in Rome in October 1956, resolved that in future cases the authorities of the waiving state should be persuaded *to agree* that waivers, when granted, shall be final and unconditional, and that the disposition of cases in *any* manner consistent with United States law shall be acknowledged as exercise of jurisdiction fulfilling the requirements of that paragraph. This was necessary because the committee thought, in agreement with the position of the two departments, that "no legal or factual basis exists for asserting that such exercise of jurisdiction is tantamount to a trial in the sense of paragraph 8 of Article VII." [50] Schuck's position in dealing with the court's inference from the double-jeopardy provision was sounder. The "unimpeachable proposition" that a purely administrative

[47] That is, the "theory" that in every case of concurrent jurisdiction in which the military authority holds the primary right (whether directly on the basis of Article VII, paragraph 3[a], or as a consequence of a waiver), the accused "must" be tried by court-martial (in order to prevent his trial in a French court) even if it is clear that he has committed no offense provable under American rules of evidence (*op. cit.*, pp. 367-68 [emphasis added]).

[48] Snee and Pye, *Report*, pp. 47-48.

[49] In explaining his draft during the London negotiations, the United States representative declared that the double-jeopardy prohibition would not prevent the other contracting party from prosecution where it was not possible for the state holding the primary right to collect sufficient evidence to prosecute (MS[J]–R[51]5, paragraph 8, quoted by Snee and Pye, *Status*, p. 72).

[50] Snee and Pye, *ibid.*, p. 68.

decision is not a sentence or an acquittal, he suggested, "serves only to negate a single bar to trial. This falls far short of establishing affirmatively a right to try the case." [51]

Thus, all concerned seemed to agree on one point, that the court had erred in assuming that nothing more is waived than the right of the public prosecutor to prosecute. But how much more *is* waived? This depends on whether the word "right" or the word "primary" is emphasized in the phrase "primary right to exercise jurisdiction" of Article VII, Section 3. When the significance of the adjective is overlooked, or, as can happen too easily, "primary jurisdiction" is substituted, it appears that nothing is left to the waiving state and that, therefore, "jurisdiction" must be "waived back" before that state can resume its exercise.[52] Although loose references to the waiving provision would thus tend to support the American military authorities' effort to establish that waivers are irrevocable, it was an American comment which made it explicit that "the waiver is a waiver of the primary right to proceed and not of the jurisdiction itself, which remains with the French authorities as a secondary or residual right." [53] Léauté, besides partly misconstruing the situation,[54] emphasizes that the waiving state is renouncing jurisdiction ("renonce à l'ensemble de son droit de juger") rather than the right of public prosecution. Consequently, although he insists that the waiver is conditional, the connection between the degree of finality and the subject matter of the waiver

---

[51] *Op. cit.*, p. 366.

[52] Schuck (*op. cit.*, pp. 362-67 (passim) uses the terms interchangeably, also omitting the adjective altogether, which, of course, is a method promoting his thesis, in that it excludes the possibility of an inference that what is being waived might be merely the priority. Rouse and Baldwin seem to be aware that the conflict between the two jurisdictions, which Article VII is intended to settle, is on the issue "who shall *first* act" (*loc. cit., supra,* n. 50 [emphasis added]), but their desire to resolve the matter "with finality" leaves no room for a secondary opportunity to act.

[53] Snee and Pye, *Status,* p. 64.

[54] He thinks that the victim was an American, indicating that the original waiver was granted because the Ministry of Justice handled the case as an *inter se* matter of the visiting forces, falling under Article VII, 3(a)(i) (*op. cit.*, p. 610).

is lost.[55] If *jurisdiction* is renounced—"in its entirety," at that—the exercise of jurisdiction can hardly be resumed unilaterally by the state that has renounced it. The dispute on the issue of whether the waiver is final or conditional is a dispute about what is being waived. To say that jurisdiction is cancelled only after the other state fulfills the requirements of Article VII, paragraph 8,[56] is to hold that the waiver itself effects nothing more than a change in the order in which the two states having concurrent rights of jurisdiction may act.

This perhaps becomes clearer when the French version of the relevant section of the agreement, which appears to support the limited-waiver theory more explicitly than the English text, is considered. In the French version,[57] first, the coexistence of two jurisdictions is clearer because each state exercises "its" jurisdiction (not merely "jurisdiction" without an adjective, as if there were only one which is shifted from state to state); second, the authorities of the receiving state are not even in possession of a transferable object called "the primary right" but simply "exercent leur jurisdiction *par priorité*" in the applicable situation, "exercise their jurisdiction first" or, possibly, "in a manner overriding any conflicting attempt of the other state to exercise its jurisdiction" ("par priorité" modifying the verb "exercent" rather than the noun "droit"); and third, the identical word "renoncer" stands for both the English "waiving" (second sentence of paragraph 3c) and

---

[55] *Ibid.*, p. 611.

[56] Snee and Pye (*loc. cit.*) seem to agree in this respect with Léauté, though they would interpret the terms of paragraph 8 broadly to include summary punishment under Article 15 UCMJ and dismissal of the case "after a careful investigation and legal analysis" (*ibid.*, p. 71).

[57] Article VII, Section 3:

"(b) Dans le cas de toute autre infraction, les authorités de l'Etat de séjour exercent par priorité leur juridiction.

"(c) Si l'Etat qui a le droit d'exercer par priorité sa juridiction decide d'y renoncer, il le notifiera aussitôt que possible aux authorités de l'autre Etat. Les authorités de l'Etat qui a le droit d'exercer par priorité sa juridiction examinent avec bienveillance les demandes de renonciation à ce droit, présentées par les authorités de l'autre Etat, lorsque celles-ci estiment que des considérations particulièrement importantes le justifient."

"deciding not to exercise" (first sentence), suggesting that what takes place in both cases (whether upon request or possibly unsolicited) is not a transaction but a refraining. Although the renunciation has consequences for the other state under the terms of the treaty, the first state does not waive anything *to* the second; it merely *waives* (without a following indirect object), that is, "refrains from taking advantage of" [58] its right to act *first* (not of its "primary right" *to act*). At that point the second state may act not because it has received something from the first state, but because it has concurrent jurisdiction. Since nothing was transferred to start with, nothing needs to be returned should the second state likewise refain from action; though, of course, the exercise of jurisdiction by the first state can now be prevented by an intervening establishment of premises of Section 8, if the second state makes use of that opportunity.

Both texts of the agreement are, of course, equally valid; and they do not necessarily contradict each other, though one is more conducive to the limited-waiver theory than the other. In the Whitley case French courts have in the end retracted.[59] But it was perhaps premature for American military spokesmen to celebrate that "we won on a significant issue." [60] For one thing, it may have been a Pyrrhic victory, because finality of waivers can simply mean that less waivers will be granted in the future, particularly in cases where a private claim has to be settled.[61] For another, both the sig-

[58] *Webster's New Collegiate Dictionary* (Springfield: Merriam, 1951), p. 960.

[59] Court of Appeal of Paris approved the decision of the Corbeil court, following the same reasoning, but with more emphasis on specific requirements of Section 8, adding, in particular, the comment that even a sentence passed by a court, if not actually served by the convicted offender, would not exclude subsequent trial. It also affirmed that the signatory parties have foreseen "solely a renunciation of the right of 'priority of exercise' of jurisdiction, without considering anywhere any waiving of jurisdiction whatever" (*Annuaire français, supra,* n. 36). The Court of Cassation reversed (*supra,* n. 36) after the claim of the civil party was settled out of court.

[60] General Hickman in *Operation Hearings* IV, p. 43.

[61] A circular of the French Ministry of Justice reserved the granting of waivers to the Minister when there is a private complaint involved. This procedure was

nificance of judicial precedent in France (and most other receiving countries) and the existence of clarity about the issue in which this particular case set a precedent can be easily overestimated. By the time the case was decided in the final instance, American military lawyers were proud because "we have thus had some part in the establishment of the French principle that a treaty is the supreme law of France." [62] But the supremacy of treaties over law as a matter of principle was never in doubt; the issue was the correct meaning of a treaty whose overriding quality was already explicitly recognized by the court of first instance.[63] The fact that the court, in a major part of its opinion, had failed to apply properly the principle it had acknowledged to start with may have provided additional motive for the highest court to reverse the decision, but it did not constitute a denial of the principle. Furthermore, it is perhaps not without significance for the outcome of the case that the injured party was a member of another visiting force, and that Whitley's insurance company changed its mind and settled the claim before the case was decided by the Court of Cassation. A dispute between an American and a Canadian is a matter of little direct interest to the French. The combined civil-criminal trial, whose main purpose is to establish civil liability by means of a nominal criminal sentence, loses its rationale once the civil claim it paid. It is hard to conceive that the Court of Cassation acted with any degree of awareness (in the sense of, say, the United States Supreme Court when deliberating on a constitutional issue) that it was "legislating" on future incidents in which Frenchmen might be killed and settlement of claims refused. Indeed, if such

followed in the Whitley case, but see *supra*, n. 54. In future, the Ministry of Justice may simply become more careful in examining requests for waivers.

[62] Hickman's statement, *loc. cit.*

[63] "Attendu que . . . application de ce principe de droit interne français doit être faite en tenant compte des dispositions du dit traité, *en conséquence de la supériorité de conventions diplomatiques régulièrement ratifiées, sur la loi du for français,* par application des articles 26 et suivants de la Constitution française de 1946 . . ." (Corbeil court, *Revue critique, op. cit.,* p. 603 [emphasis added]).

a situation ever arises, American authorities may find it hazardous to insist on the Whitley precedent.[64] However, for the time being, waivers, when granted, are technically final in France; what is waived, therefore, is jurisdiction, for "only an express waiver of jurisdiction by the United States authorities *back to* France would revive the jurisdiction of French courts over the case." [65]

## WAIVERS: REQUESTING PRACTICES AND RESULTS

It was suggested before that waivers could have represented an indispensible element of flexibility had the status-of-forces agreements also established a highly specific system of criteria for the separation of competences of the contracting states. But even under the broadly formulated terms of NATO-SFA they can serve as a useful device for preventing results which do not conform with the over-all intent of the agreement, and which may in some situations follow from a literal application of its text.[66] It would be a

[64] A decision in a case in which the victim was French did in fact intervene, setting the stage for the Whitley reversal. But the incident in the other case involved an act committed in the course of duty which had occurred before NATO-SFA became effective, and the "waiver" on the part of the lower court was something quite different from the waiver in the Whitley case. It was a declaration of the court that it was not competent to hear a case involving an offense committed by a member of the visiting force in the course of his duty and *not* a waiver by the authorities of the receiving state of their primary right to exercise jurisdiction pursuant to paragraph 3(c), Article VII, NATO-SFA. The Court of Cessation dismissed the appeal against this "waiver" of the Court of Appeal of Paris, holding that the lower court had properly applied the provision of paragraphs 3(a)(ii) of Article VII when it "released jurisdiction in favor of the American military authority exercising its right of priority of jurisdiction," since an agreement governing problems of concurrent jurisdiction is applicable to cases in progress, and the present agreement does not subject the sending state's claim of priority "to any particular condition and especially to proof that prosecutions have already been instituted" (*Affaire Labelle, veuve Gadois,* Court of Cassation, Criminal Chamber, March 7, 1957 [copy supplied by Staff Judge Advocate's office, Orléans]; cf. *Annuaire français de droit international,* IV [1958] 781-90).

[65] Hickman's statement, *loc. cit.* (Emphasis added.)

[66] This, of course, is not a reference to cases such as Girard and Gadois, where a state attempts to avoid embarrassment by waiving a right that it does not possess to start with—thereby, in effect, compounding confusion. See, however, this chapter, *supra* at n. 29, for some applicable examples.

mistake, however, to assume that waivers are relied upon primarily in such situations. It will be recalled that in the treaty itself the only standard given for waiving the primary rights to exercise jurisdiction is that the requesting state considers the waiver to be "of particular importance." Since we are not told, however, in what types of situations the waiver may appropriately be considered as particularly important, the interesting result is that the United States requesting policies seem to be based on the assumption that this distinguishing characteristic is present in the case of every single offense falling under the jurisdiction of the receiving state. Thus, one Department of Defense directive makes the Designated Commanding Officer[67] responsible "to assure that effective liaison is developed and maintained at all levels of command . . . to the end that through the use of local procedures a maximum number of waivers of jurisdiction may be obtained. Constant efforts will be made to establish relationships and methods of operation which, in the light of local judicial processes, will result in waivers wherever possible." [68] Another directive instructs the commanders exercising general court-martial jurisdiction over the accused, "whenever it appears that foreign authorities may assume jurisdiction over or take custody of United States personnel," to report the matter to the Designated Commanding Officer, who shall then see whether the accused may receive a fair trial in the country and consult with the chief of the diplomatic mission about whether to press the request for waiver through diplomatic channels.[69] The instruction, designed to implement the requirements imposed by the Senate when giving advice and consent on NATO-

[67] "Designated Commanding Officer" in each country is the single military commander, representing all three services, who is responsible for the implementation of the NATO-SFA ratification resolution.

[68] *H.R. 8704 Hearings*, p. 3496. See also S. Repts. 2558, 84th Cong., and 1162, 85th Cong., p. 3, for the finding of the Senate Subcommittee on the Operation of Article VII that the policy of the Defense Department is to request waivers "in practically all cases."

[69] Department of Defense Directive Number 5525.1, November 3, 1955, Section VIII (*Operation Hearings* II, p. 6).

SFA,[70] nominally refers to situations "where it appears probable
. . . that the accused may not obtain a fair trial or fair treatment," [71] In actuality, however, requests for waivers in some form
are made in all cases falling under the jurisdiction of the receiving
state,[72] including those that cannot be tried under the United
States jurisdiction because of the restricted authority of courts-
martial or because they involve no offense, or no provable offense,
under American law.[73] Thus, Army procedures in effect in France
prescribe, in every case of arrest or possible prosecution in a
French court, requests for release from custody and requests for
release from jurisdiction, starting at the level of the local prosecutor, with simultaneous reports to the Country Representative,[74]
who repeats the requests at the level of the Ministry of Justice,
reporting negative results to the Department of the Army. Furthermore, pending cases are placed on cumulative remainder lists
that are maintained for various categories of cases to be submitted
weekly to the Ministry until a decision on the request is received,
and the cases are also discussed in weekly conferences with the
Ministry. Procedures vary somewhat from service to service (hence,
from country to country, insofar as a different service may represent the American forces as a whole), but in any event routine procedures guarantee that a request for waiver, or requests at various

[70] *Supra,* Chapter III, n. 70.

[71] *Loc. cit.,* paragraph A.

[72] This information was obtained from the Staff Judge Advocate, USAREUR, Com Z
(Army Headquarters, Europe, Country Representative for France [Orléans]), in an
interview held in July, 1957. It confirms the continuation of the requesting practices found to be in effect by Snee and Pye in four NATO countries they had visited
one year earlier (*Report,* p. 21). In non-NATO countries, where local procedures
appear more perplexing (though, in fact, not necessarily less fair) to the military,
the policy of requesting waivers in every case applies a fortiori.

[73] Such as in the Whitley case (*supra*) or in cases of accompanying civilians over
whom the courts-martial have no jurisdiction in peacetime under American law.

[74] The "Country Representative" is the officer, appointed by the Designated
Commanding Officer (*supra,* n. 67), who actually performs day-to-day functions in
the implementing of the status-of-forces agreement at the level of the central government in each country.

contact points, follow every incident over which local authorities may decide to exercise their jurisdiction.[75]

This practice, should it be merely a consequence of concern about the fairness of local trials in pursuance of the Senate ratification resolution, invites the inference that no country guarantees in its regular courts a degree of fairness approaching that of the American courts-martial.[76] It is necessary to note, however, first, that the Senate resolution has been interpreted to require more than court-martial fairness;[77] and second, that the actual requesting policy—aside from the necessity to demonstrate sincerity in trying to satisfy the concern of Congress for the rights of servicemen—is apparently motivated by other considerations. As one military spokesman put it, "it is the position of the Department of Defense that jurisdictional arrangements prescribed by the NATO Status of Forces Agreement is [*sic*] to be considered only as an acceptable minimum. We would like to try them all, keep them all within the military conclave. Accordingly the United States have, wherever possible, sought to extend their jurisdiction." [78]

[75] Interview, Orléans, *supra*, n. 72; see, however, *infra*, n. 87. In some commands, self-restraint in requesting policy is necessary in minor cases, because the request, as Snee and Pye found (*Report*, p. 17), may precipitate prosecution in a matter that might have been disregarded by the prosecutor had the request not resulted in "starting a file" on the incident. Such restraint does not change the principle, of course.

[76] The directive quoted *supra*, n. 69, makes clear that fairness is "not to be considered as requiring such trials to be identical with United States trials" (*loc. cit.*, paragraph C).

[77] However, not as much as required in a regular federal court. Generally speaking, the American military authorities assume that the Senate had in mind the rights guaranteed by the United States Constitution in trials in American state courts. See "Supplemental Statement by Hon. Wilbur M. Brucker," *House SFA Hearings*, p. 249, and Edmund H. Schwenk, "Comparative Study of the Law of Criminal Procedure in NATO Countries under the NATO *Status* of Forces Agreement," *North Carolina Law Review*, XXXV, No. 3 (April, 1957), 358-79, on pp. 362-65.

[78] *Operation Hearings* I, p. 19.

Actually, waivers are often requested over the objection of the accused, who may expect to obtain a lesser sentence in the local court than in court-martial. The use of the waiving provision is a matter of the two states concerned, based on their own policy considerations, which may well be unrelated to the interest of the involved individual (cf. Snee and Pye, *Status*, p. 62).

In short, it was hoped that what had been conceded in negotiating the agreements could be recaptured in the course of implementing their provisions; and who in the United States would argue that any trial of an American soldier in a foreign court is not a matter of "particular importance" to the United States?

The logical expectation that the law of diminishing returns should set in and that, if all cases are declared to be particularly important, the receiving states may begin to look at the important and the less important ones with equal skepticism, is not warranted by "operation" statistics. During the first five-year period following the ratification of NATO-SFA, the "worldwide waiver rate" [79] has fluctuated only between 61 and 73 per cent, showing the largest decrease after the first, probably incomplete, annual report, and a small increase for the last year.[80] Indeed, so successful was the implementing policy of the American military authorities in pursuing exemptions from local jurisdiction "wherever possible" that to discuss the status of American forces stationed in foreign territory, if it should mean anything, should mean to refer to the status "after waivers," which is more often than not a regime exactly the opposite of the one presumed to exist on the basis of the status-of-forces agreements. In other words, it would be more correct to say that the American forces are, by and large, exterritorial than to say that they are, with certain exceptions, subject to

[79] Presumably the relation of the total number of waivers to the number of "alleged offenses subject to foreign jurisdiction"; in fact, however, it is often the relation of the number of cases subject to foreign jurisdiction but not tried, to the total (*infra,* n. 89). The waiver rate, along with the number of unsuspended sentences, is evidently considered as an important index, an increase in the former and a decrease in the latter indicating operational success (*Operation Hearings* I-IV *passim; idem,* V, pp. 7 and 16).

[80] The period covered is 1954-58, the annual reports running from December 1 of the preceding year to November 30 of the year for which the report is made. The successive waiver rates for the five years are: 73, 66, 67, 61, and 63 world-wide; 68, 58, 55, 55, and 57 for NATO countries (S. Repts. 1268 and 2558, 84th Cong., pp. 7 and 5, respectively; 1162 and 2497, 85th Cong., pp. 6 and 3, respectively; and 1110, 86th Cong., p. 4). Early reported figures may not be comparable, because the agreements were only coming into effect during the report years 1954-56.

foreign jurisdiction. There exist, as will be discussed in the last chapter, reasons for considering both ways of describing the situation inappropriate. But if the present system has to be described in one *or* the other way, it is obvious that the "exceptions," leading in practice by two to one, have a persuasive claim to being considered the rule and that the nominal rule has been in fact, only an exception. What is, by and large, in effect, a system under which military authorities retain exclusive jurisdiction over the visiting forces, except when the host state has special reasons (and the stamina) to insist on securing the contrary; though, of course, the arrangements producing this result are, as a rule, not explicit.

There are deviations from this over-all characterization in both directions. At the one extreme, American military authorities have succeeded in securing the conquered territory in the field of waiving practices by way of concluding, with some countries, supplementary agreements that formally recognize the validity of the system just described. Two such agreements, obligating the authorities of the receiving countries to waive upon request their primary right to exercise jurisdiction "except when they determine that it is of particular importance that jurisdiction be exercised" were noted before.[81] Another type of supplementary agreement contains no waiving obligation but achieves the same results through the device of creating the presumption that the waiver has been requested and granted unless the receiving state notifies the military authorities within a specified period (five or twenty days, depending on the weight of the offense) of its intention to exercise jurisdiction. This arrangement shifts the burden of acting and explaining (and acting fast enough) from the presumably requesting state to the presumably deciding state, and is a contributing factor in

---

[81] *Supra,* Chapter III, nn. 31 and 32. Greece has tried 3 out of 58 cases subject to its jurisdiction so far; the Netherlands, 2 out of a five-year reported total of 320. A similar but more generous "general waiver" formula in a non-NATO country (nn. 19 and 29, *ibid.*) eliminates the need for requests.

achieving a waiver rate of 97 per cent in Japan.[82] It is probable that some of the classified agreements contain similar provisions, since the reason for their being classified seems to be the insistence of the receiving states, because of the embarrassingly generous concessions made to the visiting forces.[83]

Near the opposite extreme is the situation in the United Kingdom, where formal requests for waivers are made "only in cases of exceptional importance," [84] though the general requesting policy described above is nominally applied inasmuch as informal oral requests are made in all cases except "petty offenses," the latter being covered by a general request intended to apply to all future incidents.[85] Though no attention seems to be paid to the general request and little to the individual requests, both formal and informal, as the British "try more cases than anyone else," this arrangement has been described by the local commander as a "continued success," and by the spokesman of the Department of Defense as a "pleasant relationship." [86]

Since it is correct only in terms of absolute numbers to say that the British "try more cases than anyone else" (and this is, then, an understatement of the full extent of the contrast between practices in the United Kingdom and those in the other receiving countries) , it may be useful to compare the waiver rates of individual countries in which major troop contingents are presumably subject to local jurisdiction (Table 1). To start with, both the mag-

[82] This is the "automatic-waiver" device agreed to in Agreed View No. 40, supplementary to SFA-Japan, quoted by Gordon B. Baldwin, "Foreign Jurisdiction and the American Soldier: 'The Adventures of Girard,' " *Wisconsin Law Review,* 1958, No. 1 (January, 1958), 52-106, n. 104 on p. 83. The Libyan agreement, referred to in the preceding note, has a similar effect (in requiring initiative on the part of the receiving state to create an exception from the general waiver granted directly by the agreement) and should really be labeled "automatic-general."

[83] Deputy Under Secretary Murphy in *House SFA Hearings,* p. 167.

[84] American Bar Association, Section on International and Comparative Law, *Proceedings* (Chicago: American Bar Center, 1957), p. 57.

[85] Snee and Pye, *Report,* pp. 20-21.

[86] *Operation Hearings* V, p. 12. Corroborated in the report to the ABA Section, *supra,* n. 84, where it was found that few difficulties and no diplomatic interventions whatever had occurred in the United Kingdom.

nitude of the total number of cases and the high degree of correlation between the annual and the over-all rate of each country should be noted. The totals refer to actual offenses of sufficient gravity to become recorded and, in the absence of successful inter-

TABLE 1

Waiver Rates under Type III Agreements*

| Country | Per Cent Waived | | Five-Year Total of Offenses Subject to Local Jurisdiction |
|---|---|---|---|
| | 1958 | 1954-58 | |
| Iceland............... | 0 | 11† | 1,065 |
| Canada............... | 8 | 17 | 2,316 |
| United Kingdom....... | 19 | 19 | 9,655 |
| Italy................. | 68 | 69‡ | 1,046‡ |
| France............... | 88** | 88 | 18,172 |
| Japan................ | 97** | 97 | 20,653 |

* Countries with a cumulative total of more than 1,000 cases. Computed from Chart E, *Operation Hearings* V, p. 20, and additional information released in country-by-country discussion in the Senate Subcommittee, *idem* I-V, except figures marked with a double asterisk, which represent rates released by the Department of Defense, rounded to the next whole number.

† 34 per cent in 1954, 24 per cent in 1955, zero in 1956-58.

‡ Two years only (agreement effective January 21, 1956).

vention by military authorities, liable to be tried in local courts under the existing agreements—not to the total number of offenses committed (i.e., not including offenses subject to the exclusive jurisdiction of the sending state, and for the most part not including those dealt with in simple police courts).[87] Correlation between the annual and the over-all rate of each country individually guarantees that we are not dealing with fortuitous numbers. Whatever the rates reveal must be the result of policies that have been solidified into a stable pattern of practices in each country,

[87] Interview, Orléans (*supra,* n. 72). There is an understandable reluctance on the part of the involved serviceman to report to his superiors an incident that he has already settled at little cost. Snee and Pye found that even in cases involving third parties and resulting in formal prosecution, the first notice of the offense may come to the commander from the Staff Judge Advocate, who has been informed by the French prosecutor (*Report*, p. 12).

and not merely an accident of human or statistical imperfection. Comparison of rates of the several countries with each other demonstrates that certain countries consistently waive a high proportion of cases subject to their jurisdiction, while others use their jurisdictional rights extensively from year to year. There is almost no middle way, even considering the countries that were not included in the first table because the number of cases is too small, or the rates, based on different types of agreement, are not comparable.[88] The validity of the conclusion that certain countries clearly have a preferred position is, incidentally, not threatened by the fact that reporting practices and the availability of information on individual countries are far from perfect.[89] The over-all NATO rate is, for example, consistently three times higher than the British waiver rate (Tables 1 and 2). Though one may be uncertain as to whether the reported figures for the United Kingdom are exaggerated or understated, the contrast is so substantial that it cannot be easily explained away.[90] Furthermore, if the special

---

[88] For some of these see *infra,* n. 91 and Appendix IV, and *supra,* n. 81.

[89] It is only for NATO countries that statistical tables prepared by the Department of Defense disclose annual and cumulative figures in absolute numbers, showing cases subject to foreign jurisdiction and those actually tried during the report period. Figures on other countries, such as Iceland and Japan, included in Table 2 above, have to be found in annual country-by-country discussions in the Senate Subcommittee, in the course of which "waivers" are sometimes, but not for all countries, distinguished from a mere "dropping of charges" (both included in waiver rates considered in this chapter); and the figures do not add up, with the number of cases tried, to the totals subject to foreign jurisdiction (because of a mostly unspecified number of pending cases, overlapping from one report period to the other, and for miscellaneous other reasons). The record shows over-all rates for NATO and the world, but seldom for individual countries with the exception of France and Japan. When the rate is shown, it seems to be based on the assumption that the number of cases subject to foreign jurisdiction less the number of cases tried by foreign courts is the number of cases waived. The possible margin of error, however, does not appear to be substantial enough to affect the conclusions made here.

[90] Because violations of British law which for one or another reason are "turned over to the American military authorities" are counted as waivers (Snee and Pye, *op. cit.,* p. 20; see also the preceding note *in fine*), the rate is probably exaggerated. The often encountered suggestion that the low waiver rate is misleading, because most offenses are minor traffic violations (presumably not tried or reported in other countries, or simply because in the United Kingdom there is that "left-handed way of arriving at the left-hand side of the road, which was the principal

situation in Iceland is disregarded, the United Kingdom is joined only by other Commonwealth countries in maintaining a regime that still reflects the basic distribution of competences foreseen in the text of the status-of-forces agreements.[91] This means that the

TABLE 2
COMPARISON OF NATO AND NON-NATO WAIVER RATES*

| AREA | PER CENT WAIVED | | FIVE-YEAR TOTAL OF OFFENSES SUBJECT TO LOCAL JURISDICTION |
|---|---|---|---|
| | 1958 | 1954-58 | |
| NATO.................. | 57** | 61 | 32,082 |
| World less NATO........ | 79 | 82 | 27,607 |
| World.............. | 63** | 69 | 59,689 |

* Computed from Charts E and F, *Operation Hearings* V, p. 20, except figures marked with a double asterisk, which represent rates released by the Department of Defense, rounded to the next whole number.

provisions of Article VII, Sections 2 and 3, NATO-SFA, are of little if any importance for at least four-fifths of the American soldiers stationed in countries where local jurisdiction over the visiting forces is theoretically recognized; and this is so in spite of the fact that the bulk of American forces in foreign territory is stationed

problem . . ." [*Operation Hearings* IV, p. 50; see also Snee and Pye, *loc. cit.*]), does not seem to be warranted by facts. Traffic offenses constitute the majority of offenses everywhere (66 per cent world-wide, 74 per cent in NATO countries during 1957 [S. Rept. 2497, 85th Cong., p. 4], the latter being just a little higher than in the United Kingdom [*Operation Hearings* III, p. 35]). The British simply try a vastly higher proportion of all offenses, including those which elsewhere are not considered worth the effort of resisting American requests, though, for reasons noted earlier (*supra*, text at nn. 4 and 30), they retain jurisdiction in an even higher proportion of traffic offenses.

[91] Besides Canada (Table 1), the Leased Bases show a sizeable total of offenses subject to local jurisdiction (2,453 for the five-year period), with an extremely small number of waivers (22 out of 583 cases during 1958, less in preceding years). This was not included in the first table above because the treaty is of Type II (see Chapter III, *supra*).

Reports are available for only three other countries in which the number of offenses subject to local jurisdiction is large enough to warrant consideration here: Panama (with no agreement in effect), Morocco (under a classified agreement, waiving about 60 per cent of whatever it has the right to try), and the Philippines (almost no "waivers" whatever, but "dropping the charges" in nearly all cases).

in countries in which that article or identical provisions are nominally in effect. Much of the debate about the so-called surrender, under NATO-SFA and similar agreements, of the constitutional rights of the servicemen and of the sovereign rights of the United States is, therefore, centered on an imaginary subject; for only a serviceman stationed in Commonwealth territory (and Iceland, at this time) should expect with a reasonable degree of probability, if he violates local law, to become subject to the exercise of local jurisdiction. In continental Europe he will probably remain exempt from local proceedings even if the offense is never considered by a court-martial; and it requires a highly unusual chain of circumstances for a member of the American forces to become subject to the exercise of local jurisdiction elsewhere.

Similar to the preferred position of the United Kingdom vis-à-vis nearly all other receiving countries is the preferred position of the NATO area as a whole in relation to the rest of the world. The percentage of offenses subject to local jurisdiction that NATO members try in their courts is more than double the percentage that non-NATO countries try in local courts (Table 2). The full scope of the contrast between NATO and non-NATO countries is, incidentally, not revealed by the statistics or waivers, since their starting point must be the universe of offenses subject to local jurisdiction, not of offenses committed. In other words, NATO countries try twice as large a proportion of the already higher proportion of offenses over which their jurisdiction is recognized by treaty provisions; this, therefore, must be a vastly higher proportion of all offenses committed within their area as contrasted to the proportion of offenses tried by local authorities in non-NATO countries. How much higher is impossible to say, because no statistics are published on the number of offenses falling under the exclusive jurisdiction of the sending state.

It is interesting to note that the ostensibly chaotic American implementation practices, relying as much as they do (in the absence of authoritative interpretations and adequate instructions)[92] upon the talents for improvisation of officers in the field, have made it possible to achieve with such regularity the results just described. Although statistical evidence is available only on one aspect of implementation of the status-of-forces agreement, it is easily the most important aspect. Furthermore, it will be remembered that our inference from the statistics on waiving practices is also supported by the fact that the British have reserved for their own courts the determination of the original scope of the American primary right under Section 3(a) of Article VII.[93] It is, therefore, with respect to the two most important provisions of the agreement that British policies were readily accepted and American procedures in the United Kingdom were adjusted to them,[94] and cheerfully so, while more generous concessions allowed by other countries were considered unsatisfactory on account of minor deviations from the American viewpoint.

It is, of course, not suggested that an official American master plan has been drawn up, prescribing different degrees of insistence on exclusive jurisdiction, according to the rank assigned to the receiving countries. But the opposite proposition, namely to ascribe the differences in the actual scope of immunities solely to the idiosyncrasies of various authorities in the receiving countries, would be even less realistic. It would imply, for example, that the British are continuously more distrustful of American intentions than the French (and the French more so than the Japanese); or that the Luxemburgers are far more stubborn than the Dutch; or that the authorities of the British West Indies have a definite inferiority complex as compared to the Portuguese authorities in

[92] Cf. *supra,* text at n. 33.

[93] By retaining, particularly, the ultimate authority on the relation of offense to duty *(supra,* nn. 3-5). See further, text at n. 30 *supra.*

[94] For requesting the waivers, see *supra,* nn. 84-85; for asserting primary jurisdiction, Snee and Pye assure us that "in the United Kingdom, our military authorities, before claiming primary jurisdiction, are careful to establish: (1) that an incident has occurred in the performance of official duty; and (2) that the incident involves an offense under military law" *(Report,* p. 44)—a policy which is in striking contrast to the one displayed in the Japanese and French cases discussed in this chapter.

the Azores. More likely, the United States had extracted larger privileges from the Japanese than from the British because the Americans distrust the former more than the latter, or assume that the British legal system is fairer or more adaptable to American soldiers.[95] Whatever the determining factor, it first shaped the intensity of determination of the United States to retain a certain level of privileges and then, through varying degrees of American pressure in receiving countries, effected the end-product. The underlying assumptions on the American side do not have to be well founded or even explicit, although the persons involved in the implementation of the agreements must have shared them in a general way in order to produce the graded results described here. One finds, consequently, an actual policy that pursues objectives more complex than the simple, declared objective of obtaining maximum immunities everywhere. Though not officially formulated, it is an effective policy—so much so that, for the citizens of the receiving countries, it is hardly distinguishable from the deliberate, official variety.

[95] This is not to say that actual fairness of local legal procedures or their similarity to American procedures generally determine United States implementation policies. If that were the case, the United States should be more willing to relinquish the exercise of jurisdiction to the Philippine than to the British authorities (the Philippine procedure being in essence American law, passed by the United States); and one would have difficulty in discovering the advantages of, say, Turkish law over that of Belgium, or of Morrocan over that of Greece and the Netherlands, etc. See also n. 78 *supra.* Along with other factors, legal considerations (possibly based on a misconception of the receiving country's law) are determining the American position; but the point here is that whatever determines that position becomes ultimately the chief determinant of the actual scope of immunities granted in the receiving country.

# V. Visiting Forces and Customary International Law

THE STATUS OF FORCES according to the rules of customary international law has received particular attention in professional literature on two occasions. During World War II, the conclusion of the Leased Bases agreement and the assimilation of the legal status of Allied forces in the United Kingdom to the status of the visiting Dominion forces by way of British domestic legislation[1] stimulated the elaboration of the so-called American view. In the formulation by its most articulate protagonist, Colonel Archibald King, this view contained the assertion that

[1] Recognizing the right of the sending states to exercise jurisdiction over members of their forces, but granting no exemption from the jurisdiction of local courts in cases of offenses against local law (Allied Forces Act, 1940, 3 & 4 Geo. VI, C. 51, applied to the American forces by the United States of America [Visiting Forces] Order, *Statutory Rules and Orders,* 1942, No. 966).

according to a principle of international law recognized by British, American, and other authorities, permission by one nation for the troops of another to enter or remain in the former's territory carries with it extraterritoriality, an exemption of the troops in question from the courts of the country and a permission for the operation of the courts-martial of the visiting army.[2]

Colonel King thought that because his analysis of relevant texts disclosed the "substantial unanimity" of judges and publicists in support of this view, and because modern warfare obliterated the distinctions of place of offense and duty condition of the soldier, exclusive jurisdiction of the sending state appeared to be the only proper solution. A concession to the receiving country was made in civil suits (for which the visiting authorities offered no forum), provided they are limited to non-duty contexts and include no enforcement measures tending to control the person of the soldier, question the authority of the commanding officer, interfere with military duties, or impound military pay. Such an arrangement, besides recognizing the rights to which the sending states were entitled, would also contribute to the military efficiency needed in winning the war. When Great Britain, by special legislation, extended the privilege of exclusive jurisdiction to the American forces,[3] Colonel King noted that she "did not fully concede and implement the rights of [her other] allies"—an omission branded "the more regrettable because the United States was at the time a great and powerful nation, whose aid was needed . . . whereas the other allies, whose rights were not so fully conceded, were smaller and weaker countries . . . homeless exiles in Great Britain." [4]

On the second occasion, during the Congressional debates on the

[2] Archibald King (Colonel, Judge Advocate General's Office, U.S. Army), "Jurisdiction over Friendly Foreign Armed Forces," *AJIL*, XXXVI, No. 4 (October, 1942), 539-67 (hereafter: King, I), 547.

[3] United States of America (Visiting Forces) Act, 1942, 5 & 6 Geo. VI, c. 31.

[4] "Further Developments Concerning Jurisdiction over Friendly Foreign Armed Forces," *AJIL*, XL, No. 2 (April, 1946), 257-79 (hereafter: King, II), 265.

adoption and continuance of NATO-SFA,[5] American authors under-took a dramatic reappraisal of the problem. One contribution, which appeared after the controversy had passed its most heated phase, explained that it became necessary—in refutation of the isolationist argument that the United States was relinquishing its rights—to discredit the theory of absolute immunity of visiting forces.[6] Indeed, it was officially contended that "there is no substantial support for any such alleged rule of international law" and that "the only immunity for which there is any substantial support is for an offense committed in the line of duty, although even this is questionable."[7] American authors supporting the official position now relied on a selection of authorities equally impressive and in part identical with the one invoked in support of the earlier view, adding, however, new interpretations, in an attempt to prove that

> although a certain immunity exists for foreign friendly visiting forces, the extent of the immunity is strictly a matter of agreement. It is for the territorial sovereign to determine the extent to which he wishes to waive the exercise of his jurisdiction. The agreements actually entered into by the nations of the world, as well as the decided cases, clearly demonstrate that the problem has always involved reconciling "the practical necessities of the situation with a proper respect for national sovereignty."[8]

More specifically, it was now asserted that from the provisions of various international agreements on the subject of visiting forces "no principle of international law can be deduced"; if anything, it appeared that "in international agreements nations have not acted upon the premise that visiting forces are entitled to immunity as

[5] *Supra*, Chapter III, nn. 4-11.

[6] Bert A. Abrams, "International Law and Friendly Foreign Forces," Note, *New York University Law Review*, XXXII, No. 2 (February, 1957), 351-76, 351.

[7] "Memorandum of the Department of Justice," Summary, *House SFA Hearings*, p. 140.

[8] Edward D. Re, "The NATO Status of Forces Agreement and International Law," *Northwestern University Law Review*, L, No. 3 (July-August, 1955), 349-94, 392.

a matter of right . . ." and that, in the practice of states and in adjudication, "absent an express agreement . . . claims of immunity have been generally rejected."[9] NATO-SFA appeared, consequently, as either granting to the United States "more immunity than they would have had but for the agreement,"[10] or at least being "essentially a codification of customary international law."[11]

The new American position was thus adapted to what had been known as the British view. The leading British authority, G. P. Barton, on whom virtually all recent American and foreign publications have relied heavily, makes the following generalizations: *First*, assuming that a state consents to the presence in its territory of a friendly foreign force, international law contains (a) "an obligation to allow the service courts and authorities of that visiting force to exercise such jurisdiction in matters of discipline and internal administration over members of that force as are derived from their own law"; but (b) no principle of international law prevents the local state from setting limits within which the visiting authorities may exercise their jurisdiction, "so long as there remains no substantial area within which the local courts may by exercise of their supervisory jurisdiction paralyse the maintenance of discipline and the government of the visiting army."[12] *Second,*

---

[9] Murray L. Schwartz, "International Law and the Status of Forces Agreement," *Columbia Law Review*, LIII, No. 8 (December, 1953), 1091-1113, on pp. 1104 and 1111.

[10] *Ibid.;* likewise, Lester B. Orfield, "Jurisdiction of Foreign Courts over Crimes Committed Abroad by American Military Personnel," *South Carolina Law Quarterly*, VIII, No. 3 (Spring, 1956), 346-54, 348.

[11] Abrams, *op. cit.,* 369; the same view is expressed in a Note, "Criminal Jurisdiction over American Armed Forces Abroad," *Harvard Law Review*, LXX, No. 6 (April, 1957), 1043-67, 1050. Rouse and Baldwin (*op. cit.* [*supra*, Chapter IV, n. 12], p. 30), Snee and Pye (*Status*, p. 8), and R. R. Baxter ("Criminal Jurisdiction in the NATO Status of Forces Agreement," *Proceedings of the Section of International and Comparative Law*, American Bar Association, 1957, p. 61), while focusing on different aspects of NATO-SFA, indicate that the evidence on the immunities of visiting forces under general international law is inconclusive.

[12] G. P. Barton, "Foreign Armed Forces: Immunity from Supervisory Jurisdiction," *British Year Book of International Law* (London: Oxford University Press, under the auspices of the Royal Institute of International Affairs), XXVI (1949), 380-413 (hereafter: Barton, I), 412-13. "Supervisory jurisdiction" is the control by local courts over the exercise of powers of the visiting force, such as would, e.g.,

with particular relevance for criminal jurisdiction, the courts of a visiting force

> are entitled as of right to exercise jurisdiction over members of that force. . . . This includes the right to try a member of those forces for offences against the local law. But it has not yet been established that this right carries with it the right to exercise *exclusive* jurisdiction over members of those forces who commit offences against the local law. On the contrary, it has been shown that there exists a rule of international law according to which members of visiting forces are, in principle, subject to the exercise of criminal jurisdiction by the local courts and that any exceptions to that general and far-reaching principle must be traced to express privilege or concession.[13]

*Third,* with reference to three special grounds for exemption from local jurisdiction,

> there is no basis for a supposed rule of international law recognizing immunity from prosecution in local courts for members of a visiting force who commit offences either within the limits of their quarters, or while on duty, or against fellow servicemen or their property.[14]

Although Barton concedes that textbook writers support *intracastral* and duty-connected immunities, their theories are brushed off on the basis of other evidence. In distinction to offenses *while*

---

occur if a member of the visiting force, confined to quarters, applied for a writ of habeas corpus or if he should sue his superior officer for false imprisonment.

While there is an indispensable minimum of immunity from such supervision by local authorities, without which the visiting force would be unable to remain an organized body and perform its functions, Barton's view is that beyond such minimum it is up to the receiving state to control, if it so wishes, the excesses of the exercise of disciplinary powers of the visiting force. The immunity of individual servicemen from local jurisdiction is not a matter at issue here.

[13] *Idem,* "Foreign Armed Forces: Immunity from Criminal Jurisdiction," *BYIL,* XXVII (1950), 186-234 (hereafter: Barton, II), 234.

[14] *Idem,* "Foreign Armed Forces: Qualified Jurisdictional Immunity," *BYIL,* XXXI (1954), 349-70 (hereafter: Barton, III), 370.

on duty, however, it is "a legitimate rule of international law" that "no person carrying out an act *as the agent* of a State should be held personally responsible before the courts of another state for the criminal or civil consequences of that act, unless the act itself should be a crime under international law." [15]

Judged on the basis of these assumptions, the status of forces of the Brussels Treaty powers appears as "a consolidation of the view that immunity from criminal proceedings does not belong as of right to members of visiting forces." NATO-SFA, while incorporating "a radically new concept of priorities in the exercise of jurisdiction for certain offenses," is credited with being "a practicable and serviceable compromise which is to be preferred to any of those which have been suggested." [16]

American authors—in view of the fact that NATO-SFA had survived the early political challenge—soon lost most of their earlier interest in the matter of the relation of the new agreements to the traditional pattern which would exist in the absence of an agreement. Turning to the problem of applying the new treaties, which after a period of crisis appeared to be here to stay, they declared that the issue of status of visiting forces under the general principles of international law has been rendered "largely academic" or "largely moot" by the ratification of NATO-SFA, for the latter "overrides those principles if it conflicts with them." [17] If any relevance was still ascribed to that issue, it was because NATO-SFA may be unilaterally terminated by one year's notice, insofar as it affects any particular party,[18] in which case, presumably, status as defined by the principles of general international law would again come into force.

There are, however, at least two more reasons why the question of general international law is not "moot." First, a challenge to the

[15] *Ibid.*, 358. (Emphasis added.)

[16] *Ibid.*, 364, 370, 365.

[17] Snee and Pye, *Status*, p. 9; Schuck, *op. cit.* (*supra*, Chapter IV, n. 44), p. 355; and Schwenk, *op. cit.* (*supra*, Chapter IV, n. 77), p. 360.

[18] Abrams, *op. cit.*, p. 351.

legitimacy of NATO-SFA cannot be answered simply by finding that the new arrangement is effectively in force.[19] Second, inasmuch as the arrangement now in force has introduced changes in status of forces as compared to the traditional pattern, their exact nature, extent, and consequences are not entirely irrelevant matters—even if it is not expected that a reversion to the old system could occur. In particular, an analysis of the difference between the new conventional rules and general international law may throw some light upon the broader question of the relation between the new global pattern of bases and alliances and the traditional Western state system. It is, therefore, with a view to the latter question that we shall examine the more important precedents involving the peaceful stay of armed forces on foreign territory.

## THE "SCHOONER EXCHANGE" AND ITS REINTERPRETATIONS

Much of the recent controversy over the customary status of visiting forces goes back to an attempt of Chief Justice Marshall to apply in the field of international law some of his methods—such as the unnecessary use of analogy and the emphatic assertion of a general rule only to make an exception to that rule more palatable —which are better known from his more famous decisions on American constitutional issues. As the oldest fully recorded decision containing a statement on the exemption of friendly foreign forces from territorial jurisdiction, *Schooner Exchange* v. *M'Faddon and Others*[20] became naturally the starting point of other judicial pronouncements and theoretical discussions in the United

---

[19] Such an attempt involves the fallacy of placing facts and values on the same plane—a procedure against which theorists of both normative and empirical disciplines (such as Hans Kelsen and Max Weber, respectively) have fought with limited success. The actual validity of NATO-SFA is a fact totally unilluminating with respect to the question whether we ought to have such an agreement.

[20] 7 Cranch 116-47 (1812).

States and abroad. Yet, what exactly it comports is still as indefinite as Marshall's statements on the distribution of authority between the various levels of the American governmental structure would be had they not been supplied with specific meaning in subsequent decisions. The actual matter at issue was the exterritoriality of warships rather than the status of soldiers stationed in a friendly foreign state. Marshall had to decide whether the original owners of a ship seized by Emperor Napoleon and commissioned as a French man-of-war could reclaim their property in an American court when the ship put in at Philadelphia for repairs. Politically and legally, at least as it would appear today, the Chief Justice had little choice. But before turning down the original owners of the ship, he discussed at some length the extent of territorial jurisdiction under the principles of customary international law. This discussion of his provided fuel for both sides in the recent controversy concerning the status-of-forces agreements. In particular, he asserted the following principles which support the primacy of local jurisdiction:

> The jurisdiction of courts is a branch of that which is possessed by the nation as an independent sovereign power.
> The jurisdiction of the nation within its own territory is necessarily exclusive and absolute. It is susceptible of no limitation not imposed by itself. Any restriction upon it, deriving validity from an external source, would imply a diminution of its sovereignty to the extent of the restriction, and an investment of that sovereignty to the same extent in that power which could impose such restriction.
> All exceptions, therefore, to the full and complete power of a nation within its own territories, must be traced up to the consent of the nation itself. They can flow from no other legitimate source.

The Chief Justice proceeded, however, to qualify his general principles in an attempt to explain the exterritoriality of warships by an analogy to cases that he considered to represent more obvious exceptions from territorial jurisdiction. The consent of the territorial sovereign to a restriction of his jurisdiction, he declared, may be either express, or implied in the permission to enter the territory. The latter is customarily found, first, in the case of the person of a visiting sovereign; second, in the case of foreign ambassadors. After that came the most important qualification of his general principles:

> A third case in which a sovereign is understood to cede a portion of his territorial jurisdiction is where he allows the troops of a foreign prince to pass through his dominions.
>
> In such case, without any express declaration waving jurisdiction over the army to which this right of passage has been granted, the sovereign who should attempt to exercise it would certainly be considered as violating the faith. By exercising it, the purpose for which the free passage was granted would be defeated, and a portion of the military force of a foreign independent nation would be diverted from those national objects and duties to which it was applicable, and would be withdrawn from the control of the sovereign whose power and whose safety might greatly depend on retaining the exclusive command and disposition of this force. The grant of a free passage therefore implies a waver of all jurisdiction over the troops during their passage, and permits the foreign general to use that discipline, and to inflict those punishments which the government of his army may require.

This, of course, is the statement on which much of the recent theorizing on the exclusive jurisdiction of the sending state over its troops relies. Was the statement necessary or even helpful in deciding the case at hand? In drawing the analogy between ships and armies, Marshall certainly had hard going. For one thing, the French warship had entered the American port without an express permission. Thus, there was no positive act on the part of the local sovereign—such as a permission given to a foreign corps of troops to pass through the territory—from which an implied consent to exemption from jurisdiction could be deduced. Representing a small power that had to be concerned with the principle of non-intervention, Marshall would be the last one to concede that foreign *armies* may pass through the territory with a merely presumed permission. The dangers inherent in the passage of an army, he declared, are so substantial that "such a practice would break down some of the most decisive distinctions between peace and war." Moreover, a foreign army entering the territory on its own "may justly be considered as committing an act of hostility; and, if not opposed by force, acquires no privileges by its irregular and improper conduct."

In short, to protect the integrity of the territorial sovereign, including the principle that *all* exemptions from territorial jurisdiction must be based on his consent, even if it be an implied consent, Marshall must distinguish as he draws his analogy. He explains, therefore, that warships are sufficiently different from armies to require merely a presumed consent to enter the territorial waters:

> But the rule which is applicable to armies, does not appear to be equally applicable to ships of war entering the ports of a friendly foreign power. The injury inseparable from the march of any army through an inhabited country, and the dangers often, indeed generally, attending it, do not ensue from admitting a ship of war, without special licence, into a friendly port. A different rule therefore with respect to this species of military force has been generally adopted. If, for reasons of state, the ports of a nation generally, or any particular ports be closed against vessels of war generally, or the vessels of any particular nation, notice is usually given of such determination. If there be no prohibition, the ports of [a] friendly nation are considered open to the public ships of all powers with whom it is at peace, and they are supposed to enter such ports and to remain in them while allowed to remain under the protection of the government of the place.

In the case of ships, then, the exemption from jurisdiction is implied in a merely presumed permission to enter the territorial waters. This, however, is precisely the construction to which the counsels for the original owners of the ship had remarked that it destroys the analogy between a foreign sovereign, his ambassador, and his army on the one side, and his "property" on the other; for "the three former cases are all founded upon consent and the latter is not." Moreover, where is the analogy to end? Could it not be extended to merchant vessels and private travelers that, like warships, may enter the territory without an express permission?

Marshall attempts to deal with these difficulties in pointing out, first, that the extent of implied exemptions from the exercise of territorial jurisdiction "must be regulated by the nature of the case and the views under which the parties requiring and conceding it must be supposed to act." Neither party would, for example, expect that merchant vessels in territorial waters would be exempt from local jurisdiction. Second, he introduces a higher category which includes both passing armies and warships, but not other foreign subjects or property. "There is a manifest distinction," he declares, "between the private property of a person who happens to be a prince, and that military force which supports the sovereign power, and maintains the dignity and the independence of a nation." This seems to support a modern interpretation, according to which "it does not follow that Marshall's statements about troops are mere dicta. . . . The essence of the decision is not that an armed public vessel, but that any public armed force, whether on land or sea, which enters the territory of another nation with the latter's permission, enjoys an extraterritorial status." [21] Yet Marshall's introduction of the category "military force" takes care of the counsel's objection only insofar as in that objection the term "property" was used to describe the ship. It does not refute the essence of the objection, namely, that men-of-war, sufficiently different from armies to enter the territorial sphere without an express permission, obtain an exemption from jurisdiction in the same way as the armies, whose exterritoriality is only presumed because they have an express permission to pass

[21] King, I, p. 541.

through the territory. Indeed, Marshall must have felt the weakness of his analogy, for in the end he justifies his decision in terms which are more earthly than finding "the nature of the case." He resorts to the positive practice of states pure and simple, which, indeed, is an irrefutable argument:

> Upon these principles, by the unanimous consent of nations, a foreigner is amenable to the laws of the place; but certainly *in practice, nations have not yet asserted* their jurisdiction over the public armed ships of a foreign sovereign entering a port open for their reception.

And with reference to a case, "cited by Bynkershoek," of Spanish men-of-war "seized in Flushing for a debt due from the king of Spain," Marshall declares:

> That this proceeding was at once arrested by the government, in a nation which appears to have asserted the power of proceeding . . . against the private property of the prince, would seem to furnish no feeble argument in support of the *universality of the opinion in favor of the exemption claimed for ships of war.* The distinction made in our own laws between public and private ships would appear to proceed from the same opinion.
>
> It seems then to the Court, to be a principle of public law, that national ships of war . . . are to be considered exempted.[22]

Today, indeed, hardly anybody would take issue with the substance of Marshall's decision. In fact, Marshall has to be credited with the authoritative statement of a rule—the exterritoriality of warships—which, it appears, was less well established at the time he asserted it.[23] The difficulties arising from the *Schooner Ex-*

---

[22] The indented quotations from John Marshall's decision in this subsection are from 7 Cranch 135-36, 139-40, 141, 144, 145-46. (The spelling is Marshall's; emphasis added in the last two quotations.) The Counsel's reasoning is from p. 131 *ibid.*

[23] Lauterpacht's statement (I, 853, n. 4) that the exterritoriality of men-of-war "became universally recognized only during the nineteenth century" is contradicted by Marshall's own final argument. See, however, Charles Cheney Hyde, *International Law Chiefly as Interpreted and Applied by the United States* (2d ed.; Bos-

*change* have their source in a part of Marshall's reasoning—not in his conclusion per se. In retrospect, the reference to the practice of states was all that was needed to justify the decision. The awkward construction of a consent implied in an implied consent merely introduces confusion. As Kelsen puts it, "this construction is a legal fiction. It is superfluous, for it is a rule of general international law by which the privilege concerned is established, without any consent of the respective states." [24]

Moreover, the confusion was magnified by subsequent reinterpretations, in which Marshall's analogy was twisted to cover situations which he could not have foreseen or had even excluded from his considerations. The problem cannot be eliminated by simply dismissing his statement on the passing corps of troops as a mere dictum.[25] For the validity of judicial pronouncements, however limited (that is, along with the teachings of publicists, only "as subsidiary means" for the discovery of what is law according to general practice of nations), remains—whether they be made in an international or a national tribunal, or even obiter.[26]

---

ton: Little, Brown, 1947), II, 824-25, and Moore, *Digest*, II, 574-75, on the early attitude of Congress and the Attorney General (though not of the President and the Secretary of State) insofar as serving of legal process to persons charged with certain crimes committed ashore is concerned, and in cases of American subjects unlawfully detained on board foreign men-of-war.

[24] Hans Kelsen, *Principles of International Law* (New York: Rinehart, 1952), p. 233 n. Cf. also F. Kalshoven, "Criminal Jurisdiction over Military Persons in the Territory of a Friendly Foreign Power," *Nederlands Tijdschrift voor Internationaal Recht*, V, No. 2 (April, 1958), 165-94, especially 170: "But since that time the legal regime of warships has developed quite independently; the general rule laid down by Marshall is nowhere to be found . . . and the exterritoriality of troops is never connected with the regime governing ships."

[25] King's view (*loc. cit.*) that Marshall's statement about troops is "an indispensable part . . . and [it] cannot be rejected without rejecting the conclusion as well" is contradicted by Abrams (*op. cit.*, p. 354), E. D. Re (*op. cit.*, pp. 364-65), and in the Note, *Harvard Law Review* (*op. cit.* [*supra*, n. 11], p. 1047, n. 24). For an acceptance of Marshall's dictum as relevant, by an opponent of King's theory of exclusive jurisdiction of the sending state, see Barton, I, pp. 383-84.

[26] See the Statute of the I.C.J., Article 38, paragraph (d), in connection with paragraph (b), and Article 59. Bishop, *op. cit.* (Chapter II, n. 19 *supra*), p. 33, warns of the lesser significance of the distinction between dictum and *ratio decidendi* in international law. Cf. also King, I, p. 542, who finds that "even dicta by Supreme Court are entitled to great weight."

But to acknowledge some significance of judicial dicta is a matter quite different from applying a particular one where it does not fit at all. What exactly was the situation Marshall had in mind in his statement on the status of troops? He writes of troops passing through foreign territory with express permission of the territorial sovereign, not of troops invading the country, or stationed in it more or less permanently, or entering without express permission whatever their intention. Passing troops, he says, are exempt from all local jurisdiction; *furthermore,* the sending state is authorized to enforce its disciplinary powers within the territory and, insofar as required by the government of the passing army, "to inflict punishment" in the territory through which the troops are passing. The situation is narrowly defined: troops located with the permission of the territorial sovereign in a limited area for a limited time. In such a situation, nothing restricts the jurisdiction of the sending state over the members of the passing army to, say, offenses committed in the course of duty or to *inter se* offenses. For that matter, "infliction of punishments" by the visiting general upon anybody, even a local resident, is not excluded *expressis verbis,* though, of course, it should be kept in mind that the emphasis of the paragraph is on exterritoriality of the passing army, rather than on the limits of the right to exercise extra-territorial jurisdiction.[27]

Marshall's doctrine was invoked in quite different situations in three other decisions by the Supreme Court. Two of these, *Coleman* v. *Tennessee*[28] and *Dow* v. *Johnson,*[29] were Civil War cases,

---

[27] In older literature, the passage of troops was often considered as a sort of occupation-by-consent of limited duration. See Raymond Robin, *Des Occupations militaires en dehors des Occupations de Guerre* (Paris: Librairie de la Société du Recueil Sirey, 1913), pp. 57-59. The expectation of the exercise of some jurisdiction of the sending state over the local residents would not have been inconsistent with the way the situation was probably envisaged at the time Marshall wrote his opinion.

[28] 97 U.S. 509-40 (1878), holding that state courts have no jurisdiction to try a former member of the United States army for murder committed in the invaded area while he was there in the military service of the United States during the Civil War.

interpreting Marshall's exterritoriality of passing troops, for obvious reasons, to include troops *stationed* in foreign territory.[30] Going on from that position, the Supreme Court declared that "a fortiori would an army invading an enemy's country be exempt." [31] Though the two cases were ultimately disposed of on the basis of rules applying to belligerent occupation, it is the expanded version of exterritoriality of friendly foreign forces asserted in them (that is, expanded from Marshall's passing corps of troops to troops stationed in foreign territory) that has entered most textbooks of international law (inasmuch as they take up the subject).[32] This version was also used during the two world wars in support of government positions taken at the time.[33]

The third Supreme Court decision often quoted in support of exclusive jurisdiction of the sending state is *Tucker* v. *Alexandroff*.[34] It concerned a case of desertion from a group of foreign seamen sent to the United States to become part of the crew of a

[29] 100 U.S. 148-95 (1879), holding that a district court of Louisiana, continued in existence and permitted by the commanding general to hear cases after the United States army had occupied the state, had no jurisdiction over a United States officer, under whose command, it was alleged, a military company carried off the property of the plaintiff in a way unauthorized by the necessities of war, the martial law, and the orders of his superiors.

[30] See 97 U.S. 515 and 100 U.S. 165. Cf. the discussion of the two cases by E. D. Re, *op. cit.*, pp. 365-69, and Barton, II, p. 218.

[31] *Coleman* v. *Tennessee*, 97 U.S., p. 516. *Dow* v. *Johnson*, 100 U.S., p. 165, agrees: "Much more must this exemption prevail where a hostile army invades an enemy's country." The argument a fortiori is clearly inappropriate where the local courts function only at the sufferance of the conquering state. As far as the local state is concerned, an invasion can hardly confer exterritoriality—a point made clear by Marshall.

[32] The fact that Supreme Court decisions are thoroughly dissected and their parts rearranged in legal chrestomathies and indices, which make its dicta readily available for reference, may account for much of the larger weight, as compared to other sources, given to such dicta by authors of general textbooks who have had no time or interest to pick out for special investigation, among the many subjects they deal with, the problem of friendly forces in foreign territory.

[33] See the "Memorandum of the United States Government to the Canadian Government" (*House SFA Hearings*, p. 412) and the "Factum of the Attorney General of Canada" (*ibid.*, p. 428) submitted in connection with the request of the Canadian government for an advisory opinion of the Canadian Supreme Court on the status of United States forces in Canada during World War II (*infra*, n. 67).

[34] 183 U.S. 424-70 (1901).

public ship being built in Philadelphia for the Russian government. While the case was decided on the basis of the provision of a treaty,[35] the Court discussed the status of foreign forces under customary international law, commenting on *Schooner Exchange* as follows:

> This case, however, only holds that the public armed vessels of a foreign nation may, upon principles of comity, enter our harbors with the presumed license of the government, and while [they are] there[,] are exempt from the jurisdiction of the local courts; and, by parity of reasoning, that, if foreign troops are permitted to enter, or cross our territory, they are still subject to the control of their officers and exempt from local jurisdiction.

Thus, by the use of the word "enter," this decision can also accommodate troops *stationed* in foreign territory under the regime envisaged by Marshall for *passing* corps of troops. But more interesting is the complete reversal of Marshall's analogy. Evidently, by 1901, there was no apprehension about exterritoriality of warships as an independently valid principle; and there must have arisen at least some uncertainty about the automatic exterritoriality of troops, if "parity of reasoning" had to be introduced to assert it.[36] Not until 1956, however, did the American courts discard both versions of the analogy, accepting as valid the assump-

[35] Justice Brown, writing for the majority, expressed doubt that, in the absence of treaty stipulation, foreign officers are authorized to call upon the local authorities for assistance in reclaiming deserters from the visiting force, although the foreign officer himself "may exercise his accustomed authority for the maintenance of discipline, and perhaps arrest a deserter *dum fervet opus.*" The court decided, however, that Alexandroff was a deserter from a ship under the terms of the treaty with Russia of 1832 (8 Stat. 444), although the ship was barely launched and Alexandroff had not yet set foot on it; Article IX of the Treaty obligated the United States to supply assistance in apprehending and detaining such deserters.

[36] "This is a strange inversion of Marshall's reasoning. Even if it be assumed that in *Schooner Exchange* v. *M'Faddon* the analogy of immunity of troops in passage was resorted to in order, ostensibly, to deduce therefrom the like immunity for foreign public armed vessels, there can be no justification in logic for taking the Chief Justice's conclusion to prove the premise of his syllogism" (Barton, II, p. 217, n. 9).

tions which underlie the new status-of-forces agreements.[37] There
were no relevant court decisions in the United States during some
three decades preceding the conclusion of these; but it is interesting to note that as late as 1944 the Senate rejected a proposal that
the Act to Implement the Jurisdiction of Service Courts of
Friendly Foreign Forces (58 Stat. 643) be amended to grant to
the sending states jurisdiction over their servicemen in the United
States, mainly on the ground that such jurisdiction is already implied in the permission to enter the territory of the United
States.[38]

At the opposite extreme is the not unimaginative attempt of
G. P. Barton to restrict the meaning of Marshall's statement concerning the troops to a scope narrower than its wording indicates.
Relying on an interpretation of *Schooner Exchange* by an Australia court,[39] he undertakes to prove that Marshall intended to assert only the immunity of visiting forces from the "supervisory
jurisdiction" [40] of the local sovereign. Assuming that the basic
proposition of Marshall's argument was "that, since all states are
equal, it is to be presumed that the absolute jurisdiction of one
state does not contemplate the sovereign rights of another state as
its object," Barton dismisses as "moot point" the question whether
it was possible to show without analogy to persons of sovereigns,
ambassadors, and passing troops that French rights over the "Exchange" were of sovereign variety which, in terms of the basic
proposition, would be exempt from local jurisdiction. Since, how-

---

[37] The Court of Appeals in the District of Columbia declared that the statements
in *Schooner Exchange* and other earlier cases are "entitled to no weight" (*Cozart
v. Wilson*, 236 F. 2d 732 at 733 [1956]). However, such recent cases, applying to the
situation after the conclusion of the new status-of-forces agreements, are not indic-
ative of the traditional status under general international law.

[38] See *Congressional Record*, XC (1944), 6490-98.

[39] *Wright* v. *Cantrell*, 44 State Reports, New South Wales, 45-54 (1943).

[40] Defined *supra*, n. 12. Abrams (*op. cit.*, p. 354) and Schwartz (*op. cit.*, p. 1105;
substituting "the right of the territorial sovereign to exercise its disciplinary [*sic*]
jurisdiction" for Barton's "supervisory jurisdiction") join Barton on this point
without elaborating.

ever, the schooner had entered Philadelphia without express permission, and the Court, Barton indicates, knew that "on analogy,
therefore, she was not entitled to immunity," we are told that
"the example of troops in passage was, accordingly, introduced
by the learned Chief Justice only to be immediately distinguished
from the case before him." Barton goes on:

> What did Chief Justice Marshall mean when he used the term
> "jurisdiction"? It is reasonable to suppose that he had in mind a
> type of jurisdiction the exercise of which by the courts of the local
> state would have results similar to those caused by the exercise
> of jurisdiction over the schooner *Exchange*. The exercise of juris-
> diction over the schooner *Exchange* would result in the complete
> withdrawal of the ship from the French naval forces. That Chief
> Justice Marshall was referring to this kind of jurisdiction emerges
> from a sentence in the above quotation. He said: "By exercising
> (jurisdiction), the purpose for which the free passage was granted
> would be defeated, and a portion of the military force of a foreign
> independent nation . . . would be withdrawn from the control
> of the Sovereign."

.     .     .     .     .     .     .     .     .     .     .     .

> Clearly, the jurisdiction the exercise of which would interfere
> with the maintenance of discipline and prohibit the foreign gen-
> eral from using "that discipline and inflicting those punishments
> which the government of his army may require" is supervisory
> jurisdiction. To give members of visiting forces access to this
> jurisdiction of the local courts would mean the frustration of the
> exercise of disciplinary powers by the foreign authorities. On the
> other hand, to suggest that the exercise of the local criminal
> jurisdiction over a visiting force would necessarily impair its effec-
> tiveness is at once to under-estimate the number of its law-abiding
> members and to over-estimate the contribution each soldier makes
> to its general efficiency.[41]

This interpretation appears to be unwarranted by the text
directly at issue,[42] the context of the argument of the Court,[43] and

[41] Barton, I, pp. 384-85.
[42] Quoted on p. 127 *supra*.
As was already suggested, the words "and permits" after the first comma in the last

the general circumstances at the time.[44] In particular, one must consider that in Marshall's time the close community of interests upon which some of the present instances of stationing of troops abroad are based, with multilateral defense schemes and forces under joint command structures assuming the character of quasi-federal institutions,[45] was utterly inconceivable. During the nineteenth century, presence of foreign troops[46] could only be con-

---

sentence of Marshall's paragraph seem to indicate addition rather than explication: Marshall might have said "in order to permit," and he might have omitted the words "all" and "and" if he had wanted to accommodate Barton's theory. Cf. *supra,* pp. 132.

[43] Marshall's attempt to save his analogy by introducing the higher category of the "military force" indicates that he had more in mind when mentioning the army than merely finding a convenient object with which to contrast the status of warships. The respondents' counsels have admitted that the personnel of the ship is subject to the sending state's jurisdiction (7 Cranch 127), centering their challenge on the ownership of the ship. What Marshall then replies, in effect, is that the ship should partake in the immunity since (together with the crew) it constitutes a man-of-war, i.e., a part of an armed force passing through with presumed permission and, therefore, entitled to what was, in terms of the thinking at the time, self-evident for a passing army. Immunity against the challenge to the title to the ship, he attempts to prove, is only a part of the immunity of passing armed forces against *"all* jurisdiction" of local authorities.

The paragraph at issue (p. 127 *supra*) is, further, immediately followed by a revealing rhetorical question: "But if, without such express permit, an army should be led through the territories of a foreign prince, might the jurisdiction of the territory be rightfully exercised *over the individuals* composing this army?" (7 Cranch 140 [emphasis added]). Marshall either does not understand what is Barton's "supervisory jurisdiction" (n. 12 *supra*) or deliberately refuses to distinguish the jurisdiction over the force from that over the soldiers.

[44] "It is obvious," Marshall states, "that the passage of an army through foreign territory will probably be at all times inconvenient and injurious, and would often be imminently dangerous to the sovereign through whose dominion it passed. Such a practice would . . . reduce a nation to the necessity of resisting by war an act not absolutely hostile in its character, or of exposing itself to the stratagems and frauds of a power whose integrity might be doubted, and who might enter the country under deceitful pretexts." This tone continues as Marshall explains why passage of troops requires express permission, while for ships, unless specifically excluded, the permission to enter the ports may be presumed; it is enough, however, to show how he envisaged the presence of foreign troops. Cf. also *supra,* the quotations in the main body of the text, p. 128.

[45] This development will be further considered in Chapter VI.

[46] Including the passage of troops (see *supra,* n. 27); Robin's monograph, published only in 1913, appears to be the first systematic attempt to distinguish between the different varieties of peaceful occupation developed during the nineteenth century (*op. cit.* [n. 27 *supra*], especially pp. 611-22 and 687-726). Only after the experience of World War I, however, is an attempt made to draw a clear line between occupation and the presence of allied troops in the course of a co-opera-

ceived in terms equivalent to occupation, even if a peaceful one, and the distinction between belligerent and "agreed" occupation was at first rather blurred. Agreed occupation, in turn, tended to amount to a disguised cession of territory.[47] Small wonder that Marshall dreaded the possibility of passage of troops without express permission and insisted on opposing it at the risk of destroying his analogy.[48] To say the least, it appears improbable that he could have in all seriousness thought of the possibility that local courts could effectively grant remedies to passing soldiers, in order to protect them from the excesses of the exercise of disciplinary powers by their officers, thereby causing a threat to the sending state, a situation "which would prevent the troops from acting as a force."[49] Barton's conception, therefore, may only prove to be useful *de lege ferenda,* particularly for arrangements among states achieving a sufficient degree of mutual confidence and integration. It will lose nothing by not being traceable to John Marshall; nor is Marshall's greatness jeopardized by the realization that he could

---

tive defense effort (Aline Chalufour, *Le Statut Juridique des Troupes Alliées pendant la Guerre 1914-1918* [Thèse, Université de Paris; Les Presses Modernes, 1927]).

[47] As is shown by Perrinjaquet, *op. cit.* (Chapter II, n. 19 *supra*), and Robin, *op. cit.,* pp. 518-27 and 715-26.

[48] He could have saved it by invoking the authority of classical authors, had he been willing to accept their restricted conception of territoriality. Vattel, for example, although concerned with the rights of the neutrals more than the older authors, states as a matter of principle that "a sovereign *must* grant an innocent passage through his territories to all nations with which it lives at peace, and the permission *must be extended to bodies of troops* as well as to individuals" (*Le droit des gens ou principes de la loi naturelle* . . . [London, 1758], III, vii, 119 [p. 274 of the Carnegie Endowment translation; emphasis added]; see also *ibid.,* paragraph 122).

Vattel's book, we are informed (by Arthur Nussbaum, *A Concise History of the Law of Nations* [New York: Macmillan, 1954], p. 161-62), was sent to Franklin in 1775 and "soon became a textbook . . . and the favorite authority in American theory of international law." Marshall quotes Vattel on another matter (7 Cranch 143) and follows his reasoning concerning the dangers inherent in the presence of foreign troops. These dangers, for Vattel, justify exceptions from the general right of free passage. But Marshall disregards the general principle retained by Vattel and asserts on the contrary: "It is for reasons like these that the general license to foreigners to enter the dominions of a friendly foreign power is *never* understood to extend to a military force" (*ibid.,* p. 140 [emphasis added]).

[49] *Wright* v. *Cantrell, loc. cit.,* p. 49.

not have provided for all exigencies of the second half of the twentieth century.

In sum then, *Schooner Exchange* has contributed to the solidification of two principles of general international law and has some relevance as the basis of a further proposition, the nature of which as a principle of general international law is still uncertain. It confirmed, first, that men-of-war are not subject to the territorial jurisdiction of a foreign state. This is still a valid rule, although the analogy between troops and warships is not. Second, it asserted the principle of territorial exclusiveness, explaining all exceptions to it in terms of a consent of the territorial sovereign. Recent status-of-forces agreements were still negotiated assuming, generally at least, the continued validity of this principle. But important qualifications (differing in their foundation as well as in content from those proposed by Marshall) have been added, and the principle itself may become transformed by the ever more widespread acceptance of novel conventional arrangements. Third, it asserted that foreign troops, passing through with permission, must be presumed by the local courts to be fully exempt from local jurisdiction, unless the territorial sovereign undertakes to destroy this presumption. The current status of this proposition is doubtful. Strictly speaking, the situation referred to by Marshall is not likely to occur, since the neutrals are now prohibited from letting the forces of belligerents pass through their territory, and there are few uncontiguous portions of state territories left to which access by military forces in pursuit of routine peacetime purposes is possible only through the territory of another state. There is, consequently, little need to ascertain whether Marshall's proposition has acquired the nature of a general rule and thus ceased to be subject to unilateral destruction. Later extensions of this proposition to situations other than passage, as well as the attempt to restrict its meaning to an exemption from the so-called supervisory jurisdiction, have no claim to Marshall's authority and must be justified by reference to other sources of international law if they are to be accepted as valid.

It follows that a tribunal faced today with the task of deciding what is the legal status of troops stationed abroad with local permission but without a status-of-forces agreement would find little specific aid in the *Schooner Exchange* decision. In the absence of more serviceable guidance from other sources, what remains is Marshall's general proposition of territorial competence. It is clear, however, that the possibility of some exceptions from local jurisdictions *without* the consent of the territorial sovereign is currently (as seen in the case of men-of-war) not excluded. Thus, there is in current theory less rigidity in the conceptualization of both the scope of the privileges of the sending state and the territorial competence of the host state. Evidently, a state can today admit that its sovereignty is not as "exclusive and absolute" as asserted in the older doctrine and still remain a state; and it needs no reassurance of its "perfect equality and independence" whenever it acts (or refrains from acting) to comply with a rule found in the general practice of nations. In this respect, Marshall's general statement on the territorial competence has also lost validity: to say that a state is "susceptible to *no* limitation not imposed by itself" is not to state the current law. What is actually decisive is the extent of such limitations—a matter which will be discussed further in Chapter VI.

### OTHER JUDICIAL OPINIONS

Aside from the four American decisions considered above, a considerable number of cases decided under various other jurisdictions, although many of them at best of marginal relevance, have figured prominently in the controversy over the status-of-forces agreements.[50] Only one decision of an international tribunal

---

[50] Another American case, the "Caroline"-McLeod affair, resulted in diplomatic correspondence recognizing a ground of immunity which is relevant but it is also both too narrow and too obvious to be useful here (see *supra*, Chapter III, n. 65 and the main body of the text there); the case was, moreover, disposed of on proof of alibi rather than on the basis of immunity.

falls into this category: *The Casablanca Case*,[51] which dealt with a conflict between two kinds of extraterritorial jurisdiction; and it is, consequently, correct that it "sheds no particular light," indeed, "does not apply at all." [52] Although "one fact stands out," we are told, namely, "that the court recognized exclusive jurisdiction . . . of a nation over its troops in a friendly foreign country," [53] the city where the incident took place, as the court found, was "occupied and guarded by French military forces which constituted the garrison," and the dispute was over the right of the German consul to interfere with the disciplinary powers of the occupying force.

Similarly doubtful is the relevance of several cases decided in national courts, such as *In re Polimeni*,[54] where a military court decided that it had jurisdiction to try a serviceman for an offense he had committed while on duty abroad as a member of an occupation force, over his objection that he should be brought before the ordinary civil courts.[55] It is somewhat less clear that *The Republic of Panama* v. *Wilbert L. Schwartzfinger* and *In re Gilbert* can be dismissed as irrelevant and erroneous.[56] In the latter case, the court assigned some relevance to the *intra-castral* and on-duty nature of the act, though it also referred to a more tangible obstacle to the exercise of jurisdiction.[57] In the Schwartzfinger

[51] *The Hague Court Reports,* ed. James Brown Scott (New York: Oxford University Press [for the Carnegie Endowment], 1916), Ser. 1, pp. 110-20.

[52] Re, *op. cit.* (n. 8 *supra*), p. 372, and Schwartz, *op. cit.* (n. 9 *supra*), p. 1110, respectively.

[53] King, I, p. 544.

[54] Italy, 1935; *Annual Digest and Reports of Public International Law Cases,* ed. H. Lauterpacht (hereafter: *Annual Digest*), 1935-37 (1941), case No. 101, p. 248.

[55] Civil courts of his country, that is, where the trial took place; not of the occupied territory (Saar). A conflict with the local jurisdiction was, therefore, not at issue. See Barton, II, p. 220, and Schwartz, *op. cit.,* p. 1107 n. But Lauterpacht (I, 848 n.) treats this case as analogous to the Schwartzfinger case *(infra)*.

[56] As is done by Barton (II, pp. 219 and 229; III, pp. 345 and 359). See also Re, *op. cit.,* pp. 372-73; Schwartz, *loc. cit.;* and Abrams, *op. cit.,* p. 355.

[57] Brazil, 1945; *Annual Digest,* 1946, No. 37.
The case involved the killing of a Brazilian by a United States marine on guard duty at the gate of a camp occupied by American forces; immunity was recognized on several grounds, including the narrow definition, by domestic legislation, of the

case,[58] the court made—unnecessarily, as it appears[59]—the following comment:

It is a principle of international law that the armed force of one state, when crossing the territory of another friendly country, with the acquiescence of the latter, is not subject to the jurisdiction of the territorial sovereign, but to that of the officers and superior authorities of its own command.

In such case the government to which the army belongs is responsible for any damages that may be caused by the passage of the force, and for any violations of local law which it may commit. But individually its members remain subject to the jurisdiction of their own officers, and to the laws of the country to which they belong.

This exemption from the local jurisdiction is recognized by all civilized nations; and is not considered a diminution of their sovereignty or independence.

The largest number of cases decided in a single country were those falling under the Mixed Courts of Egypt, which by virtue of an agreement exercised jurisdiction over British forces outside the camp areas and, during World War II, over other Allied forces in Egypt as well.[60] The cumulative effect of these cases is, first, a

---

jurisdiction of the Brazilian military court in which the legal action was started. The camp was considered "designated . . . as an *American military area* with the result that the American courts-martial have jurisdiction." The fact that the accused was *on guard duty* was regarded as "sufficient in itself to invest the accused with immunity" (Barton, II, pp. 229 and 231 [emphasis added]).

[58] Panama, 1925; *Annual Digest*, 1927-28, No. 114, pp. 180-81.
In this case, the charges against the driver of a military ambulance, involved in an accident outside the Canal Zone, were dismissed with reference to the Isthmian Convention of November 18, 1903 (33 Stat. 2234). "In accordance with the text of that treaty, the Canal Zone authorities may employ their forces . . . and in such case those forces, *when acting in the name or on behalf of the United States Government,* are subject to the authority and jurisdiction to which they belong, and not to our national authorities; *nor to both simultaneously,* because such a double jurisdiction is contrary to law" (emphasis added).

[59] See Kalshoven, *op. cit.,* p. 173. Cf. also Barton, II, p. 219, who finds that the court "gave clear recognition to a principle of qualified immunity only" (i.e., for on-duty offenses).

[60] See the Anglo-Egyptian convention of August 26, 1936, *United Kingdom Treaty Series,* 1937, No. 6, p. 24. For criticism based on two diametrically opposed viewpoints, see King, II, pp. 257-62, and Barton, III, p. 357, respectively.

liberal recognition of the on-duty exemption from the local jurisdiction, as distinguished from immunity for acts committed
strictly in pursuance of an order, that is, acts of state;[61] second,
recognition as "well settled" that *intra-castral* immunity exists as
a principle of international law, the courts apparently identifying
camps with warships, as they did sailors ashore with soldiers out
of camp.[62]

In contrast to the position of the Mixed Courts of Egypt, a
British court denied *intra-castral* immunity during World War
II in *R. v. Navratil,* declaring that to recognize it "would mean
that, wherever there are foreign armed forces stationed in this
country, there could be committed within their lines every conceivable offense against our law, which our courts would be quite
unable to entertain at all. That is not so." [63] But there appears
to have occurred no denial of immunity for an on-duty offense
where the commanding officer supported the exemption and the
claim of exempted status was at least plausible.[64]

[61] *Triandafilou c. Ministère Public (Annual Digest,* 1919-42, Supplement, No. 86,
pp. 165-69) was the first case of this nature; it involved a sailor, but applied
analogously to soldiers and airmen later (Barton, II, p. 226). In some cases, however, the courts rejected claims of on-duty status, when the accused had acted
obviously on his own (see Barton, III, pp. 351-56). In such cases, the courts
thought that "nobody is allowed to abuse what is called 'service commandé'"
(thus, *Ministère Public c. Tsoukaris, Annual Digest,* 1942-45, No. 40, pp. 150-52).
See, however, n. 64 *infra.*

[62] In *Manuel c. Ministère Public (Annual Digest,* 1943-45, No. 42, pp. 154-64),
immunity was denied because "no generally recognized rule . . . extends the principle of immunity . . . to offences against ordinary law committed outside military
establishments" (cf. Barton, III, p. 346), which was an implied recognition of
*intra-castral* immunity by virtue of general international law, and was applied to
subsequent cases. However, the value of the decisions of the Mixed Courts as a
source of general international law should be taken in the light of the fact that
they have basically interpreted the agreement of 1936. See, further, Barton, II, p.
228.

[63] *Annual Digest,* 1919-42 Supplement, No. 85, pp. 161-65, on p. 165, cited by
Barton, II, p. 229.

[64] In *Ministère Public c. Scardalos* (cited by Barton, III, p. 355), the Mixed Court
of Cassation upheld the decision of the lower court in a case of murder, accepting
as evidence of duty a certificate that the accused was at the time of the offense
"charged with certain delicate and secret missions." However, in *Wright v. Cantrell*
(cited *supra,* n. 39), one of the grounds on which immunity was claimed, namely,
that the defendant "did the act complained of [defamation of the plaintiff] in the
course and for the purpose of his duties," was rejected because "the defendant is

Two other cases require some attention. *Chung Chi Cheung v. The King*,[65] is again not directly concerned with the status of visiting forces; but it is frequently quoted because of its comments on exterritoriality in general. The case involved murder committed aboard a Chinese warship; the offender, a member of the crew, happening to find himself in British custody when transferred to a hospital ashore, was sentenced by a British court in Hong Kong to die. On appeal, Lord Atkin, speaking for the Lords in their judicial capacity, rejected the "floating-island theory" of exterritoriality, identified with the Oppenheim-Lauterpacht textbook, as a fiction, and adopted Brierly's statement that the term "exterritoriality" is misleading because "at most it means nothing more than that a person or thing has some immunity from local jurisdiction; it does not help us to determine the only important question, namely, how far this immunity extends." The court went on:

The true view is that, in accordance with the conventions of international law, the territorial sovereign grants to foreign sovereigns and their envoys, and public ships and the naval forces carried by such ships *certain immunities*. Some are well settled; others are uncertain. . . . But if the principles which their Lordships have been discussing are accepted, *the immunities which the local Courts recognize flow from a waiver by the local sovereign* of his full territorial jurisdiction, *and can themselves be waived*. [Emphasis added.]

Since the attitude of the Chinese government, in particular the absence of a request for surrender of the defendant, could be interpreted to constitute such a return-waiver, the appeal was turned down. We see here a partial revival of Marshall's doctrine

---

not alleged to have defamed another member of the forces in the course of making a report about him which it was his duty to make, but to have defamed a civilian whilst doing something in the course of his duties" (*op. cit.*, p. 53).

[65] *Appeal Cases*, House of Lords and Privy Council, 1939, pp. 160-77.

of implied waiving, which opens the possibility of a fiction within a fiction in the form of the reversed implied waiver; all on the part of a court opposed to fictions in principle. One source of the recent popularity of this decision lies, of course, in its pointing out that jurisdiction is not inevitably exclusive and permanent, whoever holds the right.[66] In this respect, in spite of the antiquated formula explaining it, the principle pronounced in the Hong Kong case is decidedly modern and supports the new status-of-forces agreements.

The last case to be considered here is important because it illustrates well the condition of the doctrine concerning the status of forces just before the period of negotiation of the postwar agreements. In *Reference as to Whether Members of the Military or Naval Forces of the United States of America Are Exempt from Criminal Proceedings in Canadian Criminal Courts*,[67] the Supreme Court of Canada was asked to advise the Canadian government on two questions: (1) whether or to what degree the United States forces stationed in Canada are exempt from local jurisdiction; (2) whether the Canadian government has the authority to exempt them, if they are not. The court was able to agree only on the second question, which it answered in the affirmative. On the first question, the five justices were hopelessly divided. Chief Justice Duff, joined by Justice Hudson, rejected the theory of automatic immunity derived from Marshall's dictum and suggested by both the American and the Canadian administration. He declared, instead, concerning land forces, that

> there is no rule of law in force in Canada which deprives the Canadian civil courts (that is to say non-military courts) of jurisdiction in respect of offences against the laws of Canada committed by the members of such forces on Canadian soil. The

[66] The opposite assumption is still reflected in *Panama* v. *Schwartzfinger* (see the quotation in n. 58 *supra, in fine*). In *In re Gilbert*, "jurisdiction" is the term used for "exclusive jurisdiction."

[67] *Canada Law Reports*, Supreme Court, 1943, pp. 483-527.

Canadian criminal courts do not in fact exercise jurisdiction in respect of acts committed within the lines of such forces, or of offences against discipline generally committed by one member of such forces against another member in cases in which the act or offence does not affect the person or property of a Canadian subject.

With respect to naval forces, the Chief Justice recognized immunity only for offenses committed aboard ship if they are *inter se* or solely concern internal discipline; he denied the existence of any exemption from local jurisdiction as a matter of right for offenses committed ashore, but thought that Canadian courts would not exercise jurisdiction for *inter se* offenses, unless requested to do so by the commander of the ship.

Justices Kerwin and Taschereau took the opposing view that

the members of the military and naval forces of the United States of America present in Canada with the consent of the Canadian Government for purposes of military operation in connection with or related to the state of war now existing, whether such members are attached to a unit or ship stationed in Canada or elsewhere or are absent on duty or on leave from their unit or ship stationed here, are exempt from criminal proceedings prosecuted in Canadian criminal courts. This immunity may be waived by the United States and in any event does not apply to members of forces who may enter Canada as tourists or casual visitors. The powers of arrest, search, entry or custody by Canadian authorities are not interfered with.

Justice Kerwin pointed also to the fact that the United States forces were invited to Canada "not merely for the benefit of the United States but for that of both parties and, in fact for the benefit of all allied nations"; hence, it must be assumed that the invitation has been "extended and accepted on the basis that complete immunity . . . would be extended to the members of the United States forces." *Schooner Exchange* and *Chung Chi Cheung,* according to this interpretation, confirm the existence of immunity as a matter of right, though the immunity be waivable and involve no literal "ex-territoriality."

The last member of the court, Justice Rand, took a third position. He found the "preponderance of the opinion" of tribunals and publicists to be in support of the proposition that immunity from jurisdiction is automatically included in the permission to enter the territory. Moreover, he recognized that "what has been invited into Canada is an army with its laws, courts and discipline," and that "it cannot be assumed that such an organization would take the invitation to mean that, once the international border was crossed, its disciplinary powers should be suspended and its functions, except for innocuous motions, come to an end." But complete immunity, he thought, would clash with the principle of the "supremacy of the civil law over the military arm." Even though it is "not foreign but domestic military usurpation against which the principle is a bastion," it "stands in the way of implied exemption when the act complained of clashes with civilian life. . . . It does not therefore stand in the way of a rule limited to the relations of members of a foreign group . . . with persons other than members of the Canadian public." The conclusion, however, is not *inter se* immunity pure and simple for there follows another qualification:

> The point of the controversy is whether the adjudication upon infractions of the local law by members of foreign forces shall be carried out by the tribunals of those forces. The principle enunciated in the *Schooner Exchange* decision has as a necessary corollary the implied *obligation* on the foreign court to accept that responsibility. The principle of immunity laid down in the case of *Chung Chi Cheung* v. *The King* is that the local jurisdiction withdraws *before the assertion* of jurisdiction by the foreign authority: if the latter fails to make that assertion, it must be taken as waiving it and in such a case the local processes are considered not to have been displaced. Likewise the foreign jurisdiction may waive the local exercise of preliminary or ancillary process. In such a conception, an act in violation of the local law is not per-

mitted an escape, jurisdictionally, from appropriate juridical action. [Emphasis added.]

Hence, there is an *intra-castral* and aboard-ship immunity, except in cases of persons not subject to the American military law; and there is an immunity for *inter se* offenses wherever committed, "but the exemption is only to the extent that the United States courts exercise jurisdiction over such offences."

Thus, in the last pre-NATO case in which the court made a detailed study of available authorities, we find a deadlock between fundamentally different views: full immunity, implied in the consent to enter or in the purpose of the presence of the foreign force; no immunity as a matter of right; and a conditional system, designed to effect legal action in all cases of violations of local law, by way of granting immunity only where the immunity is not inconsistent with assuring such action. The result is inconclusive because a majority of justices supported the existence of immunity as a principle of international law,[68] while a differently added majority denied the existence of full immunity.[69] Or to put it in other words, the outcome confirms, on the whole, *a measure* of immunity, though there was disagreement on its legal nature and its scope—which leaves us still in doubt on the question characterized by Brierly as "the only important" one.

A similar conclusion follows from the aggregate of cases considered above. That the judicature does not support a rule of absolute immunity should be clear enough. On the other hand, a single case negating *intra-castral* immunity, involving forces who were "homeless exiles"[70] in the United Kingdom during World War II, represents weak evidence for denying the existence of qualified immunity as well.[71] It appears, on the contrary, that the support for *intra-castral* and on-duty immunity is substantial,

[68] Thus, Representative Bow, statement inserted in *House SFA Hearings*, pp. 393-450, on p. 397.

[69] Thus, Barton, II, p. 224.

[70] *Supra*, n. 4. The case referred to is *R.* v. *Navratil, supra,* n. 63.

[71] Nn. 14-15 *supra* refer to a place where such an assumption is implied.

and that the courts give weight also to the *inter se* factor. The exemption for on-duty offenses is, further, not limited to the cases where the act at issue was a specifically ordered one, that is, an act of state rather than an act of the soldier. But there is considerable variation from case to case in how far the courts will go in examining the actual relation to duty when faced with a certificate asserting on-duty status.

### TEACHINGS OF PUBLICISTS

Of the two major categories in the literature of international law, the works of classical authors reveal little concern about the status of soldiers, though they are very much concerned about the right and the conditions of passage. By and large, the so-called standard texts, in their original editions, most of which were written during the nineteenth century, adapt Marshall's dicta to the various instances of "peaceful occupation" occurring in their era. The literature of the period from about World War I to the conclusion of the new status-of-forces agreements could be considered as a third category. It would represent a transitional period, inasmuch as certain novel criteria are being introduced —though not by the majority of textbook authors, who continue to expound the nineteenth-century concepts.

What was the reason for the classical authors' apparent neglect to develop a doctrine concerning the status of forces in foreign territory? The void resulted, we are instructed in a standard textbook,

either from oversight, or, as perhaps is more probable, because the exercise of exclusive control by military and naval officers not only over the internal economy of the forces under their command, but over them as against external jurisdiction, was formerly too much taken for granted to be worth mentioning.[72]

[72] William Edward Hall, *International Law,* ed. J. P. Higgins (8th ed.; Oxford: Clarendon, 1924), p. 237.

Research focusing on various instances of non-belligerent presence of troops in foreign territory indicates, however, that there were positive reasons for the presumed oversight of classical authors. Thus, Raymond Robin, who in 1913 can still think of troops in foreign territory only in terms of occupation, albeit peaceful and in some respects limited, informs us that the classical authors could not become particularly interested, because peaceful military occupation, "if not unknown in their time, was at best in an embryonic stage." As to wartime occupation, it was dominated by "the Roman notion of *occupation-conquête,* of the war authorizing immediate appropriation of the enemy's possessions," a notion which, "until the seventeenth century . . . has remained fully valid and unchallenged." [73] Grotius rebelled against the rigidity of that doctrine and demanded that a transfer of sovereignty take place before the possession of occupied territory became final. But only the later strengthening of the respect for the independence and sovereignty of states resulted in a revision of the earlier conceptions governing both wartime and peacetime occupations.[74]

Antonio Ruini, the author of an excellent recent study on the historical development of older theories concerning the status of troops, finds, moreover, that until the end of the eighteenth century "the presence of corps of troops in foreign territory did not appear as a phenomenon of the law of peace but was considered in practice as equivalent to the phenomenon of belligerent

---

[73] Robin, *op. cit.,* pp. 575 and 579. Cf. nn. 46-47 *supra.*

[74] *Ibid.,* p. 574, in connection with n. (1) there. Robin's Roman notion was not confined to the so-called civil-law countries; in fact, it was more slow to die in the Anglo-American law. See Richard R. Baxter, "The Duty of Obedience to the Belligerent Occupant," *BYIL,* XXVII (1950), 235-66 *passim,* especially 236-37, informing us' of various instances of trials of nationals of occupied territories for "treason" against the occupant, to whom they would today owe no allegiance, and of the fact that English courts held, as late as the nineteenth century, that "no point is more clearly settled in the Courts of Common Law than that a conquered country forms immediately part of the King's dominions" (*The Foltina,* 1 Dods. 450, 451 [1814]).

occupation." [75] Hence, the only possible form of peaceful presence of troops in foreign territory was the temporary one of a *transitus innoxius* of a corps of troops. In such a case, the troops were exempt from local jurisdiction indeed; but there was no occasion for the theorists of international law to become concerned about the matter. The exemption was simply the result of domestic law, that is, of the *ius commune* of the Continent, the substance of which was derived from Justinian's codification. This common law prescribed that the *milites* belong under the jurisdiction of their *dux,* to whom they must be delivered for judgment in the case of an offense or a dispute.[76] As Ruini puts it, a local judge, approached to try a case against a member of a military force, "as a matter of principle, had to declare himself incompetent to try it, not only when confronted with the authority of an indigenous *dux* but likewise in regard to a foreign *dux.* In fact, the exclusive competence attributed by the common law [i.e., common Continental European law] to a foreign *dux* should not have appeared to the local judge as that of a foreign judicial organ, but as jurisdiction of an organ operating within the same legal system." [77]

Consequently, even though the exemption from local jurisdiction may have been preceded by a permission to pass, no "implied consent," no reference to the latter in order to assure the former, was necessary. Once the troops were in the territory—and to refuse the right of passage may have been illegal, depending on the circumstances—their exemption from jurisdiction was a function of

[75] "I corpi da truppa all'estero nel diritto internazionale generale: Premesse storiche," *Communicazioni e studi* (University of Milan, Istituto di Diritto Internazionale e Straniero), VIII (1956), 253-367, on 335.

[76] For example, the Constitution of 414 A.D. confers exclusive military jurisdiction concerning military defendants in both civil and criminal matters: "Magisteriae potestatis inter militares viros *vel privato actore in reum militarem etiam civilium quaestionem* audiendi concedimus facultatem, praesertim cum id ipsum e re esse litigantium, videatur constetque *militarem reum nisi a suo iudice nec exhiberi posse, nec, si in culpa fuerit, coerceri*" (*Code* 3.13.6 [emphasis added]). See Ruini, *op. cit.,* p. 263, n. 16, for other relevant places.

[77] Ruini, *op. cit.,* p. 273 (translated from Italian).

their military rather than foreign quality. The only problem left to the theorists of *international* law was the right to enter the territory—which, indeed, was their field of interest par excellence.[78]

The immunity of corps of troops from local jurisdiction dates, thus, from a period before the territorial state took over the monopoly of the judicial process; and it was simply transformed into a principle of "inter-national" law when the "nations," in the form of integrated territorial units, were established. That is, as the imperium of the *rex* became "territorium," the imperium of the foreign *dux* over his passing *milites* became "exterritoriality." In this almost automatic process all that the theorists of international law had to do was to continue taking it for granted that immunity exists.[79] John Marshall couched the established practice in terms of reverence for the sovereign territorial state; quite likely, he may have felt the need of an explanation agreeing with the territorial conception of sovereignty more than did the classical authors, to whom a contradiction between the immunity

[78] When they did not ignore the status of the soldiers, they could deal with it by reference to Roman sources. Thus, Belli simply quotes *Digest*: "Habent etiam milites fori privilegium, neque convenientur nisi coram suo judice cum distinctione tamen. Aut est enim causa criminalis aut civilis, primo casu aut crimen est militare et ad solum militum judicem spectat cognitio" (49.16.3.pr., quoted in *De re militari et bello tractatus*, Venetiis, 1563 [photographic reproduction, "Classics of International Law"; Oxford-London: Carnegie Endowment, 1936], p. 81). Ayala, *De jure officiis bellicis et disciplina militari libri III*, Duaci, 1582 (photographic reproduction; Washington: Carnegie Endowment, 1912), p. 193, relies on the place quoted above (n. 76): "Milites non nisi suum judicem conveniri possunt, nec, si in culpa sint, coerci . . . unde capti a praeside ad proprium judicem remitti debent." See Ruini, *op. cit.*, p. 265, nn. 20 and 21. Based on what was already said, these are references to a passing army as much as to domestic *milites*. Cf. also the next note *infra*.

[79] Vattel, for example, argues for restrictions of the right of passage and then proceeds (*op. cit.*, III, vii, 134, Carnegie Endowment translation): "The troops to whom passage is granted should avoid causing the least damage to the country; they should keep to the high roads, and not enter the possessions of private persons; they should observe the strictest discipline, and pay without fail for whatever is furnished them. And if the disorderly conduct of soldiers, or certain necessary operations, such as camping or intrenching, have caused damage, the general commanding them, or their sovereign, must make reparation." It is logical that, if the sending state is responsible for the misconduct of soldiers not less than for damages caused by official acts of the army, the soldier is not assumed to be responsible to the local courts.

of passing troops and the emerging state conception may not have occurred or appeared as important.[80]

Turning from classics to the authors of "standard texts" we find a different situation—but not a clearer one as far as the substance of their doctrines is concerned. In the first place, they took their time to register the results of the practice of nations. One hundred years after Marshall, they were still repeating the statements from *Schooner Exchange,* often incorporating them into their textbooks with little if any comment, as if no change had occurred in the circumstances of the sending of troops abroad. Small wonder that the majority of textbook authors "support" automatic exterritoriality: they are referring to the situation described by Vattel, as legally reinterpreted by Marshall. Quoting each other and the cases which were not intended to apply to *friendly* forces *stationed* abroad, the authors ostensibly taking sides multiply, and are being multiplied by reinterpretations of their texts, often without any intention of their own.[81] In fact, it would be useless to offer here a compilation of excerpts from general texts, as we shall see, for more reasons than the one just mentioned.[82] As it happens, one of

[80] It should now be even clearer why Marshall's statement on the troops could have been meant neither to apply to troops *stationed* in foreign territory, nor to recognize less than exemption from "*all*" jurisdiction." The situation described by Vattel is precisely the one Marshall had in mind: a narrowly described route of passage of limited duration, to assure minimum threat to the sovereignty of the host state even though full immunity cannot be avoided. For Vattel, however, both the right of passage and the limitations on its use are still founded in natural law (Book II, paragraph 132), and it is in this respect that Marshall parts from him: no passage without an express act of will, no immunity without an implied one. The *dux* thus becomes an "organ" having no standing without the dignity of his sovereign state behind him.

[81] Thus, Henry Wheaton, *Elements of International Law* (5th English ed., Coleman Phillipson, ed.; London, 1916), paragraphs 99 and 95, relying on *Schooner Exchange* and *Coleman* v. *Tennessee,* is, in turn, quoted by others. John Westlake, for example (*International Law* [2nd ed.; Cambridge: University Press, 1910-13], I, 265), relies on Wheaton's paraphrasis of *Coleman* v. *Tennessee,* thereby qualifying as a supporter of exterritoriality of visiting forces in the controversy of the 1950's.

[82] Such compilations are, incidentally, available elsewhere. (See, the American and Canadian memoranda, *loc. cit.* [*supra,* n. 33] at pp. 405-11 and 437-50, respectively; further, Re, *op. cit.,* pp. 373-83, King, I, pp. 544-47, and *Reference re Exemption* . . . [*supra,* n. 67] pp. 512-13, 521-22.) They show, in support of automatic

these authorities had himself remarked that little can be proved by counting pro and con statements, unless all those are also polled who have neglected to volunteer their views on the specific matter in dispute.[83] In any event, the projection of the views of the textbook authors to the controversy which arose after their time merely draws attention to the degree of disorientation existing even with reference to situations which could have been analyzed at the time the texts were written.[84]

In the second place, the inconclusiveness of the views expressed in "standard texts" was not merely the result of an inertness in taking new developments into consideration. Much of the disorientation on the present subject is due to the nature of these developments, since they obliterated the conditions to which the established doctrine was applicable, while no situations conducive to the growth of new principles were apparent. The exterritoriality of corps of troops contained an almost built-in obsolescence. This was so because the affirmation of the territorial state, which had transformed the Roman-law exemption of the military from the jurisdiction of civilian courts into the international principle of

---

exterritoriality, a memorable list of authorities. Specifically, from among the authors of general textbooks, there are Hall, Wheaton, Westlake, Gallandet, Travers, Twiss, Phillimore, Holland, Lorimer, Wildman, Pitt Cobbet, Hannis Taylor, Calvo, Holtzendorff, Rivier, Hyde, Oppenheim, Lawrence, and Hackworth; and from among the specialists in related disciplines and authors of various monographs, there are, to take but a selection, Strisower, Gidel, Valery, Foelix, Travers, Adinolfi, Heyking, Clunet, Birkhimer, Chalufour, and Van Praag. On the side of the thesis of narrowly circumscribed immunities, we find Baty, Davis, and Fiore, plus the last four of the authors of general texts listed above—the latter thus playing an ambivalent role. (The relevant works are indicated in the Bibliographical Note.) Lauterpacht's and Lawrence's texts attracted attention by switching sides in successive editions, and others merely state (see, e.g., Hall, *op. cit.*, pp. 250-51) that under certain conditions military commanders "assert" or "claim" immunity, which, indeed, is not an assertion of the existence of a rule.

[83] L. van Praag, *Jurisdiction et Droit international public* (Hague: Belinfante, 1915), p. 504.

[84] That the latter condition is a persisting one, is well illustrated by the fact that even post–World War II texts occasionally discuss the stationing of friendly forces in foreign territory under the general heading of "war and military occupation." (See, e.g., Oscar Svarlien, *An Introduction to the Law of Nations* [New York–Toronto–London: McGraw-Hill, 1955].)

exterritoriality of foreign forces, was paralleled with, and assisted by, the decline of the right of passage and of its foundation, the just-war doctrine. For, once the territorial state had acquired the right of excluding the prospective transient army (a principle eventually extended into a *duty* of neutrals to prohibit passage of forces of the belligerents), the rule guaranteeing the exterritoriality of corps of troops could find no actual situations to be applied to.

It is true that the nineteenth century was an era of frequent instances of "peaceful" presence of troops in foreign or quasi-foreign territory. But these developments, generally considered under the headings of imperialism and colonial expansion, were poor material for a theorist of international law to work with. In the first place, their international nature, even in the absence of a formal annexation, was doubtful. Consequently, the extension of the old rule concerning the corps of troops to the practices of the nineteenth century would have been obviously inappropriate. Not only was the common legal foundation that had supported the old principle lacking, but the new practices were characterized by the absence of that relation of normality and reciprocity between the "sending" and the "receiving" territory which had once made the transformation of the immunity of corps of troops into a principle of international law almost automatic. Where the relation of normality and reciprocity continued, namely, in the case of men-of-war in foreign territorial waters, the extension of the doctrine was both appropriate and effective. But where the actual practices, as in the various instances of "peaceful occupation" during the nineteenth century,[85] were nearly always founded on a basic *inequality* between the sending state and the receiving

---

[85] The term "peaceful occupation" creates difficulties itself; it has nothing to do with the *occupatio pacifica* of the established terminology. But "occupation by consent" and *occupatio petita* ("requested"), two other terms used to describe non-belligerent presence of foreign troops, are equally inappropriate for obvious reasons.

territory and revealed otherwise, as Raymond Robin has found,[86] an "infinite variety" of characteristics arising out of *particular* relationships, there was no possibility for such extension of principles or for the discovery of new ones. The particular circumstances—the various purposes for the sending of troops, under various formal and informal arrangements, with various quantities of admixture of force—were by themselves an obstacle to the formulation of generally applicable principles. The chief common characteristic, inequality between the two parties, meant that principles limiting the sending power would not apply; and to talk about rules of international law in the absence of limitations would be self-contradictory. Consequently, the authors of the nineteenth century could only deal with individual practices of their era under *ad hoc* titles: intervention, garrison rights, administrative concessions, protectorates and zones, and the stationing of troops to guarantee the fulfillment of an "alliance," or the payment of a debt, or to disguise a cession of territory, etc. The development of a general theory applying to the status of forces was precluded by the nature of the situations which it would have to cover.

In sum, whereas the classical theorists had paid little attention to the status of forces because no problem was posited by the kind of situation they had known, the authors of the standard texts appear to have been disoriented or to have sought solutions in antiquated formulae by necessity, because they were confronted with an unsolvable problem. That is, they not only are a poor source for providing guidance in the present situation, but they were also in no condition to formulate principles applying to the circumstances of their own era: these were neither conducive to theoretical generalization, nor susceptible to legal limitation.

[86] *Op. cit.,* p. viii, of the Carnegie Endowment's translated excerpts. Robin's work reveals the variety well. It discovers three "fundamental" characteristics of "peaceful occupation" (provisional, pacific, and not transferring sovereignty) and one "general" (mostly treaty-based), all of which are subsequently qualified so much that no substance is left (cf. p. 612 with pp. 614-21 and 630-32 [in the original edition]). The last of these indicates absence of principles by definition.

### CUSTOMARY STATUS OF FORCES AND THE
### STATUS-OF-FORCES AGREEMENTS

What follows then from the discussion in the present chapter is that neither the literature of international law nor judicial opinions reveal a "general practice of nations accepted as law" that regulates the status of forces stationed in a friendly foreign country. This is not to say that one must become reconciled with the "logically not possible" [87] or "untenable" [88] discovery of a void in international law; it is merely to say that—as the outcome of the last important pre-NATO case, the advisory opinion of the Canadian Supreme Court, demonstrates—finding what exactly the law is may still prove to be an unsolvable task.

For our purpose, however, it is not indispensable to determine what the status of forces would be in the hypothetical situation of their deployment in allied foreign territory without a status-of-forces agreement. It is enough to point to the trend which can already be discovered in some of the sources of customary international law preceding the current conventional system. In particular, the period since about World War I is characterized by progressively more careful differentiating between the various circumstances of presence of friendly foreign forces in the territory of a state. The earlier practice of confusing different situations—war with peace, ships with military camps, passage with stationing, and occupation with the performance of co-operative tasks by an allied force—occurs less and less frequently. At the beginning of this period stands an attempt to classify in various categories of peaceful occupation all incidences of non-belligerent presence of foreign troops in the territory of a state (Robin). Occupation is soon distinguished from joint conduct of military operations in allied territory (Chalufour), and both from station-

---

[87] Kelsen, *op. cit.* (n. 24 *supra*), p. 305.
[88] Brierly, *op. cit.* (*supra,* Chapter I, n. 21), p. 68.

ing in the territory of an allied state at large, i.e., without reference to areas of military operations or defined camp zones but simply to be present "wherever needed" (Canadian Supreme Court). Furthermore, judges and theorists began to define more carefully the criteria determining the scope of immunities and to relate them to the purposes of the deployment of forces. Thus, not only is the exercise of local enforcement processes now clearly distinguished from the obligatory force of the substantive local law, but an exemption from the former began to be considered as being conditional upon the enforcement of the latter by the sending state's authorities (Justice Rand in the Canadian case). This means, in fact, that the differentiation of the concept of extra-territorial jurisdiction from the concept of immunity from territorial processes has been brought to its logical conclusion, which allows for the existence of concurrent powers of two states over the same subject matter in the same territory—a feature incorporated into the postwar agreements explicitly. At the same time, in progressively more precise usage of terms, not only are acts of state distinguished from the broader concept of on-duty acts, but the latter from acts done only "while doing something in the course of duties" (*Wright* v. *Cantrell*) or from acts done in abuse of duty (*Ministère Public* c. *Tsoukaris*). Finally, various aspects of the nature of an offense which raises conflicting claims of jurisdiction are scrutinized, and it is asserted that they should determine who shall exercise jurisdiction regardless of other considerations.[89] No general agreement was reached on the relative significance of these criteria; but the fact that they began to be distinguished, defined, and considered, at least in some sources, was a step in the direction of the current conventional status.

Indeed, some of the problems encountered in the application

---

[89] "Nature of the offense" includes the relative interests of the states involved, based on object or gravity of the offense, as contrasted with systems settling the conflict of competences solely on the basis of location or personal status of the offender. Cf. *supra*, Chapter III, pp. 80-81; also, *R.* v. *Navratil, Chung Chi Cheung* v. *The King*, and the opinions of Rand, Duff, and Hudson in the Canadian advisory case, discussed earlier in this chapter.

of NATO-SFA had been discovered in court decisions preceding it, since the courts had already begun to rely on criteria which were later incorporated into that agreement. In other words, the conventional development has as yet not achieved significant progress in clarifying its criteria beyond the views expressed in some of the pre-NATO decisions; and its most general tendency, that is, increased reliance on the nature of the offense, is the direct continuation of what was already in process of affirmation before the adoption of the new agreements.

It should not be forgotten, however, that our transitional pre-NATO development is clearly reflected only in a few opinions, which have drawn distinctions neglected elsewhere and, to that extent, have anticipated the current agreements. Indeed, in the absence of general recognition of the new criteria, customary status of friendly forces in foreign territory could still be derived only negatively, that is, from the general principle which permits the territorial sovereign to exercise all powers not specifically prohibited by established rules. If anything came close to such prohibition, it was the *intra-castral* and the on-duty immunities of foreign forces. In the postwar conventional system, however, the *intra-castral* immunity has been abandoned (after its importance had already been reduced in the Leased Bases agreement); and the conventional transformation of the on-duty exemption involved both broadening the concept[90] and making it less compelling.[91] Otherwise, the new conventional system formally recognizes the overriding quality of the territorial competence, so that the privileges of the visiting forces are still deduced from the consent of the receiving states.

A different result obtains, however, if we compare the customary status with the new conventional system as reflected in the actual application of the new agreements. The fact that the actual scope

---

[90] By inclusion of non-duty acts, particularly in practice (*supra,* Chapter IV).

[91] Because it merely produces concurrent, though primary, right to exercise jurisdiction (*supra,* Chapter III).

of privileges of the visiting forces largely depends, as we have seen in Chapter IV, upon the considerations made by the sending state indicates that the recognition of the supreme authority of the receiving state is more nominal than real. Consequently, the principle of territorial sovereignty is undermined on two levels: first, in the formal recognition of concurrent powers of foreign authorities in the territory of the receiving states; second, in the actual deviation from the principle that all exemptions from territorial competence must be based on the consent of the territorial state.

Although exemptions from the exercise of territorial powers have occurred before, they normally meant the transfer of exclusive rights in a defined field to another state—not a system of concurrent powers, requiring further redefinition in the course of their use. It is precisely because the new exemptions from the territorial competence occur in such a form as to require additional decisions before their scope is known—decisions which are in actuality often not made by the receiving state—that it would stretch the old fiction of implied consent too far if it were used to explain the new conventional status. The fiction may have been successful in supporting the principle of territorial exclusiveness at a time when the principle itself appeared to be more realistic and the legal construction of exceptions from it (which were narrower than today, unless there was a *de facto* cession) was not too far fetched to appear immediately implausible. Once the exceptions have grown out of proportion, an attempt to salvage the principle of territorial exclusiveness by stretching the old legal construction is both unmanageable and unnecessary because, in the last analysis, the principle has outlived—for more reasons than the actual status of forces—whatever usefulness it may have had in the past.

## VI. American Forces Abroad and the Sovereign Territorial State

THOUGH THE BASIC INSTITUTION of the Westphalian era, the sovereign territorial state, remains, its viability has become uncertain. As a guarantor of security, the state has been rendered obsolete by technology. Its territory is penetrable from without. Its domestic order is threatened by transterritorial loyalties and new techniques of attack from within. As the chief agent in world politics, the state has often been denounced for misusing its surplus of power; now, however, it has become dangerous because of the disproportion between its limited capabilities and its absolutist pretensions. What, then, is the significance of the postwar arrangements pertaining to bases and to the stationing of forces abroad? Do they signal the surrender of the state's prerogatives that were derived from seventeenth-century conditions, or are they merely an unpromising attempt to carry the traditional state model through a period of crisis?

Both seem to be true, since the states of the world, although reluctant to admit that a fundamental change has occurred in their traditional role, simultaneously attempt to develop novel methods to take care of problems that have ceased to be susceptible to traditional treatment. This ambiguous situation has a particular significance for the states of the Western alliance-system, which becomes apparent when their traditional attributes are re-examined in the light of the new arrangements.

### SYMPTOMS OF DETERRITORIALIZATION

Both conditions for admitting alien forces to the territory of a state and the status of such forces, once admitted, contain evidence of deviation from the Westphalian model. It will be recalled that under the most recent type of agreement forces are admitted to the territory of a state at large, rather than to a geographically defined "leased" portion. They share facilities with the local forces, and they are responsible, with forces of the host and of third states, for defending an "area"—that is, more than just the territory of the sending and the receiving states. Their function, moreover, is not necessarily restricted to checking an attack from without the territory or the area. They may assist the local forces in maintaining domestic order, although this is seldom openly stipulated. Thus, there is an implied recognition of the need for larger forces and larger territory than any single state can supply. At the same time, foreign forces stationed within the territory of a state have ceased to represent an inherent threat to its sovereignty. In short, the traditional identification of security with territorial exclusiveness has lost its former credibility.

Soldiers stationed abroad are subject to a jurisdictional regime that (1) involves sharing of responsibilities by the authorities of the sending and the receiving state under a system of concurrent prerogatives; (2) is in principle identical throughout the territory of the receiving state and possibly in several adjoining states under a multilateral agreement; (3) resolves jurisdictional conflicts on the basis of substantive criteria, such as the nature of an offense over which jurisdiction is to be exercised; and (4) relies on actual accommodation in the course of applying the agreements more than on precision of definition. This is in contrast to the older system, which (1) assigned exclusive rights to one or the other state, often obliterating the distinction between extraterritorial jurisdiction and exterritoriality, because one could not occur without the other; (2) drew a sharp distinction between the status of soldiers in the garrisoned and transit areas on the one hand and the remaining territory on the other, while a multilateral agreement was altogether inconceivable; (3) paid little attention to the nature of the offense, relying, aside from geography, chiefly on the personal status of the individual involved; and (4) insisted on reconciling non-territorial realities with the principle of territorial jurisdiction by fabricating legal fictions. In sum, the abandonment of territorial exclusiveness as the basic postulate of security is complemented by a yielding of traditional rights of jurisdiction.

However, are not the current status-of-forces agreements reaffirming the territorial principle when they allow local authorities the exercise of concurrent jurisdiction over visiting forces? Assuming that the old system contained an implied grant of immunity from the exercise of territorial jurisdiction, the new agreements may appear to have undermined the privileges of the sending state. But we have seen that the actual jurisdiction of the sending state is greater than what one would expect from the text of the new agreements. Even where the status of forces is defined in a multi-lateral convention, it is given specific meaning only in the course of its application, which is bilateral and generally facilitates disproportionate influence on the part of the sending state. Furthermore, the sending state has traded partial subjection of its soldiers to local law enforcement (in the reduced extent remaining when the agreements are actually applied) for access to the entire territory of the receiving state. The effect is to make the new, "conjurisdictional" [1] system a medium of restriction of local rights. The sending state now has its share of concurrent jurisdiction in parts of the receiving state's territory which, being ungarrisoned, would have remained, according to the old system, under the exclusive authority of the host. On balance, therefore, it cannot be said that the status-of-forces agreements have strengthened the territorial rights. Rather, there was some yielding on both sides at the level of negotiation; but at the level of implementation, the host state has yielded the most.

It is not difficult to trace the characteristic features of the old and new regimes regarding alien forces to the particular circumstances of the old and new eras. One may consider, for example, the shift from resolving jurisdictional conflicts *ratione loci* to the new system based on *ratio materiae*. What was the purpose of armed forces in the heyday of the territorial principle? In the absence of permanent friends or foes identifiable in terms of non-territorial criteria, every state represented a potential threat to all others. Foreign forces, then, necessarily were suspected of annexation designs—regardless of which state they represented. Indeed, in a hypothetical world of ideal-type territorial states, even occupation—as a regime distinct from outright possession—would be inconceivable. A political unit defined solely in terms of territorial domination cannot hold territory without making that

[1] The origin of the term is ascribed to Professor Julius Stone, University of Sidney, by Snee and Pye, *Status*, p. 10 n.

territory a part of its domain. In the real world of the Westphalian era, which represented as close an approximation to the pure territorial system as had ever become practical, the presence of foreign forces meant war and belligerent occupation, or something almost indistinguishable from the latter. Small wonder that no state-wide conjurisdictional processes could be developed during an era when military forces "carried territory" of the sending state with them. A state unwilling or unable to resist penetration by foreign forces could only hope to keep them restricted to defined garrison and transit areas, leaving them undisturbed there but denying any privileged status to soldiers found in the remaining territory. The best the "host" state could make out of the situation within the garrisoned area was to attempt to save its dignity by theorizing that its "ultimate" sovereignty over the area was still in effect. Hence, the privileges of the foreign force were traced to an implied license on the part of the territorial sovereign, extended as a tribute to "sovereign dignity" and the "perfect equality and independence" of states—a tour de force to keep the "absolute and exclusive" nature of territorial jurisdiction well isolated from contrary facts.

The motive for such theorizing disappears as the significance of territoriality decreases and the purpose of forces changes. At the turn of the century, after various transterritorial factors had transformed the state from a nearly pure territorial to a hybrid institution,[2] the old legal formulas began to be discarded. It was then possible to class passage and garrison rights as subcategories of occupation, and to expose specific instances of the so-called

[2] Transterritorial elements in the Western state system are, of course, older than the bomb-carrying plane and the peacetime stationing of friendly foreign forces in the territory of a state. One may consider such early signals of deterritorialization as the progressive coming into disuse of schemes of religious ("cuius regio, illius religio") and economic territoriality (e.g., plans of autarky); and, further, the impact of the "nation-ization" of the state (insofar as states and nations only approximately share the same territory)—not to speak of the rise of social and political movements that are deliberately both transnational and transterritorial.

occupation by consent as "disguised annexations" and "displacements of sovereignty," simply because occupation not implying automatic annexation had also become conceivable.

Since that time we have moved so far away from Westphalian conditions that the theoretical categories of the transitional period have become as obsolete as the older legal fictions. Thus, forces do not pursue control of territory per se but seek the defense of a transterritorial way of life against a transterritorial threat. No legal fiction is necessary to avoid a "diminution of sovereignty," since the alien forces cannot sensibly accomplish their chief task if they are also employed to plunder the receiving territory. In the absence of an inherent threat of annexation, the distinction between *intra-castral* and *extra-castral* events becomes unimportant. The new criteria for the separation of rights of jurisdiction reflect instead the division of labor, which the states concerned have adopted to serve their common goals more effectively. The hypothetical end product is not a military force that cannot move about without expanding the territorial boundaries of the sending state, but a condition in which local and visiting forces become indistinguishable from each other.

Altogether, the new arrangements for the stationing of forces reveal more than the decreasing effectiveness of the sovereign territorial state. They reflect a change in the purpose of forces, and they demonstrate that the state is, in its most elementary function, being divorced from its traditional territorial foundation. However, official support of the traditional concepts of state sovereignty and territorial jurisdiction continues. Outdated legal formulas survive in more places than court records and the arguments of groups opposing the entire alliance system. The very provisions that renounce some of the traditional prerogatives are camouflaged with assurances in the language of seventeenth-century legal fiction. The result is, indeed, an incipient deterritorialization of the state. But it is just that: incipient and short of what is needed and, frequently, short even of what was intended. Nowhere is this more apparent than in the case of NATO.

The NATO system represents the most radical deviation from the traditional patterns governing forces abroad. It is difficult, however, to determine its full significance, because the working of the joint military command structure—as distinguished from the legal status—is not a matter of open record. Particularly in the early years of NATO the picture was incomplete; it was largely a matter of conjecture from unilluminative official communiques or analogy. Thus, the division of competences *ratione materiae,* which happens to be a typical device of federalism, has been interpreted by some writers to mean that the alliance has already progressed beyond mere confederation. One authority proposed that

> the bases examined . . . are not foreign bases in the current sense of this modifier; they do not, in fact, depend on a foreign country, but on a *federal organization* in which the receiving country participates; hence they do not constitute, strictly speaking, military bases installed in foreign territory, but *federal bases* on which foreign troops may stay. . . . The signatory states authorize each other to receive in their territory and to install on bases established for that purpose the *troops of the Alliance* which are necessary for collective security. No privilege is accorded by the state A to state B; rather states A, B, and C consent to mutual privileges.[3]

Various examples of the use of federal techniques, besides the new division of competences, have been invoked in support of this view. Military and civil "federal" (NATO) authorities are

---

[3] Flory, *op. cit.* (*supra,* Chapter II, n. 60), pp. 6-8 (translation [emphasis added]).

presumed to exercise command over the bases and to decide all non-military problems that may arise at a NATO base. The disposition of forces appears to be, according to NATO-SFA, a NATO matter.[4] The Organization, equipped with legal personality,[5] contracts and acquires, and distributes the proceeds of sale of abandoned installations, crediting the accounts of member states according to their cost-sharing rate,[6] which is also set by the Organization.[7] Article VII of NATO-SFA, according to this view, does not provide for concessions of one state to another but "establishes a system of distribution of powers between two states of a federation."[8]

Official interpretations of the nature of military arrangements in the North Atlantic Treaty area have been ambiguous. National and NATO officials often insist that "NATO is not a transnational organization."[9] Indeed, the Senate was told originally that NATO is not even an "old-fashioned alliance," since it avoids "automatic commitments to go to war in the event the other parties become involved."[10] It is clear, however, that some of the official assurances along this line can be discounted as attempts to appease domestic opposition. For example, that NATO is not an old-fashioned alliance

[4] According to Article III, NATO-SFA (cited *supra*, Chapter III, n. 4), members of a force are exempt from passport and visa regulations, etc., if they are in possession of an "individual or collective *movement order* . . . issued by an appropriate agency of the sending state or *of the North Atlantic Treaty Organization* . . ." (paragraph 2 b [emphasis added]).

[5] Agreement on the Status of the North Atlantic Treaty Organization, National Representatives, and International Staff, Ottawa, September 20, 1951 (5 UST 1087; TIAS 2882), Article 4. That the Organization also possesses an international juridical personality is evidenced by the conclusion of a formal agreement between the North Atlantic Council and the United States on February 25, 1953 (5 UST 890; TIAS 2978).

[6] Protocol on the Status of International Military Headquarters, Paris, August 22, 1952 (5 UST 870; TIAS 2978), Article 9. According to Article 10, "each Supreme Headquarters shall possess juridicial personality" as does the Organization.

[7] Lord Ismay, *NATO: The First Five Years, 1949-54* (Paris: NATO, 1955), pp. 61, 115-18.

[8] Flory, *op. cit.*, p. 11.

[9] *The NATO Handbook* (Paris: NATO, 1959), p. 11.

[10] Senate Executive Report No. 8, 81st Cong., 1st Sess., p. 23; *North Atlantic Treaty*, Hearings, Senate Committee on Foreign Relations, 81st Cong., 1st Sess., Pt. I, Administration Witnesses, April 27-May 3, 1949, pp. 14, 173, and 334-37.

is still correct only because the verbal commitments of traditional alliances could easily be broken; the new type of commitment is binding regardless of the formula describing the *casus foederis.* If it was true before the North Atlantic Treaty was ratified that "without this pact, had war broken out we would have found ourselves fighting in the center of Europe because we have troops there,"[11] it became more so afterwards. Thus, our question is not whether NATO is an alliance, but how much more, even, than a new-fashioned alliance it is.

Two successive administrations in the United States have informed the Senate, respectively, that "forces of various nations which form part of the integrated force for the defense of the North Atlantic Treaty area [must be] free to move from one country to another in accordance with the demands of strategy"[12] and that certain supplementary agreements serve "to carry forward" the program of "integrated defense forces *of* the . . . Organization" and its "integrated operations."[13] Such statements also appear to supply evidence in favor of the federative conception of NATO arrangements: if the organization decides on deployment of forces and directs their integrated operations, it is not unreasonable to see in this pattern the use of techniques of federalism—at least insofar as the military decision-making machinery of NATO is distinguishable from the organs of the largest member states.[14] The same conclusion follows from several bilateral agreements implementing NATO decisions, as noted in Chapter II

---

[11] General Bradley in *North Atlantic Treaty,* Hearings, *op. cit.,* p. 295; cf. *idem* in *Assignment Hearings* (Chapter I, n. 22 *supra*), p. 145, and General Clay, *ibid.,* p. 768.

[12] Report of the Secretary of State, attached to President Truman's transmittal to the Senate of NATO-SFA, June 13, 1952 (*ibid.,* p. 95).

[13] President Eisenhower, Message to the Senate, February 27, 1953 (*SFA Ratification Hearings,* p. 109 [emphasis added]).

[14] Evidence of formal differentiating exists. Thus, Admiral Jerauld Wright, United States Navy, representing the Headquarters of the Supreme Allied Commander Atlantic, and Secretary of Defense Charles E. Wilson, representing the United States, concluded an Agreement Regarding the Headquarters . . . , Washington, October 22, 1954 (5 UST 2519; TIAS 3113).

above. We have been told, in fact, that the early decisions relating to the defense of the North Atlantic Treaty area resulted in military headquarters "both international and integrated. The headquarters would not function like a committee made up of a number of national delegations, but rather as a single unified organization in which all officers, regardless of nationality, worked for the common mission." [15]

Nevertheless, the federative interpretation of NATO arrangements is exaggerated. Most of the sources supporting it date from the early period of implementation of Article 3 of the North Atlantic Treaty. Compared with the preceding military vacuum, even a modest build-up of forces and a minimum of integrative efforts appeared to be great progress. Other sources reflected plans rather than achievement. By 1956, American military spokesmen began to complain that "we have more trouble with bases now than we did have two or three years ago," [16] and that "Russian propaganda" was influencing American allies, "causing them either—not yet, of course—to withdraw from the organization, but certainly to take steps which affect the effectiveness of the organization itself." [17] Meanwhile, the Algerian, Suez, and Berlin crises demonstrated the lack of co-ordination of policies as well as insufficient integration of forces. The organization may well rely on federal techniques insofar as it makes decisions. But how far is that? Collective decisions "subject to separate arrangements" [18] mean little if the members can in fact arrange away the results at their pleasure. As it stands now, forces can be withdrawn from the system unilaterally, restrictions incidental to inter-allied

[15] Colonel Andrew J. Goodpaster, "The Development of SHAPE; 1950-1953," *International Organization*, IX, No. 2 (May, 1955), 258.

[16] General Twining, *Airpower Hearings, op. cit.*, VII, Pt. XXIII, 1812.

[17] General Bradley, *ibid.*, I, Pt. 1, 30.

[18] Cf. Protocol on the Status of Headquarters, Preamble; NATO-SFA, Preamble and Articles III, 1 and 2b *in fine;* further, Article I(1) of the American-Greek agreement and Preamble of the Greenland agreement (quoted *supra*, Chapter II, text at nn. 63 and 65).

bargaining can be imposed on the deployment of forces, agreed plans can remain unfinanced—all of which has happened recently —leaving the "federal" overhead without substance. A federation must fulfill its quantitative requirement not less than the qualitative. Without it, NATO is appropriately characterized as being "located at a relatively low point of the integrative continuum" [19] and, as an early diagnosis suggested, it may be open to doubt how real it is.[20]

The North Atlantic Treaty was adopted with the optimistic comment that "the reality which is set down here is not created here. The reality is the unity of belief, of spirit, of interest, of the community of nations represented here. It is a product of many centuries." [21] The treaty was given specific meaning by the American decision to deploy additional forces in the area covered by it, and by the collective decision to unify the military instrumentalities of the member states in peacetime. Yet, the initial momentum of these decisions was lost as soon as it appeared that the barest military necessity had been met. Could it be that "Russian propaganda" has prevented the creation of an adequate machinery for the expression of the unity of belief, spirit, and interest of the member nations?

A more convincing obstacle is domestic politics. Owing to the public's sensitivity to deviations from traditional patterns of world politics, the early implementation of NATO plans took the form of "disguised integration." Thus a vicious circle was started, and what emerged was a rudimentary transnational regime, confined to the military field, with no policy to accompany it. Only a political organization, "integrated and international," can provide the

[19] George Liska, *International Equilibrium* (Cambridge: Harvard University Press, 1957), p. 167.

[20] Alfred J. Hotz, "NATO: Myth or Reality," *Annals*, No. 288 (July 1953), pp. 126-33.

[21] Secretary of State Acheson, at the signing of the North Atlantic Treaty, April 4, 1949.

permanent support necessary for a unified military structure. The NATO Council, with its narrow authority,[22] its closed sessions, and its National Representatives several levels removed from the locus of public consensus-making in their respective states is far from providing it. In short, an adequate political organization could not be developed without full public discussion of the authority with which it should be equipped. This the governments of the member states are still unwilling to attempt because it would conflict with certain imbedded concepts—and misconceptions— inherited from the Westphalian era. The result is that the joint machinery, far from being of a federal variety, lacks authority where it needs it most and, indeed, is cut off from any meaningful way of asking for it.

### INTEGRATION, SOVEREIGNTY, AND TERRITORIALITY

Though its jurisdiction is far too narrow to provide the necessary political foundation for its military machinery, the NATO Council can exercise it only by unanimous vote. This is a typical example of how a widespread misconception—not simply the survival of an obsolescent legal principle, but a persisting misconception—can obstruct the development of new institutions, though it cannot revitalize what has in fact become obsolete. The misconception in this case is the absolute definition of sovereignty, which accounts for the belief that integration involves loss of independence with the very first step, regardless of how small the matter in which a state becomes subject to "limitations not imposed by itself." [23] In consequence, NATO appears to be constantly faced with the dilemma between the rule of unanimity,

[22] The Council can create subsidiary bodies, including international headquarters, but it can only "consider" matters of implementation of the North Atlantic Treaty (Article 9 of the Treaty).

[23] The *Schooner Exchange* (see the entire quotation *supra*, Chapter V, p. 126).

"the constitutional bulwark of the rights of the smaller nations," on the one side and a degree of integration which would "presuppose a surrender of national independence and sovereignty" on the other.[24]

In fact, however, no such apocalyptic dilemma exists. This, incidentally, is perceived more clearly by the smaller members of the alliance. As it happens, it is not Luxemburg that prevents the broadening of the integrative process for fear of being outvoted by the larger nations. Rather, it is such members as the United Kingdom, which is unwilling to abandon its preferred position in the current system; or France, which demands similar privileges; or the United States, which fears such imaginary dangers as that its allies might pool their forces to repeal the Bill of Rights. Principle of unanimity or not, the small nations, speaking as units, have less to say than their share. But their people *may* obtain proportionate influence as members of a larger community if integration takes place in an appropriate form. The apparent concern of the larger members for the rights of the smaller ones is here obviously focused on the wrong aspect.

More fundamentally, sovereignty has nothing to do with the postulate of unrestricted authority raised by Hegelian (and Blackstonian) jurists. For sovereignty, both in the sense of a requirement and in the sense of a characteristic, was always something substantially less than not being subject to any limitations. The original proponent of the concept, extreme as his position was, had defined it to mean not more than "suprema potestas *in subditos*" and merely *"legibus soluta"* (i.e., merely a power unrestricted by domestic, positive law).[25] But a maximal concept such as this is neither informative nor practical. It is far more realistic to focus on the minimum level of effectiveness and independence below which a state cannot fall and still remain a state. It then

---

[24] Ben T. Moore, *NATO and the Future of Europe* (New York: Harper [for the Council on Foreign Relations], 1958), pp. 217, 221.

[25] Bodin, *De republica*, i. 8. (Emphasis added.)

becomes at once evident that "diminution of sovereignty" does not occur with every restriction. There can be increases and decreases, but in that event we are talking of power, and the quantity of power that a state possesses is per se not sovereignty. Increases and decreases of power not crossing the critical point are irrelevant. Falling below it at once eliminates sovereignty. But a state is not more state if it has more than the indispensable minimum of effectiveness and independence. Nor can a state cease to be a state by installments. As Kelsen puts it, sovereignty, being a quality, is not divisible.[26]

It is true that the required minimum of effectiveness is not small. It cannot be less than that possessed by any other organization or individual in the same domain. It means supremacy over the wide front of activities and relationships normally controlled by public authority. It must be characterized by sufficient continuity and regularity to constitute an effective order. If this exists, independence from the outside is already a fact. But effective supremacy means something quite different from unrestricted authority or absolute independence in all matters. Two dimensions are involved but neither is unlimited. Thus—to recall an illustration also dating from the Westphalian era—a Committee of Fools attempting from a distance to regulate, down to minute details, the lives of citizens of the Chinese Empire is not sovereign, because its "order" is in fact not supreme there. But neither is a gang in the city of East Utopia, though it collects protection money with a high degree of effectiveness from tavern-owners in its "territory," because of the narrow scope of matters with respect to which it *is* supreme. The sovereignty of the Chinese Emperor is not affected if his subjects obey some of the "laws" of our committee regularly, or all of them only occasionally. For the same reason, the gang in the city of East Utopia does not affect the status of the United States as a sovereign state. Nor is that status affected when, for instance, the Universal Postal Union or the Interna-

---

[26] *Op. cit. (supra,* Chapter V, n. 24), p. 113.

tional Civil Aviation Organization effectively regulate American behavior, thus demonstrating supremacy over the government in Washington in their respective fields; nor when Iceland exercises its jurisdiction over an American soldier; nor when a French officer claims exemption from United States jurisdiction in the case of an accident occurring in Washington, D.C.; nor when a NATO international headquarters, under a British officer, directs military exercises in which American forces participate.

This suggests that the sovereign quality of the Westphalian state remains unaffected by the current NATO arrangements—or plans. The only conceivable conflict is with a maximal conception of sovereignty, which, when it was first invented, was nothing more than a political postulate, and is now nothing more than an irrational fear of losing something that was never possessed. Since no state was ever so powerful as not to be partially ineffective and partially subordinated to rules or decisions not derived from its own consent, the absolute concept was never descriptive of reality. But it likewise never was a valid legal principle, for a state can only be assigned maximal authority within its territory if rules assigning that authority exist and bind the states regardless of their individual acceptance. Conflicting with both reality and the fundamental assumption on which the legal system of the Westphalian era had been built, the absolute concept of sovereignty remains an obstacle only as long as the governments concerned lack determination to expose it for what it always was—a myth.

The sovereign aspect of the state represents thus a different problem than the principle of territoriality. The latter once had a tangible basis and has become a valid legal principle. Formal deterritorialization presupposes, therefore, the comprehension and acceptance of a change, rather than merely the discarding of what was a misconception to start with. In reality, however, more has been achieved in transcending territoriality than in overcoming the obstacle of the absolute conception of sovereignty.

Nevertheless, the territorial aspect also involves a misconception, namely, that territory is a *necessary* component of the concept "state." From what has been said about sovereignty, it is obvious that a state represents a relationship of a particular kind among people rather than between a sovereign authority and a parcel of land. Territory enters into the picture only because during the last three hundred years it has been used as the main criterion to determine with which particular people each particular state is concerned. But that states have for the most part been established in a given territory no more makes territory a part of the concept "state" than the field on which wheat usually grows is a part of the concept "wheat." Wheat, for example, can be grown in a laboratory, and the type of relationship characterized by the two dimensions indicated above[27] can exist among people identified by criteria other than territory and, indeed, has existed.[28]

This being the case, it is obvious that the widespread identification of the state with a piece of territory under the exclusive jurisdiction of a single government deepens the gulf between outdated formal concepts and current facts and needs—a gulf which we have already found to exist due to the maximalist myth of sovereignty. Before the current arrangements can be developed into an adequate substitute method for the performance of functions that now surpass the potential of the Westphalian state, both myths will have to be dispelled. This may not be an easy or popular task; but no inherent difficulty exists. A state *can* be semi-territorial and, while it cannot be non-sovereign, it may well

[27] Whether the state is conceived as a social fact or as a normative order is irrelevant in this context. The state as an order is valid where the two dimensions (sufficiently effective supremacy on a sufficiently broad front) exist.

[28] For example, in the case of nomadic states; in the case of medieval coexistence of several systems, each supreme with reference to a different, but territorially not identifiable, category of people or relationships; and in the case of all states of marginal effectiveness, when groups within a state's territory successfully defy the nominal state authority on such a wide front that they become in fact "states within the state." Examples of a merely supplementary use of non-territorial criteria are numerous: all forms of extraterritorial jurisdiction, jurisdiction on the high sea, and now, conceivably, extraterrestrial jurisdiction.

"surrender" a part of its traditional authority to joint organs without incurring any impairment of its sovereign status.

## THE FUTURE OF THE SOVEREIGN TERRITORIAL STATE

Military integration, then, is not self-sufficient, and the broadening of its base requires more than anything else initiative in creating a realistic consensus on the related fundamentals. It is not merely a dialectical trick to say that the survival of the actual states of the world depends on the speed with which the state as an institution can be stripped of some of its traditional prerogatives. At least in the case of the states of the Atlantic alliance, it appears to be clear that discarding their outdated formal attributes would make them more viable. This, of course, does not presuppose that they can achieve security in the traditional sense by any amount of integration. It does, however, presuppose, in the first place, that a collective effort offers them a better chance of maintaining the precarious balance on which their continued existence depends. In the second place, integration means genuine federal techniques rather than the broadening of the responsibilities of one state at the expense of the others. A one-way integration, pointing to the model of an empire rather than to that of a federation,[29] cannot but be ineffective. It can only breed opposition, which, considering the actual relevance of democratic postulates in the area at issue here, before long must mean failure and reversal of the process.

Yet, if the practices in matters of military command are analogous to the application of jurisdictional agreements[30]—and

---

[29] Though the comparison is tempting, a configuration in which the United States would stand for the central government and the receiving countries for the member states would, of course, represent the opposite of the use of federal techniques.

[30] See the third subsection in Chapter IV *supra*.

there is some testimony available to that effect[31]—integration, as far as it goes, is being attempted by the ineffective method. The fact that there was initially little objection to this method is perhaps sufficiently explained by the realization on the part of participating governments that, to insure immediate, tangible American commitments, it was best to make the entire project appear as an American one. Recent developments, however, demonstrate the impracticality of this method in the long run.[32]

It is true that integration by means of genuine federal techniques may in the end progress to the point where sovereignty (in the relative sense discussed in the preceding subsection) becomes the adjective of the joint organs. But this creates no difficulty, for in that event—again considering the validity of democratic postulates in the NATO area—nothing would be lost to the people whom the member states represent. Certainly, however, it is a long way to that point, and integration can be arrested whenever it effectively fulfills its intended functions.

All this is, incidentally, not without significance for areas, bases, and forces that are now outside the NATO system but are, in fact, dependent on it. Two major categories are directly involved. First, there are now forces, bases, and weapons that are physically within the NATO area but organizationally outside the NATO military structure. These forces are nevertheless subject to such agreements as NATO-SFA. Second, the NATO area is surrounded by bases

---

[31] Thus, President de Gaulle has declared that integration of NATO military forces is "a system in which, in fact, everything is under the command of Americans and in which the Americans decide on the use of principal weapons" (news conference of September 5 [*Le Monde,* September 7, 1960]).

[32] What was here only extrapolated when this section was written seems to be receiving additional support from the 1962-63 debate on control of nuclear weapons within the Western alliance as the book is coming off the press. The rapid succession of reversals of U.S. proposals with which the attempt to assure a permanent U.S. monopoly was accompanied, the French reaction of January, 1963, more drastic than De Gaulle's statement of 1960 cited above, and the immediately following U.S.–Canadian misunderstanding, in its political consequences analogous, exemplify the type of difficulties that are likely to result from "one-way integration" or, more specifically, from any urge to assert a leadership for which the political and psychological foundations (as distinguished from the technical and military requirements) have not been laid or preserved.

located in non-NATO countries, to which neither NATO command nor NATO-type status of forces applies. Unless these can be effectively employed in support of the Western-alliance system as a whole, there is little sense in having them. Some co-ordination is, of course, possible through the efforts of states that participate in several subsystems. Along this line, as was noted in a preceding chapter, a number of recent American agreements with non-NATO countries permit the use of local facilities by forces of third states which are under American auspices. But the United States is not the only NATO country with bases outside the NATO area, or forces and weapons outside NATO jurisdiction. In the last analysis only the main alliance, once its integration has progressed, can make the subsystems useful by absorbing the internal and co-ordinating the peripheral.[33]

The alternative would be to consider the NATO arrangement as a subsystem, presupposing a sort of world-wide *Pax Americana*—an idea having sufficient support in the United States to constitute another obstacle to truly joint decision-making within the Atlantic alliance itself[34] and to invite misleading interpretations of collective responsibilities as unilateral matters.[35] But this is hardly a very promising idea. Unilateral co-ordination of non-NATO areas

[33] For a nominal recognition of this, see the Communiqué of the Ministerial Meeting of December, 1957, noting that "our Alliance cannot . . . be concerned only with the North Atlantic area . . ." (*The NATO Handbook*, Appendix 5).

[34] Thus, during the troops-to-Europe debate, the opposition, while in principle conceding the need for sending American forces abroad, centered the attack against their placement under joint headquarters, though the actual Allied commander was an American officer (*Assignment Hearings* [*supra*, Chapter I, n. 13] *passim*, especially pp. 631, 695, and 698 ff.). Opposition to NATO-SFA (*supra*, Chapter III) took an analogous course.

[35] Thus, Secretary of State Acheson, who generally preferred, "as do many Americans, to give great emphasis to our intangible ties with Western Europe" rather than to potential loss of resources should it not be defended (*Assignment Hearings*, p. 81), was on one occasion willing to agree that the North Atlantic Treaty represents simply an extension of the Monroe Doctrine (*NAT Hearings* [*supra*, n. 12], Pt. 1, p. 30).

The widespread practice of referring to joint bases and weapons as "American" (even when a local officer literally guards the key that must be turned before they can be used) is in the same vein. It only breeds anti-integrative sentiment on both sides.

and forces must be as self-defeating as is one-way integration of NATO. Being already committed because of the presence of American (or other NATO) forces, the periphery may become an active participant as its own capacity is increased. Attempts in that direction, however, can hardly succeed unless it is first demonstrated that NATO itself is a co-operative rather than a manipulated organization, and that between NATO and non-NATO allies there is no trace left of the type of relationship that once existed between some of the former and most of the latter. For a prerequisite even more important than technological capacity is the elimination of psychological obstacles which, though residual from a closed era, are still standing in the way of an effective implementation of current common interests.

To those of the peripheral countries that were once objects of the colonial expansion of Western powers, the "imperialists" may not, of course, appear more palatable collectively than individually.[36] But collective policy-making within NATO may be a more efficient way of formulating policies whose substance can appeal to a wider clientele. For the psychological obstacles exist on both sides. In the case of some of the members of the Western alliance, a restored self-confidence, which ought to result from the increased potential of the alliance, is the obvious prerequisite of more enlightened policies. In short, NATO need not, but it may, accomplish what its members, acting individually, are demonstrably unable to do. This, indeed, is *mutatis mutandis* also valid with regard to countries that are not hosts to Western forces or recipients of Western military assistance.

Thus, broadening of collective processes within NATO, provided it is effected in an appropriate way, may well represent the key to the future of the state as an institution. For where this institution still exists—within the Western alliance system and in the so-called uncommitted zone—its continuation depends, directly or

---

[36] The periphery is, of course, heterogeneous, and this type of suspicion does not exist everywhere.

indirectly, on the continued ability of the Western alliance to extend its protection. To maintain this ability, the member states of the Atlantic alliance must scrap their obsolete prerogatives and pretentions. But their choice is not between the rule of unanimity and the loss of sovereignty. Rather, it is between an effective and an ineffective organization of states whose power and *raison d'être* as separate security-communities have largely disappeared.

*Appendixes*

# Appendix I: Collective-Defense Agreements

## (A)

*North Atlantic Treaty* (63 Stat. [2] 2241; TIAS 1964)

Washington April 4, 1949; entered into force for the United States August 24, 1949.

*Protocol on the Accession of Greece and Turkey* (3 UST 43; TIAS 2390)

London October 17, 1951; entered into force for the United States February 15, 1952.

*Protocol on the Accession of Germany* (6 UST 5707; TIAS 3428)

Paris October 23, 1954; entered into force for the United States May 5, 1955.

*NATO Status of Forces Agreement* (4 UST 1792; TIAS 2846)

London June 19, 1951; entered into force for the United States August 23, 1953 (cited: NATO-SFA).

*Agreement on the Status of the North Atlantic Treaty Organization, National Representatives, and International Staff* (5 UST 1087; TIAS 2992)

Ottawa September 20, 1951; entered into force for the United States May 18, 1954.

*Protocol on the Status of International Military Headquarters* (5 UST 870; TIAS 2978)

Paris August 28, 1952; entered into force for the United States April 10, 1954.

*Agreement for Co-operation Regarding Atomic Information* (7 UST 397; TIAS 3521)

Paris June 22, 1955; entered into force for the United States March 29, 1956.

States which have become parties:

| | North Atlantic Treaty | Accession of Greece and Turkey | Accession of Germany | NATO Status of Forces | Agreement on the Status of NATO | Status of International Military Headquarters | Co-operation regarding Atomic Information |
|---|---|---|---|---|---|---|---|
| Belgium | * | * | * | * | * | * | * |
| Canada | * | * | * | * | * | | * |
| Denmark | * | * | * | * | * | * | * |
| France | * | * | * | * | * | * | * |
| Germany | * | | | | | | * |
| Greece | * | | * | * | * | * | * |
| Iceland | * | * | * | | * | * | * |
| Italy | * | * | * | * | * | * | * |
| Luxemburg | * | * | * | * | * | * | * |
| Netherlands | * | * | * | * | * | * | * |
| Norway | * | * | * | * | * | * | * |
| Portugal | * | * | * | * | * | * | * |
| Turkey | * | | * | * | * | * | * |
| United Kingdom | * | * | * | * | * | * | * |
| United States | * | * | * | * | * | * | * |

(B)

*Inter-American Treaty of Reciprocal Assistance* (62 Stat. [2] 1681; TIAS 1838)

Rio de Janeiro September 2, 1947; entered into force for the United States December 3, 1948.

States which have become parties:

| | |
|---|---|
| Argentina | Haiti |
| Bolivia | Honduras |
| Brazil | Mexico |
| Chile | Nicaragua |
| Colombia | Panama |
| Costa Rica | Paraguay |
| Cuba | Peru |
| Dominican Republic | United States |
| Ecuador | Uruguay |
| El Salvador | Venezuela |
| Guatemala | |

## (C)

[*ANZUS*] *Security Treaty* (3 UST 3420; TIAS 2493)

San Francisco September 1, 1951; entered into force for the United States April 29, 1952.

States which have become parties:

Australia
New Zealand
United States

## (D)

*South East Asia Collective Defense Treaty* (6 UST 81; TIAS 3170)

Manila September 8, 1954; entered into force for the United States February 19, 1955.

States which have become parties:

| | |
|---|---|
| Australia | Philippines |
| France | Thailand |
| New Zealand | United Kingdom |
| Pakistan | United States |

## (E)

*Declaration Relating to the Baghdad Pact* [CENTO] (9 UST 1077; TIAS 4084)

London July 28, 1958; entered into force for the United States July 28, 1958.

States which have become parties:

| | |
|---|---|
| Iran | United Kingdom |
| Pakistan | United States |
| Turkey | |

## (F)

*Mutual Defense Treaty between the United States and the Republic of the Philippines* (3 UST 3947; TIAS 2529)

Washington August 30, 1951; entered into force August 27, 1952.

## (G)

*Treaty of Mutual Cooperation and Security between the United States and Japan* (11 UST 1632; TIAS 4509)

Washington January 19, 1960; entered into force June 23, 1960 (replacing the Security Treaty of September 8, 1951 [3 UST 3329; TIAS 2491]).

## (H)

*Mutual Defense Treaty between the United States and the Republic of Korea* (5 UST 2368; TIAS 3097)

Washington October 1, 1953; entered into force November 17, 1954.

## (I)

*Mutual Defense Treaty between the United States and the Republic of China* (6 UST 433; TIAS 3178)

Washington December 2, 1954; entered into force March 3, 1955.

# Appendix II: Countries with Which the United States Has Agreements Concerning Jurisdiction over United States Forces or Military Personnel Stationed in Those Countries*

Belgium
Bolivia
Brazil
Burma
Canada
Chile
China
Colombia
Costa Rica
Denmark (including Greenland)
Ecuador
El Salvador
Ethiopia
France
Germany
Great Britain (including Antigua, Bermuda, British Guiana, Jamaica, St. Lucia, Trinidad, Bahamas, including Turks and Caicos Islands, Newfoundland)
Greece
Guatemala
Haiti
Honduras
Iceland
Indochina
Indonesia
Iran
Iraq
Italy
Japan
Korea
Liberia
Libya
Luxemburg
Mexico
Netherlands
Nicaragua
Norway
Pakistan
Panama
Paraguay
Peru
Philippines
Portugal
Saudi Arabia
Spain
Thailand
Turkey
Uruguay
Venezuela
Yugoslavia

* Source: *House SFA Hearings*, Part 1, p. 159.

# Appendix III: Representative Status-of-Forces Agreements

## (A) TYPE I*

*Mutual Defense Assistance Agreement between the United States of America and Norway* (1 UST 106; TIAS 2016)

. . . . . . . . . . . . . . . . . .

### ARTICLE V

1. The two Governments will, upon the request of either of them, consult regarding any matter relating to the application of this Agreement or to operations or arrangements carried out pursuant to this Agreement.

2. Each Government agrees to receive personnel of the other Government who will discharge in its territory the responsibilities of the other Government under this Agreement and who will be accorded facilities to observe the progress of assistance furnished pursuant to this Agreement. Such personnel who are nationals of that other country, including personnel temporarily assigned, will, in their relations with the Government of the country to which they are assigned, operate as a part of the Embassy under the direction and control of the Chief of the Diplomatic Mission of the Government of such country.

. . . . . . . . . . . . . . . . . .

* See supra, Chap. III, p. 53 for the classification basis.

## Annex D

.   .   .   .   .   .   .   .   .   .   .   .   .   .   .

The personnel will be divided by the Government assigning such personnel into 3 categories:

(a) Upon appropriate notification of the other, full diplomatic status will be granted to the senior military member and the senior Army, Navy and Air Force officer assigned thereto, and to their respective immediate deputies.

(b) The second category of personnel will enjoy privileges and immunities conferred by international custom, as recognized by each Government, to certain categories of personnel of the Embassy of the other, such as the immunity from civil and criminal jurisdiction of the host country, immunity of official papers from search and seizure, right of free egress, exemption from customs duties or similar taxes or restrictions in respect of personally owned property imported into the host country by such personnel for their personal use and consumption, without prejudice to the existing regulations on foreign exchange, exemption from internal taxation by the host country upon salaries of such personnel. Privileges and courtesies incident to diplomatic automobile license plates, inclusion on the "Diplomatic List," and social courtesies may be waived by both Governments for this category of personnel.

(c) The third category of personnel will receive the same status as the clerical personnel of the Diplomatic Mission.

It is understood between the two Governments that the number of personnel in the 3 categories above will be kept as low as possible.

The status as described above will be substituted by such status for appropriate officials and agents of the countries parties to the North Atlantic Treaty as may be agreed by those countries.

*Agreement between the United States of America and the Republic of Korea Relating to Jurisdiction over Criminal Offenses Committed by the Members of the United States Forces* (5 UST 1408; TIAS 3012)

The American Embassy presents its compliments to the Ministry of Foreign Affairs of the Republic of Korea and has the honor to state that in the absence of a formal agreement defining and setting forth the respective rights, duties and jurisdictional limitations of the military forces of the United States (excepting the United States Military Advisory Group to Korea, which is covered by the agreement signed in Seoul on January 26, 1950) and the Government of the Republic of Korea, it is proposed that exclusive jurisdiction over members of the United States Military Establishment in Korea will be exercised by courts-martial of the United States.

It is further proposed that arrests of Korean nationals will be made by United States forces only in the event Korean nationals are detected in the commission of offenses against the United States forces or its members. In the event that arrests of Korean nationals are made under the circumstances set forth above, such persons will be delivered to the civil authorities of the Republic of Korea as speedily as practicable.

The Ministry of Foreign Affairs and the Government of the Republic of Korea will understand that in view of prevailing conditions, such as the infiltrations of north Koreans into the territory of the Republic, United States forces cannot be submitted, or instructed to submit, to the custody of any but United States forces. Unless required, owing to the nonexistence of local courts, courts of the United States forces will not try nationals of the Republic of Korea.

The American Embassy would be grateful if the Ministry of Foreign Affairs would confirm, in behalf of the Government of the Republic of Korea, the above-stated requirements regarding the status of the military forces of the United States within Korea.

·     ·     ·     ·     ·     ·     ·     ·     ·     ·     ·     ·     ·

*Agreement between the United States of America and Ethiopia Concerning the Utilization of Defense Installations within the Empire of Ethiopia* (5 UST 749; TIAS 2964)

·     ·     ·     ·     ·     ·     ·     ·     ·     ,     ·     ·     ·

## Article XVII

1. Members of the United States forces shall respect the laws of Ethiopia and abstain from any activities inconsistent with the spirit of this Agreement. The Government of the United States shall take appropriate measures to this end.

2. The United States military authorities shall have right to exercise within Ethiopia all jurisdiction and control over United States forces conferred on the United States military authorities by the laws and regulations of the United States, except as limited by this Article.

3. Members of the United States forces shall be immune from the criminal jurisdiction of Ethiopian courts, and, in matters arising from the performance of their official duties, from the civil jurisdiction of Ethiopian courts, provided that, in particular cases, the United States authorities may waive such immunity. In all other cases, Ethiopian courts shall have jurisdiction.

4. Whenever United States authorities exercise jurisdiction or control pursuant to paragraph 2 of this Article, the judicial proceedings shall be conducted within the Installations or outside of Ethiopia. In such cases the appropriate authorities of the Imperial Ethiopian Government shall, upon request, assist in the collection of evidence and in the carrying out of all necessary investigations. Necessary arrangements will be made by the appropriate authorities of Ethiopia to secure the presence of Ethiopian nationals and other persons in Ethiopia (except members of the United States forces) as witnesses for official investigations and for military tribunals, and, in appropriate cases, to seize and hand over evidence, exhibits and objects connected with the offense. The United States authorities shall, in like manner, carry out the collection of evidence from members of the United States forces and assist the Ethiopian authorities in the case of an offense to be tried in the Ethiopian courts.

5. Ethiopian authorities may arrest members of the United States forces outside the Installations for the commission or attempted commission of an offense, but, in the event of such an arrest, the member

or members shall be immediately turned over to the United States authorities. Except for Ethiopian nationals and other persons normally resident in Ethiopia, any person fleeing from the jurisdiction of the United States forces and found in any place outside the Installations may, on request, be arrested by the Ethiopian authorities and turned over to the United States authorities.

6. The United States authorities shall deliver to the Ethiopian authorities for trial and punishment all Ethiopian nationals and other persons normally resident in Ethiopia who have been charged by the Ethiopians or the United States authorities with having committed offenses within the limits of the Installations.

7. The Government of the United States shall have the right to police the Installations and to take all appropriate measures to assure the maintenance of discipline, order and security in such Installations.

8. Outside the Installations, members of the United States forces may be employed for police duties by arrangement with the appropriate authorities of the Imperial Ethiopian Government insofar as such employment is necessary to maintain discipline and order among the United States forces. In such cases, Ethiopian security forces with whom members of the United States forces may be serving on police duty shall have paramount authority with respect to the person or property of persons subject to Ethiopian jurisdiction.

9. Each Government undertakes that persons subject to the jurisdiction of its courts who commit contempt or perjury in connection with courts-martial proceedings or proceedings of other military tribunals, shall be subjected to appropriate punitive action by its courts.

10. The Imperial Ethiopian Government undertakes to establish such measures of control or zones of access adjacent to such Installations as may, from time to time, in the opinion of the two Governments be essential for maintenance of the internal and external security of the Installations as well as the sanitation and health conditions of those Installations.

## (B) TYPE II

*Agreement between the United States and the United Kingdom Amending Articles IV and VI of the Leased Bases Agreement of March 27, 1941 (1 UST 585; TIAS 2105)*

.   .   .   .   .   .   .   .   .   .   .   .   .   .   .   .   .

### ARTICLE IV

### Jurisdiction

(1) The Government of the United States of America shall have the right to exercise the following jurisdiction over offences committed in the Territory:

(a) Where the accused is a member of a United States force,

(i) if a state of war exists, exclusive jurisdiction over all offences wherever committed;

(ii) if a state of war does not exist, exclusive jurisdiction over security offences wherever committed and United States interest offences committed inside the Leased Areas; concurrent jurisdiction over all other offences wherever committed.

(b) Where the accused is a British subject or a local alien and a civil court of the United States is sitting in the Territory, exclusive jurisdiction over security offences committed inside the Leased Areas.

(c) Where the accused is not a member of a United States force, a British subject or a local alien, but is a person subject to United States military or naval law,

(i) if a state of war exists, exclusive jurisdiction over security offences committed inside the Leased Areas; and United States interest offences committed inside the Leased Areas; concurrent jurisdiction over all other offences wherever committed;

(ii) if a state of war does not exist and there is no civil court of the United States sitting in the Territory, exclusive jurisdiction over security offences which are not punishable under the law of the Territory; concurrent jurisdiction over all other offences committed inside the Leased Areas.

(iii) if a state of war does not exist and a civil court of the United States is sitting in the Territory, exclusive jurisdiction over security offences committed inside the Leased Areas; concurrent jurisdiction over all other offences wherever committed.

(d) Where the accused is not a member of a United States force, a British subject or a local alien, and is not a person subject to United States military or naval law, and a civil court of the United States is sitting in the Territory, exclusive jurisdiction over security offences committed inside the Leased Areas; concurrent jursdiction over all other offences committed inside the Leased Areas and, if a state of war exists, over security offences committed outside the Leased Areas.

(2) Wherever, under paragraph (1) of this Article, the Government of the United States of America has the right to exercise exclusive jurisdiction over security offences committed inside the Leased Areas, such right shall extend to security offences committed outside the Leased Areas which are not punishable under the law of the Territory.

(3) In every case in which under this Article the Government of the United States of America has the right to exercise jurisdiction and the accused is a British subject, a local alien or, being neither a British subject nor a local alien, is not a person subject to United States military or naval law, such jurisdiction shall be exercisable only by a civil court of the United States sitting in the Territory.

(4) In every case in which under this Article the Government of the United States of America has the right to exercise exclusive jurisdiction, the following provisions shall have effect:

(a) The United States authorities shall inform the Government of the Territory as soon as is practicable whether or not they elect to exercise such jurisdiction over any alleged offences which may be brought to their attention by the competent authorities of the Territory or in any other case in which the United States authorities are requested by the competent authorities of the Territory to furnish such information.

(b) If the United States authorities elect to exercise such jurisdiction, the accused shall be brought to trial accordingly, and the courts of the Territory shall not exercise jurisdiction except in aid of a court or authority of the United States, as required or permitted by the law of the Territory.

(c) If the United States authorities elect not to exercise such jurisdiction, and if it shall be agreed between the Government of the Territory and the United States authorities that the alleged offender shall be brought to trial, nothing in this Article shall affect the exercise of jurisdiction by the courts of the Territory in the case.

(5) In every case in which under this Article the Government of the United States of America has the right to exercise concurrent jurisdiction, the following provisions shall have effect:

(a) The case shall be tried by such court as may be arranged between the Government of the Territory and the United States authorities.

(b) Where an offence is within the jurisdiction of a civil court of the Territory and of a United States military or naval court, conviction or acquittal of the accused by one such court shall not exclude subsequent trial by the other, but in the event of such subsequent trial the court in awarding punishment shall have regard to any punishment awarded in the previous proceedings.

(c) Where the offence is within the jurisdiction of a civil court of the Territory and of a civil court of the United States, trial by one shall exclude trial by the other.

(6) Notwithstanding anything contained elsewhere in this Article, when a state of war exists in which the Government of the United Kingdom is, and the Government of the United States of America is not, engaged, then in any case in which the Government of the United

States of America would, but for this paragraph, have exclusive jurisdiction, that jurisdiction shall be concurrent in respect of any of the
following offences against any part of His Majesty's dominions committed outside the Leased Areas or, if not punishable by the Government of the United States of America in the Territory, inside the
Leased Areas:

(a) treason;

(b) any offence of the nature of sabotage or espionage or against
any law relating to official secrets;

(c) any other offence relating to operations, in the Territory, of the
Government of any part of His Majesty's dominions, or to the
safety of His Majesty's naval, military or air bases or establishments or any part thereof or of any equipment or other property of any such Government in the Territory.

(7) Nothing in this Article shall give the Government of the United
States of America the right to exercise jurisdiction over a member of
a United Kingdom Dominion or Colonial armed force, except that,
if a civil court of the United States is sitting in the Territory and a
state of war does not exist or a state of war exists in which the Government of the United States of America is, and the Government of
the United Kingdom is not, engaged, the Government of the United
States of America shall have the right, where the accused is a member
of any such force, to exercise concurrent jurisdiction over security offences committed inside the Leased Areas.

(8) Nothing in this Article shall affect the jurisdiction of a civil court
of the Territory except as expressly provided in this Article.

(9) In this Article the following expressions shall have the meanings
hereby assigned to them:

(a) "British subject" shall not include a person who is both a British subject and a member of a United States force.

(b) "local alien" means a person, not being a British subject, a
member of a United States force or a national of the United
States, who is ordinarily resident in the Territory.

(c) "member of a United States force" means a member (entitled to wear the uniform) of the naval, military or air forces of the United States of America.

(d) "security offence" means any of the following offences against the United States and punishable under the law thereof:

   (i) treason;

   (ii) any offence of the nature of sabotage or espionage or against any law relating to official secrets;

   (iii) any other offence relating to operations, in the Territory, of the Government of the United States of America, or to the safety of the United States Naval or Air Bases or establishments or any part thereof or of any equipment or other property of the Government of the United States of America in the Territory.

(e) "state of war" means a state of actual hostilities in which either the Government of the United Kingdom or the Government of the United States of America is engaged and which has not been formally terminated, as by surrender.

(f) "United States interest offence" means an offence which (excluding the general interest of the Government of the Territory in the maintenance of law and order therein) is solely against the interests of the Government of the United States of America or against any person (not being a British subject or local alien) or property (not being property of a British subject or local alien) present in the Territory by reason only of service or employment in connection with the construction, maintenance, operation or defence of the Bases.

## (C) TYPE III

*Agreement between the Parties to the North Atlantic Treaty Regarding the Status of Their forces [NATO-SFA]* (4 UST 1792; TIAS 2846)

The Parties to the North Atlantic Treaty signed in Washington on 4th April, 1949.

Considering that the forces of one Party may be sent, by arrangement, to serve in the territory of another Party;

Bearing in mind that the decision to send them and the conditions under which they will be sent, in so far as such conditions are not laid down by the present Agreement, will continue to be the subject of separate arrangements between the Parties concerned;

Desiring, however, to define the status of such forces while in the territory of another Party;

Have agreed as follows:

## ARTICLE I

1. In this Agreement the expression—

(a) "force" means the personnel belonging to the land, sea or air armed services of one Contracting Party when in the territory of another Contracting Party in the North Atlantic Treaty area in connexion with their official duties, provided that the two Contracting Parties concerned may agree that certain individuals, units or formations shall not be regarded as constituting or included in a "force" for the purposes of the present Agreement;

(b) "civilian component" means the civilian personnel accompanying a force of a Contracting Party who are in the employ of an armed service of that Contracting Party, and who are not stateless persons, nor nationals of any State which is not a Party to the North Atlantic Treaty, nor nationals of, nor ordinarily resident in, the State in which the force is located;

(c) "dependent" means the spouse of a member of a force or of a civilian component, or a child of such member depending on him or her for support;

(d) "sending State" means the Contracting Party to which the force belongs;

(e) "receiving State" means the Contracting Party in the territory of which the force or civilian component is located, whether it be stationed there or passing in transit;

(f) "military authorities of the sending State" means those authorities of a sending State who are empowered by its law to enforce the military law of that State with respect to members of its forces or civilian components;

(g) "North Atlantic Council" means the Council established by Article 9 of the North Atlantic Treaty or any of its subsidiary bodies authorised to act on its behalf.

2. This Agreement shall apply to the authorities of political subdivisions of the Contracting Parties, within their territories to which the Agreement applies or extends in accordance with Article XX, as it applies to the central authorities of those Contracting Parties, provided, however, that property owned by political sub-divisions shall not be considered to be property owned by a Contracting Party within the meaning of Article VIII.

## ARTICLE II

It is the duty of a force and its civilian component and the members thereof as well as their dependents to respect the law of the receiving State, and to abstain from any activity inconsistent with the spirit of the present Agreement, and, in particular, from any political activity in the receiving State. It is also the duty of the sending State to take necessary measures to that end.

## ARTICLE III

1. On the conditions specified in paragraph 2 of this Article and subject to compliance with the formalities established by the receiving State relating to entry and departure of a force or the members thereof, such members shall be exempt from passport and visa regulations and immigration inspection on entering or leaving the territory of a receiving State. They shall also be exempt from the regulations of the receiving State on the registration and control of aliens, but shall not be considered as acquiring any right to permanent residence or domicile in the territories of the receiving State.

2. The following documents only will be required in respect of members of a force. They must be presented on demand:

(a) personal identity card issued by the sending State showing names, date of birth, rank and number (if any), service, and photograph;

(b) individual or collective movement order, in the language of the sending State and in the English and French languages, issued by an appropriate agency of the sending State or of the North Atlantic Treaty Organization and certifying to the status of the individual or group as a member or members of a force and to the movement ordered. The receiving State may require a movement order to be countersigned by its appropriate representative.

3. Members of a civilian component and dependents shall be so described in their passports.

4. If a member of a force or of a civilian component leaves the employ of the sending State and is not repatriated, the authorities of the sending State shall immediately inform the authorities of the receiving State, giving such particulars as may be required. The authorities of the sending State shall similarly inform the authorities of the receiving State of any member who has absented himself for more than twenty-one days.

5. If the receiving State has requested the removal from its territory of a member of a force or civilian component or has made an expulsion order against an ex-member of a force or of a civilian component or against a dependent of a member or ex-member, the authorities of the sending State shall be responsible for receiving the person concerned within their own territory or otherwise disposing of him outside the receiving State. This paragraph shall apply only to persons who are not nationals of the receiving State and have entered the receiving State as members of a force or civilian component or for the purpose of becoming such members, and to the dependents of such persons.

## Article IV

The receiving State shall either

(a) accept as valid, without a driving test or fee, the driving permit or licence or military driving permit issued by the sending State or a sub-division thereof to a member of a force or of a civilian component; or

(b) issue its own driving permit or licence to any member of a force or civilian component who holds a driving permit or licence or military driving permit issued by the sending State or a sub-division thereof, provided that no driving test shall be required.

## ARTICLE V

1. Members of a force shall normally wear uniform. Subject to any arrangement to the contrary between the authorities of the sending and receiving States, the wearing of civilian dress shall be on the same conditions as for members of the forces of the receiving State. Regularly constituted units or formations of a force shall be in uniform when crossing a frontier.

2. Service vehicles of a force or civilian component shall carry, in addition to their registration number, a distinctive nationality mark.

## ARTICLE VI

Members of a force may possess and carry arms, on condition that they are authorised to do so by their orders. The authorities of the sending State shall give sympathetic consideration to requests from the receiving State concerning this matter.

## ARTICLE VII

1. Subject to the provisions of this Article,

(a) the military authorities of the sending State shall have the right to exercise within the receiving State all criminal and disciplinary jurisdiction conferred on them by the law of the sending State over all persons subject to the military law of that State;

(b) the authorities of the receiving State shall have jurisdiction over the members of a force or civilian component and their dependents with respect to offences committed within the territory of the receiving State and punishable by the law of that State.

2. (a) The military authorities of the sending State shall have the right to exercise exclusive jurisdiction over persons subject to the military law of that State with respect to offences, including offences relating to its security, punishable by the law of the sending State, but not by the law of the receiving State.

(b) The authorities of the receiving State shall have the right to exercise exclusive jurisdiction over members of a force or civilian component and their dependents with respect to offences, including offences relating to the security of that State, punishable by its law but not by the law of the sending State.

(c) For the purposes of this paragraph and of paragraph 3 of this Article a security offence against a State shall include

(i) treason against the State;

(ii) sabotage, espionage or violation of any law relating to official secrets of that State, or secrets relating to the national defence of that State.

3. In cases where the right to exercise jurisdiction is concurrent the following rules shall apply:

(a) The military authorities of the sending State shall have the primary right to exercise jurisdiction over a member of a force or of a civilian component in relation to

(i) offences solely against the property or security of that State, or offences solely against the person or property of another member of the force or civilian component of that State or of a dependent;

(ii) offences arising out of any act or omission done in the performance of official duty.

(b) In the case of any other offence the authorities of the receiving State shall have the primary right to exercise jurisdiction.

(c) If the State having the primary right decides not to exercise jurisdiction, it shall notify the authorities of the other State as soon as practicable. The authorities of the State having the primary right shall give sympathetic consideration to a request from the authorities of the other State for a waiver of its right in cases where that other State considers such waiver to be of particular importance.

4. The foregoing provisions of the Article shall not imply any right for the military authorities of the sending State to exercise jurisdiction over persons who are nationals of or ordinarily resident in the receiving State, unless they are members of the force of the sending State.

5. (a) The authorities of the receiving and sending States shall assist each other in the arrest of members of a force or civilian component or their dependents in the territory of the receiving State and in handing them over to the authority which is to exercise jurisdiction in accordance with the above provisions.

(b) The authorities of the receiving State shall notify promptly the military authorities of the sending State of the arrest of any member of a force or civilian component or a dependent.

(c) The custody of an accused member of a force or civilian component over whom the receiving State is to exercise jurisdiction shall, if he is in the hands of the sending State, remain with that State until he is charged by the receiving State.

6. (a) The authorities of the receiving and sending States shall assist each other in the carrying out of all necessary investigations into offences, and in the collection and production of evidence, including the seizure and, in proper cases, the handing over of objects connected with an offence. The handing over of such objects may, however, be made subject to their return within the time specified by the authority delivering them.

(b) The authorities of the Contracting Parties shall notify one another of the disposition of all cases in which there are concurrent rights to exercise jurisdiction.

7. (a) A death sentence shall not be carried out in the receiving State by the authorities of the sending State if the legislation of the receiving State does not provide for such punishment in a similar case.

(b) The authorities of the receiving State shall give sympathetic consideration to a request from the authorities of the sending State for assistance in carrying out a sentence of imprisonment pronounced by the authorities of the sending State under the provision of this Article within the territory of the receiving State.

## ARTICLE VIII

1. Each Contracting Party waives all its claims against any other Contracting Party for damage to any property owned by it and used by its land, sea or air armed services, if such damage—

(i) was caused by a member or an employee of the armed services of the other Contracting Party in the execution of his duties in connexion with the operation of the North Atlantic Treaty; or

(ii) arose from the use of any vehicle, vessel or aircraft owned by the other Contracting Party and used by its armed services, provided either that the vehicle, vessel or aircraft causing the damage was being used in connexion with the operation of the North Atlantic Treaty, or that the damage was caused to property being so used.

Claims for maritime salvage by one Contracting Party against any other Contracting Party shall be waived, provided that the vessel or cargo salvaged was owned by a Contracting Party and being used by its armed services in connexion with the operation of the North Atlantic Treaty.

2. (a) In the case of damage caused or arising as stated in paragraph 1 to other property owned by a Contracting Party and located in its territory, the issue of the liability of any other Contracting Party shall be determined and the amount of damage shall be assessed, unless the Contracting Parties concerned agree otherwise, by a sole arbitrator selected in accordance with subparagraph (b) of this paragraph. The arbitrator shall also decide any counter-claims arising out of the same incident.

(b) The arbitrator referred to in subparagraph (a) above shall be selected by agreement between the Contracting Parties concerned from amongst the nationals of the receiving State who hold or have held high judicial office. If the Contracting Parties concerned are unable, within two months, to agree upon the arbitrator, either may request the Chairman of the North Atlantic Council Deputies to select a person with the aforesaid qualifications.

(c) Any decision taken by the arbitrator shall be binding and conclusive upon the Contracting Parties.

(d) The amount of any compensation awarded by the arbitrator shall be distributed in accordance with the provisions of paragraph 5 (e) (i), (ii) and (iii) of this Article.

(e) The compensation of the arbitrator shall be fixed by agreement between the Contracting Parties concerned and shall, together with the necessary expenses incidental to the performance of his duties, be defrayed in equal proportions by them.

(f) Nevertheless, each Contracting Party waives its claim in any such case where the damage is less than:

| | |
|---|---|
| Belgium: B.fr. 70,000. | Luxembourg: L.fr. 70,000. |
| Canada: $1,460. | Netherlands: Fl. 5,320. |
| Denmark: Kr. 9,670. | Norway: Kr. 10,000. |
| France: F.fr. 490,000. | Portugal: Es. 40,250. |
| Iceland: Kr. 22,800. | United Kingdom: £500. |
| Italy: Li. 850,000. | United States: $1,400. |

Any other Contracting Party whose property has been damaged in the same incident shall also waive its claim up to the above amount. In the case of considerable variation in the rates of exchange between these currencies the Contracting Parties shall agree on the appropriate adjustments of these amounts.

3. For the purposes of paragraphs 1 and 2 of this Article the expression "owned by a Contracting Party" in the case of a vessel includes a vessel on bare boat charter to that Contracting Party or requisitioned by it on bare boat terms or seized by it in prize (except to the extent that the risk of loss or liability is borne by some person other than such Contracting Party).

4. Each Contracting Party waives all its claims against any other Contracting Party for injury or death suffered by any member of its armed services while such member was engaged in the performance of his official duties.

5. Claims (other than contractual claims and those to which paragraphs 6 or 7 of this Article apply) arising out of acts or omissions of members of a force or civilian component done in the performance of official duty, or out of any other act, omission or occurrence for which a force or civilian component is legally responsible, and causing damage in the territory of the receiving State to third parties, other than any of the Contracting Parties, shall be dealt with by the receiving State in accordance with the following provisions:

(a) Claims shall be filed, considered and settled or adjudicated in accordance with the laws and regulations of the receiving State with respect to claims arising from the activities of its own armed forces.

(b) The receiving State may settle any such claims, and payment of the amount agreed upon or determined by adjudication shall be made by the receiving State in its currency.

(c) Such payment, whether made pursuant to a settlement or to adjudication of the case by a competent tribunal of the receiving State, or the final adjudication by such a tribunal denying payment, shall be binding and conclusive upon the Contracting Parties.

(d) Every claim paid by the receiving State shall be communicated to the sending States concerned together with full particulars and a proposed distribution in conformity with sub-paragraphs (e) (i), (ii) and (iii) below. In default of a reply within two months, the proposed distribution shall be regarded as accepted.

(e) The cost incurred in satisfying claims pursuant to the preceding sub-paragraphs and paragraph 2 of this Article shall be distributed between the Contracting Parties, as follows:

(i) Where one sending State alone is responsible, the amount awarded or adjudged shall be distributed in the proportion of 25 per cent. chargeable to the receiving State and 75 per cent. chargeable to the sending State.

(ii) Where more than one State is responsible for the damage, the amount awarded or adjudged shall be distributed equally among them: however, if the receiving State is not one of the States responsible, its contribution shall be half that of each of the sending States.

(iii) Where the damage was caused by the armed services of the Contracting Parties and it is not possible to attribute it specifically to one or more of those armed services, the amount awarded or adjudged shall be distributed equally among the Contracting Parties concerned: however, if the receiving State is not one of the States by whose armed services the damage was caused, its contribution shall be half that of each of the sending States concerned.

(iv) Every half-year, a statement of the sums paid by the receiving State in the course of the half-yearly period in respect of every case regarding which the proposed distribution on a percentage basis has been accepted, shall be sent to the sending States concerned, together with a request for reimbursement. Such reimbursement shall be made within the shortest possible time, in the currency of the receiving State.

(f) In cases where the application of the provisions of sub-paragraphs (b) and (e) of this paragraph would cause a Contracting Party serious hardship, it may request the North Atlantic Council to arrange a settlement of a different nature.

(g) A member of a force or civilian component shall not be subject to any proceedings for the enforcement of any judgment given against him in the receiving State in a matter arising from the performance of his official duties.

(h) Except in so far as sub-paragraph (e) of this paragraph applies to claims covered by paragraph 2 of this Article, the provisions of this paragraph shall not apply to any claim arising out of or in connexion with the navigation or operation of a ship or the loading, carriage, or discharge of a cargo, other than claims for death or personal injury to which paragraph 4 of this Article does not apply.

6. Claims against members of a force or civilian component arising out of tortious acts or omissions in the receiving State not done in the performance of official duty shall be dealt with in the following manner:

(a) The authorities of the receiving State shall consider the claim and assess compensation to the claimant in a fair and just manner, taking into account all the circumstances of the case, including the conduct of the injured person, and shall prepare a report on the matter.

(b) The report shall be delivered to the authorities of the sending State, who shall then decide without delay whether they will offer an *ex gratia* payment, and if so, of what amount.

(c) If an offer of *ex gratia* payment is made, and accepted by the claimant in full satisfaction of his claim, the authorities of the sending State shall make the payment themselves and inform the authorities of the receiving State of their decision and of the sum paid.

(d) Nothing in this paragraph shall affect the jurisdiction of the courts of the receiving State to entertain an action against a member of a force or of a civilian component unless and until there has been payment in full satisfaction of the claim.

7. Claims arising out of the unauthorized use of any vehicle of the armed services of a sending State shall be dealt with in accordance with paragraph 6 of this Article, except in so far as the force or civilian component is legally responsible.

8. If a dispute arises as to whether a tortious act or omission of a member of a force or civilian component was done in the performance of official duty or as to whether the use of any vehicle of the armed services of a sending State was unauthorised, the question shall be submitted to an arbitrator appointed in accordance with paragraph 2 (b) of this Article, whose decision on this point shall be final and conclusive.

9. The sending State shall not claim immunity from the jurisdiction of the courts of the receiving State for members of a force or civilian component in respect of the civil jurisdiction of the courts of the receiving State except to the extent provided in paragraph 5 (g) of this Article.

10. The authorities of the sending State and of the receiving State shall co-operate in the procurement of evidence for a fair hearing and

disposal of claims in regard to which the Contracting Parties are concerned.

## ARTICLE IX

1. Members of a force or of a civilian component and their dependents may purchase locally goods necessary for their own consumption, and such services as they need, under the same conditions as the nationals of the receiving State.

2. Goods which are required from local sources for the subsistence of a force or civilian component shall normally be purchased through the authorities which purchase such goods for the armed services of the receiving State. In order to avoid such purchases having any adverse effect on the economy of the receiving State, the competent authorities of that State shall indicate, when necessary, any articles the purchase of which should be restricted or forbidden.

3. Subject to agreements already in force or which may hereafter be made between the authorized representatives of the sending and receiving States, the authorities of the receiving State shall assume sole responsibility for making suitable arrangements to make available to a force or a civilian component the buildings and grounds which it requires, as well as facilities and services connected therewith. These agreements and arrangements shall be, as far as possible, in accordance with the regulations governing the accommodation and billeting of similar personnel of the receiving State. In the absence of a specific contract to the contrary, the laws of the receiving State shall determine the rights and obligations arising out of the occupation or use of the buildings, grounds, facilities or services.

4. Local civilian labour requirements of a force or civilian component shall be satisfied in the same way as the comparable requirements of the receiving State and with the assistance of the authorities of the receiving State through the employment exchanges. The conditions of employment and work, in particular wages, supplementary payments and conditions for the protection of workers, shall be those laid down by the legislation of the receiving State. Such civilian

workers employed by a force or civilian component shall not be regarded for any purpose as being members of that force or civilian component.

5. When a force or a civilian component has at the place where it is stationed inadequate medical or dental facilities, its members and their dependents may receive medical and dental care, including hospitalization, under the same conditions as comparable personnel of the receiving State.

6. The receiving State shall give the most favourable consideration to requests for the grant to members of a force or of a civilian component of travelling facilities and concessions with regard to fares. These facilities and concessions will be the subject of special arrangements to be made between the Governments concerned.

7. Subject to any general or particular financial arrangements between the Contracting Parties, payment in local currency for goods, accommodation and services furnished under paragraphs 2, 3, 4 and, if necessary, 5 and 6, of this Article shall be made promptly by the authorities of the force.

8. Neither a force, nor a civilian component, nor the members thereof, nor their dependents, shall by reason of this Article enjoy any exemption from taxes or duties relating to purchases and services chargeable under the fiscal regulations of the receiving State.

## ARTICLE X

1. Where the legal incidence of any form of taxation in the receiving State depends upon residence or domicile, periods during which a member of a force or civilian component shall not be considered as periods of residence therein, or as creating a change of residence or domicile, for the purposes of such taxation. Members of a force or civilian component shall be exempt from taxation in the receiving State or on any tangible movable property the presence of which in the receiving State is due solely to their temporary presence there.

2. Nothing in this Article shall prevent taxation of a member of a force or civilian component with respect to any profitable enterprise,

other than his employment as such member, in which he may engage in the receiving State, and, except as regards his salary and emoluments and the tangible movable property referred to in paragraph 1, nothing in this Article shall prevent taxation to which, even if regarded as having his residence or domicile outside the territory of the receiving State, such a member is liable under the law of that State.

3. Nothing in this Article shall apply to "duty" as defined in paragraph 12 of Article XI.

4. For the purposes of this Article the term "member of a force" shall not include any person who is a national of the receiving State.

## ARTICLE XI

1. Save as provided expressly to the contrary in this Agreement, members of a force and of a civilian component as well as their dependents shall be subject to the laws and regulations administered by the customs authorities of the receiving State. In particular the customs authorities of the receiving State shall have the right, under the general conditions laid down by the laws and regulations of the receiving State, to search members of a force or civilian component and their dependents and to examine their luggage and vehicles, and to seize articles pursuant to such laws and regulations.

2.—(a) The temporary importation and the re-exportation of service vehicles of a force or civilian component under their own power shall be authorised free of duty on presentation of a triptyque in the form shown in the Appendix to this Agreement.

(b) The temporary importation of such vehicles not under their own power shall be governed by paragraph 4 of this Article and the re-exportation thereof by paragraph 8.

(c) Service vehicles of a force or civilian component shall be exempt from any tax payable in respect of the use of vehicles on the roads.

3. Official documents under official seal shall not be subject to customs inspection. Couriers, whatever their status, carrying these documents must be in possession of an individual movement order

issues in accordance with paragraph 2 (b) of Article III. This movement order shall show the number of despatches carried and certify that they contain only official documents.

4. A force may import free of duty the equipment for the force and reasonable quantities of provisions, supplies and other goods for the exclusive use of the force and, in cases where such use is permitted by the receiving State, its civilian component and dependents. This duty-free importation shall be subject to the deposit, at the customs office for the place of entry, together with such customs documents as shall be agreed, of a certificate in a form agreed between the receiving State and the sending State signed by a person authorised by the sending State for that purpose. The designation of the person authorised to sign the certificates as well as specimens of the signatures and stamps to be used, shall be sent to the customs administration of the receiving State.

5. A member of a force or civilian component may, at the time of his first arrival to take up service in the receiving State or at the time of the first arrival of any dependent to join him, import his personal effects and furniture free of duty for the term of such service.

6. Members of a force or civilian component may import temporarily free of duty their private motor vehicles for the personal use of themselves and their dependents. There is no obligation under this Article to grant exemption from taxes payable in respect of the use of roads by private vehicles.

7. Imports made by the authorities of a force other than for the exclusive use of that force and its civilian component, and imports, other than those dealt with in paragraphs 5 and 6 of this Article, effected by members of a force or civilian component are not, by reason of this Article, entitled to any exemption from duty or other conditions.

8. Goods which have been imported duty-free under paragraphs 2 (b), 4, 5 or 6 above—

(a) may be re-exported freely, provided that, in the case of goods imported under paragraph 4, a certificate, issued in accordance with that paragraph is presented to the customs office: the customs authorities, however, may verify that goods re-exported are as described in the certificate, if any, and have in fact been imported under the conditions of paragraphs 2 (b), 4, 5 or 6 as the case may be;

(b) shall not normally be disposed of in the receiving State by way of either sale or gift: however, in particular cases such disposal may be authorised on conditions imposed by the authorities concerned of the receiving State (for instance, on payment of duty and tax and compliance with the requirements of the controls of trade and exchange).

9. Goods purchased in the receiving State shall be exported therefrom only in accordance with the regulations in force in the receiving State.

10. Special arrangements for crossing frontiers shall be granted by the customs authorities to regularly constituted units or formations, provided that the customs authorities concerned have been duly notified in advance.

11. Special arrangements shall be made by the receiving State so that fuel, oil and lubricants for use in service vehicles, aircraft and vessels of a force or civilian component, may be delivered free of all duties and taxes.

12. In paragraphs 1-10 of this Article—

"duty" means customs duties and all other duties and taxes payable on importation or exportation, as the case may be, except dues and taxes which are no more than charges for services rendered;

"importation" includes withdrawal from customs warehouses or continuous customs custody, provided that the goods concerned have not been grown, produced or manufactured in the receiving State.

13. The provisions of this Article shall apply to the goods concerned not only when they are imported into or exported from the receiving State, but also when they are in transit through the territory of a Contracting Party, and for this purpose the expression "receiving

State" in this Article shall be regarded as including any Contracting Party through whose territory the goods are passing in transit.

## ARTICLE XII

1. The customs or fiscal authorities of the receiving State may, as a condition of the grant of any customs or fiscal exemption or concession provided for in this Agreement, require such conditions to be observed as they may deem necessary to prevent abuse.

2. These authorities may refuse any exemption provided for by this Agreement in respect of the importation into the receiving State of articles grown, produced or manufactured in that State which have been exported therefrom without payment of, or upon repayment of, taxes or duties which would have been chargeable but for such exportation. Goods removed from a customs warehouse shall be deemed to be imported if they were regarded as having been exported by reason of being deposited in the warehouse.

## ARTICLE XIII

1. In order to prevent offences against customs and fiscal laws and regulations, the authorities of the receiving and of the sending States shall assist each other in the conduct of enquiries and the collection of evidence.

2. The authorities of a force shall render all assistance within their power to ensure that articles liable to seizure by, or on behalf of, the customs or fiscal authorities of the receiving State are handed to those authorities.

3. The authorities of a force shall render all assistance within their power to ensure the payment of duties, taxes and penalties payable by members of the force or civilian component or their dependents.

4. Service vehicles and articles belonging to a force or to its civilian component, and not to a member of such force or civilian component, seized by the authorities of the receiving State in connection with an offence against its customs or fiscal laws or regulations shall be handed over to the appropriate authorities of the force concerned.

## ARTICLE XIV

1. A force, a civilian component and the members thereof, as well as their dependents, shall remain subject to the foreign exchange regulations of the sending State and shall also be subject to the regulations of the receiving State.

2. The foreign exchange authorities of the sending and the receiving States may issue special regulations applicable to a force or civilian component or the members thereof as well as to their dependents.

## ARTICLE XV

1. Subject to paragraph 2 of this Article, this Agreement shall remain in force in the event of hostilities to which the North Atlantic Treaty applies, except that the provisions for settling claims in paragraphs 2 and 5 of Article VIII shall not apply to war damage, and that the provisions of the Agreement, and, in particular of Articles III and VII, shall immediately be reviewed by the Contracting Parties concerned, who may agree to such modifications as they may consider desirable regarding the application of the Agreement between them.

2. In the event of such hostilities, each of the Contracting Parties shall have the right, by giving 60 days' notice to the other Contracting Parties, to suspend the application of any of the provisions of this Agreement so far as it is concerned. If this right is exercised, the Contracting Parties shall immediately consult with a view to agreeing on suitable provisions to replace the provisions suspended.

## ARTICLE XVI

All differences between the Contracting Parties relating to the interpretation or application of this Agreement shall be settled by negotiation between them without recourse to any outside jurisdiction. Except where express provision is made to the contrary in this Agreement, differences which cannot be settled by direct negotiation shall be referred to the North Atlantic Council.

## ARTICLE XVII

Any Contracting Party may at any time request the revision of any Article of this Agreement. The request shall be addressed to the North Atlantic Council.

## ARTICLE XVIII

1. The present Agreement shall be ratified and the instruments of ratification shall be deposited as soon as possible with the Government of the United States of America, which shall notify each signatory State of the date of deposit thereof.

2. Thirty days after four signatory States have deposited their instruments of ratification the present Agreement shall come into force between them. It shall come into force for each other signatory State thirty days after the deposit of its instrument of ratification.

3. After it has come into force, the present Agreement shall, subject to the approval of the North Atlantic Council and to such conditions as it may decide, be open to accession on behalf of any State which accedes to the North Atlantic Treaty. Accession shall be effected by the deposit of an instrument of accession with the Government of the United States of America, which shall notify each signatory and acceding State of the date of deposit thereof. In respect of any State on behalf of which an instrument of accession is deposited, the present Agreement shall come into force thirty days after the date of the deposit of such instrument.

## ARTICLE XIX

1. The present Agreement may be denounced by any Contracting Party after the expiration of a period of four years from the date on which the Agreement comes into force.

2. The denunciation of the Agreement by any Contracting Party shall be effected by a written notification addressed by that Contracting Party, to the Government of the United States of America which

shall notify all the other Contracting Parties of each such notification and the date of receipt thereof.

3. The denunciation shall take effect one year after the receipt of the notification by the Government of the United States of America. After the expiration of this period of one year, the Agreement shall cease to be in force as regards the Contracting Party which denounces it, but shall continue in force for the remaining Contracting Parties.

## ARTICLE XX

1. Subject to the provisions of paragraph 2 and 3 of this Article, the present Agreement shall apply only to the metropolitan territory of a Contracting Party.

2. Any State may, however, at the time of the deposit of its instrument of ratification or accession or at any time thereafter, declare by notification given to the Government of the United States of America that the present Agreement shall extend (subject, if the State making the declaration considers it to be necessary, to the conclusion of a special agreement between that State and each of the sending States concerned), to all or any of the territories for whose international relations it is responsible in the North Atlantic Treaty area. The present Agreement shall then extend to the territory or territories named therein thirty days after the receipt by the Government of the United States of America of the notification, or thirty days after the conclusion of the special agreements if required, or when it has come into force under Article XVIII, whichever is the later.

3. A State which has made a declaration under paragraph 2 of this Article extending the present Agreement to any territory for whose international relations it is responsible may denounce the Agreement separately in respect of that territory in accordance with the provisions of Article XIX.

In witness whereof the undersigned Plenipotentiaries have signed the present Agreement.

Done in London this nineteenth day of June, 1951, in the English and French languages, both texts being equally authoritative, in a single original which shall be deposited in the archives of the Government of the United States of America. The Government of the United States of America shall transmit certified copies thereof to all the signatory and acceding States.

.    .    .    .    .    .    .    .    .    .    .    .    .    .    .

## U.S. SENATE RESOLUTION OF RATIFICATION

Resolved (two-thirds of the Senators present concurring therein), That the Senate advise and consent to the ratification of Executive T, 82d Congress, 2d session, an agreement between the parties to the North Atlantic Treaty regarding the status of their forces, signed at London on June 19, 1951.

It is the understanding of the Senate, which understanding adheres in its advice and consent to the ratification of the agreement, that nothing in the agreement diminishes, abridges, or alters the right of the United States of America to safeguard its own security by excluding or removing persons whose presence in the United States is deemed prejudicial to its safety or security, and that no person whose presence in the United States is deemed prejudicial to its safety or security shall be permitted to enter or remain in the United States.

In giving its advice and consent to ratification, it is the sense of the Senate that:

1. The criminal jurisdiction provisions of Article VII do not constitute a precedent for future agreements;

2. Where a person subject to the military jurisdiction of the United States is to be tried by the authorities of a receiving state, under the treaty the commanding officer of the Armed Forces of the United States in such state shall examine the laws of such state with particular reference to the procedural safeguards contained in the Constitution of the United States;

3. If, in the opinion of such commanding officer, under all the circumstances of the case, there is danger that the accused will not be protected because of the absence or denial of constitutional rights he would enjoy in the United States, the commanding officer shall request the authorities of the receiving state to waive jurisdiction in accord-

ance with the provisions of paragraph 3 (c) of Article VII (which requires the receiving state to give "sympathetic consideration" to such request), and if such authorities refuse to waive jurisdiction, the commanding officer shall request the Department of State to press such request through diplomatic channels and notification shall be given by the executive branch to the Armed Services Committees of the Senate and House of Representatives;

4. A representative of the United States to be appointed by the Chief of Diplomatic Mission with the advice of the senior United States military representative in the receiving state will attend the trial of any such person by the authorities of a receiving state under the agreement, and any failure to comply with the provisions of paragraph 9 of Article VII of the agreement shall be reported to the commanding officer of the Armed Forces of the United States in such state who shall then request the Department of State to take appropriate action to protect the rights of the accused, and notification shall be given by the executive branch to the Armed Services Committees of the Senate and House of Representatives.

# Appendix IV: Exercise of Foreign Criminal Juris

| Country and Effective Date | Cases Subject to Foreign Jurisdiction | | | | | |
|---|---|---|---|---|---|---|
| | 1954 | 1955 | 1956 | 1957 | 1958 | Total† |
| Belgium (Aug. 23, 1953) | 20 | 7 | 16 | 24 | 127 | 195 |
| Canada (Sept. 27, 1953) | 312 | 505 | 528 | 477 | 493 | 2,317 |
| Denmark (June 27, 1955) | | 0 | 0 | 0 | 1 | 1 |
| France (Aug. 23, 1953) | 2,600 | 3,172 | 3,981 | 3,829 | 4,323 | 18,172 |
| Greece (July 26, 1954) | 0 | 0 | 0 | 22 | 36 | 58 |
| Italy (Jan. 21, 1956) | | | 86 | 374 | 586 | 1,046 |
| Luxemburg (July 23, 1954) | 0 | 27 | 34 | 36 | 31 | 128 |
| Netherlands (Aug. 23, 1953) | 5 | 11 | 69 | 104 | 129 | 320 |
| Norway (Aug. 23, 1953) | 1 | 2 | 5 | 1 | 6 | 15 |
| Portugal (Dec. 22, 1955) | | 0 | 0 | 0 | 0 | 0 |
| Turkey (June 17, 1954) | 12 | 18 | 36 | 54 | 55 | 175 |
| United Kingdom (Jan. 13, 1954) | 492 | 1,235 | 2,735 | 2,783 | 2,410 | 9,655 |
| Total NATO | 3,442 | 4,977 | 7,490 | 7,704 | 8,197 | 32,082 |
| World-wide | 7,416 | 10,249 | 14,394 | 13,971 | 13,659 | 59,689 |

* Source: *Operation Hearings* V, p. 20. Figures run from December 1 of the preceding
† Including the following figures for 1953: Belgium, 1; Canada, 2; France, 267;
‡ Including the following figures for 1953: Belgium, 1; France, 21.
§ Including 15 cases in France in 1953.

| | CASES TRIED | | | | | | CONFINEMENT NOT SUSPENDED | | | | | |
|---|---|---|---|---|---|---|---|---|---|---|---|---|
| 1954 | 1955 | 1956 | 1957 | 1958 | Total‡ | 1954 | 1955 | 1956 | 1957 | 1958 | Total§ |
| 0 | 2 | 2 | 1 | 0 | 6 | 0 | 0 | 0 | 0 | 0 | 0 |
| 249 | 426 | 406 | 372 | 453 | 1,906 | 6 | 0 | 0 | 5 | 1 | 12 |
| | 0 | 0 | 0 | 0 | 0 | 0 | 0 | 0 | 0 | 0 | 0 |
| 283 | 439 | 471 | 445 | 479 | 2,138 | 31 | 28 | 42 | 28 | 30 | 174 |
| 0 | 0 | 0 | 0 | 3 | 3 | 0 | 0 | 0 | 0 | 2 | 2 |
| | | 64 | 126 | 138 | 328 | | | 9 | 3 | 2 | 14 |
| 0 | 6 | 17 | 27 | 11 | 61 | 0 | 0 | 1 | 3 | 1 | 5 |
| 1 | 0 | 1 | 0 | 0 | 2 | 1 | 0 | 0 | 0 | 0 | 1 |
| 0 | 1 | 3 | 1 | 6 | 11 | 0 | 0 | 0 | 0 | 2 | 2 |
| | 0 | 0 | 0 | 0 | 0 | | 0 | 0 | 0 | 0 | 0 |
| 8 | 12 | 22 | 43 | 38 | 123 | 0 | 1 | 2 | 2 | 5 | 10 |
| 271 | 1,225 | 2,208 | 2,124 | 1,961 | 7,789 | 6 | 31 | 35 | 34 | 12 | 118 |
| 812 | 2,111 | 3,194 | 3,139 | 3,089 | 12,367 | 44 | 60 | 89 | 75 | 55 | 338 |
| 1,475 | 3,142 | 4,437 | 4,980 | 4,263 | 18,297 | 77 | 120 | 108 | 124 | 96 | 525 |

year to November 30 of the stated year.
Netherlands, 2.

# Bibliographical Note

## GENERAL

The following list is provided to identify those sources that have been cited in an arbitrary abbreviated form that is not generally understandable:

*Airpower Hearings*

U.S. Senate, Committee on Armed Services, Subcommittee on the Air Force, *Study of Airpower*, Hearings, 84th Cong., 2d Sess., April 16–July 19, 1956.

Barton I

"Foreign Armed Forces: Immunity from Supervisory Jurisdiction," *British Yearbook of International Law*, XXVI (1949), 380-413.

II

"Foreign Armed Forces: Immunity from Criminal Jurisdiction," *British Yearbook of International Law*, XXVII (1950), 186-234.

III

"Foreign Armed Forces: Qualified Jurisdictional Immunity," *idem*, XXXI (1954), 341-70.

*Girard Hearing*

U.S. Senate, Committee on Armed Services, *William S. Girard Case: Testimony of Department of Defense and Department of State,* Hearing, 85th Cong., 1st Sess., June 5, 1957.

*House SFA Hearings*

U.S. House of Representatives, Committee on Foreign Affairs, *Status of Forces Agreements,* Hearings on H. J. Res. 309 and Similar Measures. . . . Pt. I: 84th Cong., 1st Sess., July 13-26, 1955; Pt. 2: 84th Cong., 2d Sess., January 31–February 2, 1956.

*H. R. 8704 Hearings*

U.S. House of Representatives, Committee on Armed Services, *Full Committee Hearings on H. R. 8704 (Hearings on Sundry Legislation Affecting the Naval and Military Establishments,* No. 56) 85th Cong., 1st Sess., July 24–August 1, 1957.

King I

"Jurisdiction over Friendly Foreign Armed Forces," *American Journal of International Law,* XXXVI, No. 4 (October, 1942), 539-67.

II

"Further Developments Concerning Jurisdiction over Friendly Foreign Armed Forces," *American Journal of International Law,* XL, No. 2 (April, 1946), 257-79.

| | |
|---|---|
| Lauterpacht I | *International Law: A Treatise* by L. Oppenheim, Vol. I: *Peace,* 8th ed. London, New York, Toronto: Longmans, Green, 1955. |
| *NATO-SFA* | Agreement between the Parties to the North Atlantic Treaty Regarding the Status of Their Forces (4 UST 1792; TIAS 3846) London, June 19, 1951. |
| *Operation Hearings* I | U.S. Senate, Committee on Armed Services, *Operation of Article VII, NATO Status of Forces Treaty,* Hearings, 84th Cong., 1st Sess., March 29–June 21, 1955. |
| II | *Idem,* 84th Cong., 2d Sess., February 9, 1956. |
| III | *Idem,* 85th Cong., 1st Sess., April 9, 1957. |
| IV | *Idem,* 85th Cong., 2d Sess., July 29, 1958. |
| V | *Idem,* 86th Cong., 1st Sess., August 18, 1959. |
| *Senate Supplementary Hearing* | U.S. Senate, Committee on Foreign Relations, *Agreement Regarding Status of Forces of Parties of the North Atlantic Treaty,* Supplementary Hearing, 83d Cong., 1st Sess., June 24, 1953. |

*SFA Ratification Hearings*    U.S. Senate, Committee on Armed Services, *Agreements Relating to the Status of the North Atlantic Treaty Organization, Armed Forces and Military Headquarters,* Hearings, 83d Cong., 1st Sess., April 7-8, 1953.

Snee and Pye, *Report*    "Report on the Actual Operation of Article VII of the Status of Force Agreement," Washington: Georgetown University Law Center, 1957 (mimeographed).

Snee and Pye, *Status*    *Status of Forces Agreements and Criminal Jurisdiction,* New York, Oceana Publications, 1957.

CHAPTER II

Historical material on the acquisition of bases is scattered in works on other subjects. Any standard history, such as JULIUS W. PRATT, *A History of United States Foreign Policy* (Englewood Cliffs: Prentice-Hall, 1955), THOMAS A. BAILEY, *A Diplomatic History of the American People* (4th ed., New York: Appleton-Century-Crofts, 1950), or ARTHUR S. LINK, *The American Epoch: A History of the United States since the 1890's* (New York: Knopf, 1955) can serve for general orientation; but there is no work devoted to the topic per se. GEORGE WELLER's *Bases Overseas* (New York: Harcourt, 1944) is not a general survey but an argument in favor of acquiring a world-wide net of permanent bases as opposed to leasing bases or merely being permitted to use them for the duration of the war. BUEL W. PATCH, "American Naval and Air Bases," *Editorial Research Reports,* Vol. 1939-I, No. 7 (February 16, 1939), pp. 109-28, and "Atlantic Islands and American Defense," *idem,* Vol. 1941-I, No. 24 (June 27, 1941), pp. 439-55, are much more informative journalistic contributions of that period, and so is his "Anti-Americanism and Soldiers Overseas," *idem,* Vol. 1957-II (July 3, 1957), pp. 481-502, on an aspect of the postwar arrangements. For details, however, one must turn to U.S. Department of State, *Foreign Relations of the United States: Diplomatic Papers,* 1933 ff. (Papers Relating to Foreign Relations of the United States, 1870-1932; Papers Relating to Foreign Affairs: Diplomatic Correspondence, 1861-78 [Washington: Government Printing Office, 1862 ff.]), now extending to World War II, and to other original sources—a task which can be often simplified by using JOHN BASSETT MOORE, *A Digest of International Law,* 8 vols. (U.S. 56th Cong., 2d Sess.; H. Doc. 551 [Washington: Government Printing Office, 1906]), and GREEN HAYWOOD HACKWORTH, *Digest of International Law,* 8 vols. (Washington: Government Printing Office, 1940-44) as guides to earlier documentation.

Several older legal studies, listed below with the sources relating to Chapter V, are largely descriptive and contain extensive information on past instances of the stationing of forces abroad by all major powers. U.S. Navy Department, Statutory Board on Submarine, Destroyer, Mine, and Naval Air Bases [Hepburn Board], *Report on Need of Additional Naval Bases to Defend the Coast of the United States, Its Territories, and Possessions,* H. Doc. 65., 76th Cong., 1st Sess., January 3, 1939; U.S. Senate, *The Army of the United States,* S. Doc. 91, 76th Cong., 1st Sess., June 7, 1939; and U.S. War Department, *Report of the Secretary of War, 1939* (Washington: Government Printing Office, 1939) reflect the military position of the United States on the eve of the outbreak of World War II. See, further, NICHOLAS SPYKMAN, *America's Strategy in World Politics* (New York: Harcourt, Brace, 1942) and EUGENE STALEY, "The Myth of the Continents," *Foreign Affairs,* XIX, No. 3 (April, 1941), 481-94.

For wartime plans and acquisitions, the multi-volumed histories of the three services—U.S. Office of Air Force History, *The Army Air Forces in World War II* (Chicago: University of Chicago Press, 1948), *United States Army in World War II* (Washington: Department of the Army, Office of the Chief of Military History, 1953), and S. E. MORRISON, *History of the United States Naval Operations in World*

*War II* (Boston: Little, Brown, 1947)—are valuable, even though no particular volume focuses on the bases. A shorter work in the same category, DUNCAN S. BALLANTINE, *U.S. Naval Logistics in the Second World War* (Princeton: Princeton University Press, 1947), is also illuminative. Among the general histories covering that period, WILLIAM L. LANGER and S. EVERETT GLEASON, *The Challenge to Isolation, 1937-1940*, "The World Crisis and American Foreign Policy" (New York: Harper [for the Council on Foreign Relations], 1952), and by the same authors, *The Undeclared War, 1940-41*, "The World Crisis and American Foreign Policy" (New York: Harper [for the Council on Foreign Relations], 1953), are indispensable. They discuss, in particular, the "destroyers-for-bases" deal at some length; so does the leading unorthodox study, C. C. TANSILL, *Back Door to War* (Chicago: Regnery, 1952); and, as a participant, WINSTON CHURCHILL also discusses it in his *Their Finest Hour*, Vol. II of *The Second World War* (Boston: Houghton Mifflin, 1949). Legal aspects of this and another wartime acquisition are discussed by QUINCY WRIGHT, "The Transfer of Destroyers to Great Britain," *American Journal of International Law*, XXXIV (1940), 680-89, HERBERT W. BRIGGS, "Neglected Aspects of the Destroyer Deal," *idem*, XXXIV (1940), 569-87, EDWIN BORCHARD, "The Attorney General's Opinion on the Exchange of Destroyers for Naval Bases," *idem*, XXXIV (1940), 590-97, and BRIGGS, "The Validity of the Greenland Agreement," *idem*, XXXV (1941), 506-13 (Editorial Comment).

Postwar arrangements are generally registered in the official treaty collections of the participating states and the UN. I have used the texts of the agreements as they appear in the American series, giving references to both *Treaties and Other International Acts Series* (TIAS) and the *United States Treaties and Other International Agreements* (UST) where available. The State Department's annual *Treaties in Force* is now the only practical guide to these and the earlier American series (since the *United States Treaty Developments*, regrettably, died of budgetary attrition); the standard abbreviations indicated there are used throughout this book. In many cases, however, only the basic agreement on general conditions for the establishment of bases or the stationing of troops is published, not the implementing arrangements concerning particular installations.

Information on major installations and areas of concentration of American troops can be found in the daily press, by using the standard indexes (see, for example, HANSON W. BALDWIN, "Overseas Bases Keys to All U.S. Strategy," *New York Times,* February 17, 1957, and "A Guide to American Bases Overseas," London *Times,* July 13, 1956); further, in the various periodicals connected with the three services (a convenient guide to the latter is the *Air University Periodical Index* [Maxwell Air Force Base, Alabama: Air University Library]) and in the press published for the servicemen on location. Country-wide surveys attempted in the press of the receiving countries are sometimes more informative than the global summaries in the American press. The *Annuaire français de droit international* (Paris: Centre National de la Recherche Scientifique, 1955——), *L'Année politique* (Paris: Presses Universitaires, 1945——), and *Chronique de politique étrangère* (Brussels: Institut des Relations Internationales, 1948——) are less widely used, but in this field they are more useful than *Facts on File* or *Keesing's Contemporary Archives,* which have a more general coverage. For an attempt at a comprehensive summary with broad theoretical conclusions based on postwar arrangements, see MAURICE FLORY, "Les bases militaires à l'étranger," *Annuaire français de droit international,* I (1955), 3-30.

Congressional hearings on military appropriations (aside from special hearings on the status of troops, listed in the next section) and their foreign equivalents, such as *Parliamentary Debates* and *Parliamentary Papers,* are another source, however unwieldy, on particular major bases. See also U.S. Senate, Committee on Armed Services, *Study of Airpower,* Hearings, 84th Cong., 2d Sess., April 16—July 19, 1956, and U.S. Senate, Committee on Armed Services, *The Panama Treaty,* Hearings on Executive F, 84th Cong., 1st Sess., July 15-20, 1955.

## CHAPTERS III AND IV

As a result of the public controversy on the NATO Status of Forces Agreement, congressional papers contain ample materials interpreting the new agreements and their implementation. Besides the original *SFA Ratification Hearings,* the *Senate Supplementary Hearing,* the *House SFA Hearings, the H.R. 8704 Hearings,* and the *Girard Hearing,* there are developments in the field that are reviewed annually in *Operation Hearings* (see the list of abbreviations above). The annual reports on the same subject are: S. Rept. 1288, 84th Cong., 1st Sess.; S. Rept. 2558, 84th Cong., 2d Sess.; S. Rept. 1162, 85th Cong., 1st Sess.; S. Rept. 2497, 85th Cong., 2d Sess.; S. Rept. 1010, 86th Cong., 1st Sess.; S. Rept. 1774, 86th Cong., 2d Sess.; S. Rept. 1041, 87th Cong., 1st Sess.; and S. Rept. 2122, 87th Cong., 2d Sess. See, further, S. Exec. Rept. No. 1, 83d Cong., 1st Sess. (on the ratification of NATO-SFA); H. Rept. 678, 85th Cong., 1st Sess. (on a revision proposal, H. J. Res. 16).

The opposition produced too many documents for a comprehensive listing. For example, the revision proposals of a single year, 1957, included H. J. Res. 11, 16, 39, 61, 134, 149, 177, 211, 349, 365, 371, 389, 398, and S. J. Res. 40, all of which propose the withdrawal of troops if their legal status is not changed; and, suggesting various other measures that would have similar effect, H. Con. Res. 36, 187, 209, and 210, S. Con. Res. 15 and 38, H. J. Res. 40, H. Res. 15, 145, and 319; finally, S. Res. 144, 145, and 155, in addition to six bills intended to prevent fulfillment of the agreements by various unilateral actions on the part of the United States: H. R. 8658, 8820, 8681, 8704, 8957, and S. 2761. Representative of the views of pressure groups are: "Resolution of the Wheel of Progress," presented by Mrs. Ernest W. Howard, Women's Patriotic Conference, *House SFA Hearings,* pp. 127-28, *Operation Hearings* II, p. 45; statements of Brig. Gen. Merritt B. Curtis, American Coalition, *House SFA Hearings,* pp. 121-22, and Eugene C. Pomeroy, Defenders of the American Constitution, *ibid.,* 123-27 and *Operation Hearings* I, pp. 63-76; statements submitted for the record by the National Society of the Daughters of the American Revolution, the National Society of Women Descendent of the Ancient and Honorable Artillery Company, and the National Society of New England Women, House SFA Hearings, pp. 133-36; and the letter of Frank E. Holman, past president of the American Bar Association, *ibid.,* 157. For the American Legion, see the resolution of its Executive Committee of May 6, 1955 (*House SFA Hearings,* pp. 92-93) and subsequent statements to the Senate subcommittee (*Operation Hearings*

I, pp. 76-77; *idem*, III, pp. 44-45), and for Veterans of Foreign Wars, *House SFA Hearings*, pp. 107 and 115. See also digest of letters received by Senator Bricker, *Senate Supplementary Hearing*, pp. 59-62.

The official position is reflected, aside from the testimony of administration witnesses in the hearings cited above, in the Memorandum of the Department of Justice, "International Law and the Status of Forces Agreement," *Senate Supplementary Hearing*, pp. 38-55, *Congressional Record* CXCIX (July 14, 1953), 9062-70, *House SFA Hearings*, pp. 139-57 (summarized *ibid.*, 245-48), and, under the identical title, the article by Murray L. Schwartz, Special Assistant to the Attorney General, *Columbia Law Review*, LIII (1953), 1091-1113; further, the Memorandum of the Department of Defense, prepared November 17, 1953 (on constitutional procedural safeguards), *House SFA Hearings*, pp. 249-56, introducing the country studies submitted by the Department to the House Committee on Foreign Affairs (not included with the published material). See also the letter of the President to Senator Knowland, July 14, 1953, *Congressional Record* CXCIX (1953), 8779; the statement of the Senate Committee on Foreign Relations on NATO-SFA criminal jurisdiction, S. Exec. Rept. No. 1, 83d Cong., 1st Sess., April 28, 1953, pp. 11-12; the memoranda of the departments of Defense and State in H. Rept. 678, 85th Cong., 1st Sess., pp. 8-19, 19-22; Robert Murphy, "Basic Issues in NATO Status of Forces Agreement," *Department of State Bulletin*, XXXIII (1955, II), 178-85; and *NATO Status of Forces Agreement Criminal Jurisdiction Provisions*, prepared by the Legislative Reference Service, Library of Congress, for the Committee on Foreign Relations, 85th Cong., 1st Sess., March 28, 1957 (Committee Print).

Professional literature on the new status-of-forces agreements centers on NATO-SFA and may be divided into three categories: general interpretations of the agreements; studies dealing with implementation, often focusing on individual cases; and studies focusing on the relation of the new agreements to the rules of customary international law. The last category is considered below among the sources related to Chapter V. In the first category, the anonymous Note, "Criminal Jurisdiction Over American Armed Forces Abroad," *Harvard Law Review*, LXX, No. 6 (April, 1957), 1043-67, is an excellent, though mainly theoretical, introduction to the various legal problems arising from the new agreements; JOSEPH H. ROUSE and GORDON B. BALDWIN, "The Exercise of Criminal Jurisdiction under the NATO Status of Forces Agreement," *American Journal of International Law*, LI, No. 1 (January, 1957), 29-62, is similar in scope. SNEE and PYE, *Status* (see the abbreviations list) is the most detailed analysis of the text; it is arranged in the form of a running commentary on the key provisions of NATO-SFA, and has, like the preceding study, benefited from cases which have arisen under the agreement. See, further, RICHARD R. BAXTER, "Criminal Jurisdiction in the NATO Status of Forces Agreement," *International and Comparative Law Quarterly*, VII, Pt. 1 (January, 1958), 72-81, and the identical paper published in the *Proceedings* of the A.B.A. Section of International and Comparative Law, 1957, pp. 61-66; F. KALSHOVEN, "Criminal Jurisdiction Over Military Persons in the Territory of a Friendly Foreign Power," *Nederlands Tijdschrift voor Internationaal Recht*, V, No. 2 (April, 1958), 165-94; FREDERICK T. MOORE, "Criminal Jurisdiction in Overseas Areas," *Journal of Politics*, XXI, No. 2 (May, 1959), 276-302; LESTER B. ORFIELD, "Jurisdiction of Foreign Courts over Crimes Committed Abroad by American Military Personnel," *South Carolina Law Quarterly*, VIII, No. 3 (Spring, 1956), 346-54; and JONKHEER H. F. VAN PANHUYS, "Some Recent Developments of International Law in Respect of the Conflict of Jurisdiction Resulting from the Presence of Foreign Armed Forces in the Territory of a State," *Nederlands Tijdschrift voor Internationaal Recht*, II (1955), 253-78. Association of the Bar of the City of New York, Committee on International Law, *Report on Status of Foreign Agreements* (New York, 1958), the discussions in the various committees of the A.B.A. Section of International and Comparative Law, *Proceedings*, 1954-57, and the 1958 *Proceedings* of the American Society of International Law also contain illuminative comments.

The main work on the "operational" aspects of NATO-SFA is the *Report* by SNEE and PYE, based on observations in France, Italy, Turkey, and Great Britain. Professional literature centering on particular issues raised by the application of the agreements in individual cases includes EDWIN G. SCHUCK, "Concurrent Jurisdiction under the NATO Status of Forces Agreement," *Columbia Law Review*, LVII, No. 3 (March, 1957), 355-71, and JACQUES LÉAUTÉ, "Compétence criminelle—Traité de l'Atlantique Nord . . . ," Jurisprudence (*Aitchison c. Whitley*), *Revue critique de droit international privé*, XLIII (1954), 602-12, on the effect of waivers; GORDON B. BALDWIN, "Foreign Jurisdiction and the American Soldier: 'The Adventures of Girard,' " *Wisconsin Law Review*, Vol. 1958, No. 1 (January, 1958), pp. 52-106, and DANIEL VIGNES, "L'Affaire Girard et le Statut des forces américaines stationnées en territoire étranger," *Annuaire français de droit international*, III (1957), 304-14, on the determination of "on-duty" status and related problems raised by the widely publicised Japanese case; "Criminal Jurisdiction over Civilians Accompanying American Armed Forces Overseas," Note, *Harvard Law Review*, LXXI, No. 4 (February, 1958), 712-27, on the effect of the current scope of courts-martial jurisdiction upon the distribution of jurisdictional rights among the contracting parties of NATO-SFA; and EDMUND H. SCHWENK, "Comparative Study of the Law of Criminal Procedure in NATO Countries under the NATO Status of Forces Agreement," *North Carolina Law Review*, XXXV, No. 3 (April, 1957), 358-79, on the effect of the Senate ratification resolution. I have also gained valuable insights on the practices under the agreements from interviews in the Staff Judge Advocate's office, Headquarters, U.S. Army, Europe, the Country Representative for France, Orléans, and from discussion at the fifty-second annual meeting of the American Society of International Law.

## CHAPTER V

Fundamental are the three studies by G. P. BARTON (see the abbreviation list). American literature comparing the new agreements with the status of forces under the rules of customary international law is represented mainly, aside from the study of SCHWARTZ that has already been cited, by BERT A. ABRAMS, "International Law and Friendly Foreign Forces," Note, *New York University Law Review*, XXXII, No. 2 (February, 1957), 351-76, and EDWARD D. RE, "The NATO Status of Forces Agreement and International Law," *Northwestern University Law Review*, L, No. 3 (July-August, 1955), 349-94; but most of the general reviews and the official papers on NATO-SFA cited before contain some pertinent comments. See, further, RICHARD R. BAXTER, "Jurisdiction over Visiting Forces and the Development of International Law," address at the annual meeting of the American Society of International Law, Washington, D.C., April 25, 1958 (mimeographed). The earlier American views are reflected in the two studies by ARCHIBALD KING and also in CHARLES FAIRMAN and ARCHIBALD KING, "Taxation of Friendly Foreign Armed Forces," *American Journal of International Law*, XXXVIII, No. 2 (April, 1944), 258-77, and M. E. BATHURST, "Jurisdiction over Friendly Foreign Armed Forces: The American Law," *British Yearbook of International Law*, XXII (1946), 338-41.

World War II conditions are also discussed in EGON SCHWELB, "The Jurisdiction over the Members of Allied Forces in Great Britain," *Czechoslovak Yearbook of International Law* (London), 1942, 147-71, and "The Status of United States Forces in English Law," *American Journal of International Law*, XXXVIII, No. 1 (January, 1944), 50-73; and in the two articles by JASPER Y. BRINTON, "Jurisdiction over Members of Allied Forces in Egypt," *American Journal of International Law*, XXXVIII, No. 3 (July, 1944), 375-82, and "The Egyptian Mixed Courts and Foreign Armed Forces," *American Journal of International Law*, XXXVIII, No. 4 (October, 1946), 737-41.

ALINE CHALUFOUR, *Le Statut Juridique des Troupes Alliées pendant la Guerre 1914-1918* (Thèse, Université de Paris, Faculté de Droit), (Paris: Les Presses Modernes, 1927) is a thoughtful analysis, not encumbered by much documentation, of the World War I status of Allied forces in France; on the same, see also EDUARD CLUNET, "La présence en France des Alliés et l'Exterritorialité," *Journal du Droit international*, XLV (1918), 514-34. For the nineteenth-century varieties of "peaceful occupation," RAYMOND ROBIN, *Des Occupations militaires en dehors des Occupations de Guerre*, Etude d'histoire diplomatique et du droit international (Paris: Recueil Sirey; Larose & Tenin, 1913) is essential, although more descriptive than analytical. Also helpful on concepts developed in that period are JEAN PERRIN-JAQUET, "Des annexions déguisées de territoire," *Revue générale de Droit international public*, XVI (1909), 316-49; L. CAVARÉ, "Quelques notions générales sur l'occupation pacifique," *Revue générale de Droit international public*, XXXI (1924), 339-71; HELEN DWIGHT REID,

*International Servitudes in Law and Practice* (Chicago: University of Chicago Press, 1932); and RUDOLF WAHL, *Die Kohlenstation* (Greifswald, 1906). The older automatic-conquest occupation is illustrated in numerous case studies in IRÉNÉE LAMEIRE, *Théorie et Pratique de la Conquête dans l'ancien Droit,* 4 vols. (Paris: Rousseau, 1903-8); and some of the contrast between the former and more recent situations is revealed in RICHARD R. BAXTER, "The Duty of Obedience to the Belligerent Occupant," *British Yearbook of International Law,* XXVII (1950), 235-66.

The cases discussed in Chapter V, cited to the standard collections, require no further explanation. See, however, GILBERT CHARLES GIDEL, "L'arbitrage de Casablanca," *Revue générale de Droit international public,* XVII (1910), 326-407, and R. Y. JENNINGS, "The *Caroline* and McLeod Cases," *American Journal of International Law,* XXXII, No. 1 (January, 1938), 82-99, on two cases that are only marginally relevant. The works of publicists referred to on page 154 are, in the category of general texts, THOMAS BATY, *The Canons of International Law* (London: J. Murray, 1930), CHARLES CALVO, *Le Droit International théoretique et pratique* (5 éd., revised, Paris: Rousseau, 1896), PITT COBBETT, *Cases on International Law* (5th ed., 2 vols., London: Sweet & Maxwell, 1931-37), GEORGE BRECKENRIDGE DAVIS, *The Elements of International Law* (4th ed., revised by Gordon E. Sherman, New York and London: Harper, 1916), EDWARD MINER GALLAUDET, *A Manual of International Law* (4th ed., New York: H. Holt, 1892), WILLIAM EDWARD HALL, *International Law* (8th ed., edited by A. P. Higgins, Oxford: Clarendon Press, 1924), SIR THOMAS ERSKINE HOLLAND, *Lectures on International Law* (London: Sweet & Maxwell, 1933), FRANZ VON HOLTZENDORFF (ed.), *Handbuch des Völkerrechts,* 4 vols. (Berlin: C. Habel, 1885-89), CHARLES CHENEY HYDE, *International Law Chiefly as Interpreted and Applied by the United States* (2d ed., 3 vols., Boston: Little, Brown, 1945-57), THOMAS JOSEPH LAWRENCE, *The Principles of International Law* (1st ed., Boston: Heath, 1895), JAMES LORIMER, *The Institutes of the Law of Nations* (Edinburgh and London: W. Blackwood, 1883-84), LASSA FRANCIS LAWRENCE OPPENHEIM, *International Law* (5th ed., edited by H. Lauterpacht), Vol. I: *Peace;* Vol. II: *Disputes, War, and Neutrality* (London: Longmans, Green, 1937, 1935), SIR ROBERT JOSEPH PHILLIMORE, *Com-*

*mentaries upon International Law* (3d ed., 4 vols., London: Butterworth, 1879-89), ALPHONSE PIERRE OCTAVE RIVIER, *Principles du Droit des Gens* (Paris: A. Rousseau, 1896), HANNIS TAYLOR, *A Treatise on International Public Law* (Chicago: Callaghan, 1901), SIR TRAVERS TWISS, *The Law of Nations Considered as Independent Political Communities* (new edition, revised and enlarged, Oxford: Clarendon, 1884), JOHN WESTLAKE, *International Law* (2d ed., 2 vols., Cambridge: Cambridge University Press, 1910-13), HENRY WHEATON, *Elements of International Law* (5th English ed., edited by Coleman Phillipson, London: Stevens, 1916), and RICHARD WILDMAN, *Institute of International Law*, 2 vols. (London: W. Benning, 1849-50); and, in the category of related special studies, WILLIAM EDWARD BIRKHIMER, *Military Government and Martial Law* (Washington: J. J. Chapman, 1892), JEAN JACQUES GASPARD FOELIX, *Traité du Droit international privé* (4 éd., revisée et augmentée par Charles Demangeat), GILBERT CHARLES GIDEL, *Le Droit international public de la Mer* (Chateauroux: Mellotée, 1932), ALFONS ALFONSOVICH HEYKING, Baron, "L'exterritorialité et ses applications en Extrême-Orient," *Recueil des Cours de L'Académie de Droit international de la Haye*, VII (1925-II), 237-339, LEO STRISOWER, "L'exterritorialité et ses principales applications," *Recueil des Cours de l'Académie de Droit international de La Haye*, I (1923), 229-87, MAURICE TRAVERS, *Le Droit Pénal International et sa mise en oeuvre au temps de paix et en temps de guerre*, 5 vols. (Paris: Librairie de la Société du Recueil Siry, 1920-22), JULES VALERY, *Manuel de Droit international privé* (Paris: Fontemoing, 1914), and L. VAN PRAAG, *Juridiction et Droit international public*, La juridiction nationale d'après le droit international public coutumier en temps de paix (Hague: Belinfante Frères, 1915), insofar as they have not been cited already. Cf. HERSCH LAUTERPACHT (ed.), *International Law: A Treatise by L. Oppenheim*, Vol. I: *Peace* (7th ed., London, New York, Toronto: Longmans, Green, 1948), p. 759, with LAUTERPACHT, I (8th ed. of the same), p. 849; and THOMAS JOSEPH LAWRENCE, *The Principles of International Law* (7th ed., Boston: Heath, 1923), p. 225, with the first edition (*idem*, 1895). See, further, from among the more recent texts containing relevant comments: WILLIAM W. BISHOP, JR., *International Law, Cases and Materials* (New York: Prentice-Hall, 1953), J. L. BRIERLY, *The Law of Nations: An*

*Introduction to the International Law of Peace* (5th ed., Oxford: Clarendon, 1955), PAUL GUGGENHEIM, *Traité de Droit international public*, avec mention de la pratique internationale et suisse, 2 vols. (Geneva: Georg, 1953-54), HANS KELSEN, *Principles of International Law* (New York: Rinehart, 1952), ARTHUR NUSSBAUM, *A Concise History of the Law of Nations* (New York: Macmillan, 1954), F. A. VALI, *Servitudes of International Law: A Study of Rights in Foreign Territory* (2d ed., London: Stevens, 1958), and ALFRED VON VERDROSS, *Völkerrecht*, Vol. XXX of *Enzyklopädie der Rechts- und Staatswissenschaft* (Berlin: Springer, 1937).

I have quoted VATTEL, *Le Droit des gens ou principes de la loi naturelle, Appliqués à la conduite et aux affaires des Nations et des Souverains*, 2 vols. (London, 1758), "Classics of International Law" (Washington: Carnegie Endowment, 1916, photographic reproduction; also, translation by C. G. Fenwick), in connection with John Marshall's decision and on earlier concepts relating to the right of passage. Concerning the latter, all "classics" are of some relevance: notably, GROTIUS, TEXTOR, KOCH, and WOLF, in addition to AYALA and BELLI whom I have quoted on a still older tradition. An important guide to their theories and a careful analysis of the transition from their era of the corps of troops in passage to the latter era of "peaceful occupation" is ANTONIO RUINI's study, "I corpi da truppa all'estero nel diritto internazionale generale: Premesse storiche," *Communicazioni e studi* (University of Milan, Istituto di Diritto Internazionale e Straniero), VIII (1956), 253-367, from which point RAYMOND ROBIN and the other sources cited above carry on.

## CHAPTERS I AND VI

Besides FLORY's article and general information sources noted above in connection with Chapter II, *The NATO Letter* (Paris: NATO, monthly), *NATO Handbook* (7th ed.; *ibid.*, 1959), and Lord ISMAY's *NATO 1949-54: The First Five Years* (*ibid.*, 1955) are essential. *NATO 1945-59: The First Ten Years* is a more popularly written pamphlet of the Public Services Division, Department of State (Publication 6783;

Washington: Government Printing Office, 1959). See also U.S. Senate, Committee on Foreign Relations, *North Atlantic Treaty*, Hearings on Executive L, 81st Cong., 1st Sess.: Part I, *Administration Witnesses*, April 27-May 3, 1949; Part II, *Private Witnesses*, May 4-11, 1949; Part III, *Private Witnesses*, May 12-18, 1949 (with S. Exec. Rept. No. 8, 81st Cong., 1st Sess.), and *idem*, Committees on Foreign Relations and Armed Services, *Assignment of Ground Forces of the United States to Duty in the European Area*, Hearings, 82nd Cong., 1st Sess., February 1-28, 1951, in addition to the more recent hearings already cited.

From among many articles on related subjects, I have found enlightening those by TOWNSEND HOOPES, "Overseas Bases in American Strategy," *Foreign Affairs*, XXXVII, No. 1 (October, 1958), 69-82, ANDREW J. GOODPASTER, "The Development of SHAPE: 1950-1953," *International Organization*, IX, No. 2 (May, 1955), 257-62, WILLIAM A. KNOWLTON, "The Early Stages of the Organization of 'SHAPE,'" *ibid.*, XIII, No. 1 (Winter, 1959), 1-18, and ROBERT J. WOOD, "The First Year of SHAPE," *ibid.*, VI, No. 2 (May, 1952), 175-91, all written by former insiders. See, further, RICHARD R. BAXTER, "Constitutional Forms and Some Legal Problems of International Military Command," *British Yearbook of International Law*, XXIX (1952), 325-59, on NATO headquarters, their antecedents, and the proposed structure of the European Defense Community. ARTHUR E. ROWSE, "Foreign Bases: Declining Asset," *Editorial Research Reports*, 1960-II (September 14, 1960), 665-82, is a journalistic survey, bringing the accounts by PATCH cited with the material for Chapter II up to date.

M. MARGARET BALL, *NATO and the European Union Movement* (London: Stevens [for the London Institute of World Affairs], 1959), BEN T. MOORE, *NATO and the Future of Europe* (New York: Harper [for the Council of Foreign Relations], 1958), and KARL W. DEUTSCH *et al.*, *Political Community and the North Atlantic Area* (Princeton: Princeton University Press, 1957) are ground-breaking studies, using different approaches, on a subject on which more work needs to be done. Along with JOHN HERZ's thoughtful book *International Politics in the Atomic Age* (New York: Columbia University Press, 1959), and the texts by WRIGHT, BRIERLY, and MORGENTHAU cited in the first chapter, they have served as sources of general enlightenment in many ways.

For further study, the reader may find initial assistance in two specialized annotated bibliographies, *U.S. Overseas Bases: Present Status and Future Prospects* (Washington: Department of the Army, Pamphlet 20-63, January, 1963) and *The Atlantic Community*, 2 vols., prepared by the Conference on Atlantic Community, Bruges (Leiden: A. W. Sythoff, 1961).

# Index

Abrams, B. A., 121n, 237

Acheson, D., 171n

Adinolfi, S., 154n

Africa, 25, 26, 27n

Air Bases; see Bases

Air Force, 5n, 23; see Military forces

Aitchison c. Whitley, 97-106, 108n

Alaska, 23, 24

Alliances: contemporary, see NATO, SEATO, etc.; nineteenth-century, 156; unequal, 37

American Bar Association, 50n

Annexations, 17-19, 155, 164, 166; "disguised," 21n, 22, 23; see also Cession of territory

Antigua: status-of-forces agreement, 61; U.S. base rights, 27

ANZUS Treaty, 4n, 187

Army, 4n, 23, 108; see also Military forces

Ascension Island, status of forces, 61

Atlantic Ocean, 24-26

Ayala, B., 152n

Azores, 25, 118; status-of-forces agreement, 60, 78; U.S. base rights, 43-45

Baghdad Pact; see CENTO

Bahamas: status-of-forces agreement, 61n; U.S. base rights, 27

Bailey, T. D., 17n, 230

Baldwin, G. B., 112n, 237; see also Rouse and Baldwin

Baldwin, H. W., 5n, 233

Ball, M. M., 242

Ballantine, D. S., 16n, 232, 22n

Barbados, status-of-forces agreement, 61n

Barton, G. P., 76, 122-23, 135-36, 227, 237

Bases: acquisition of, 8, 15-46; allied, 27, 178-79; Axis powers, 17, 24, 26-27; categories of current arrangements, 33-46; and "installations," 5; joint use of, 8, 33, 34, 39, 163, 167-68; leased, 8, 17-21, 27-29, 66n; legal nature of, 18, 19, 21-22, 29, 32; and mutual defense commitments, 33, 36-49; NATO, 167-68; need of, 7, 15, 16-17n, 25-26; neutral, 27; nineteenth-century, 8, 15-19, 154-55; non-NATO, 179; number of, 4-5, 8, 23; operating cost, 5; payment for, 35; pre–World War II, 15-22; purpose of, agreed, 28, 32, 35, 37; security of, guaranteed by local authorities, 64-65; and stationing of forces in foreign territory, 7-8; in U.S. outlying possessions, 23, 26; World War II, U.S., 22-32; see also: Military forces; Passage of troops; and listings of individual countries and territories

Bathurst, M. E., 238

Baty, T., 154n, 239

Baxter, R. R., 71n, 150n, 236, 238, 239, 242

Bayard, Senator T. F., 16n

Belgium, 24; status-of-forces agreement, 67n, 118n

Belli, P., 152n

Bermuda, 25; status-of-forces agreement, 61n; U.S. base rights, 27

Birkhimer, W. E., 154n, 240

Bishop, W. W., 21n, 240

Blackstone, W., 173